Drowning in Data?

How to Collect, Organize, and Document Student Performance

Mary Shea
Rosemary Murray
Rebecca Harlin

HEINEMANN
Portsmouth, NH

Heinemann
A division of Reed Elsevier Inc.
361 Hanover Street
Portsmouth, NH 03801–3912
www.heinemann.com

Offices and agents throughout the world

The authors and publisher wish to thank those who have generously given permission to reprint borrowed material:

"Heroes Around Us" by Mary E. Shea. From "Read, Write, Think: Lesson Plan Index." Copyright © by the International Reading Association. *www.readwritethink.org/lessons*

"No More Pencils" by Akiko Atsuda from *The Journal-Register*, June 14, 2004. Used by permission of The Journal-Register.

"Paul Revere: An American Patriot" by Mary E. Shea. From "Read, Write, Think: Lesson Plan Index." Copyright © by the International Reading Association. *www.readwritethink.org/lessons*

Excerpt from *Taking Running Records* by Mary Shea. Copyright © 2000 by Mary Shea. Published by Scholastic, Inc. Used by permission of the publisher.

"Tenement Life: Mapping Texts and Making Models" by Mary E. Shea. From "Read, Write, Think: Lesson Plan Index." Copyright © by the International Reading Association. *www.readwritethink.org/lessons*

Library of Congress Cataloging-in-Publication Data
Shea, Mary (Mary E.).
    Drowing in data? : how to collect, organize, and document student performance / Mary Shea, Rosemary Murray, Rebecca Harlin.
        p. cm.
    Includes bibliographical references and index.
    ISBN 0-325-00650-4 (alk. paper)
    1. Educational evaluation.   I. Murray, Rosemary.   II. Harlin, Rebecca.   III. Title.
LB2822.75.S55 2005
371.26—dc22   2004030796

Editor: Lois Bridges
Production: Vicki Kasabian
Cover design: Night & Day Design
Typesetter: Publishers' Design and Production Services, Inc.
Manufacturing: Louise Richardson

Printed in the United States of America on acid-free paper
09 08 07 06 05 VP 1 2 3 4 5

To all the wonderful teachers and

students who contributed to this project.

They inspire belief in the strength of our schools.

Contents

Acknowledgments

We firmly believe that our accomplishments in life are collaborative—that we stand on the shoulders of all who have supported us along the journey toward our goals. There are many kind people with strong shoulders who have held us up in this effort, and we offer our deepest appreciation to every one of them. However, we'd like to single out the following people.

First, we especially thank Lois Bridges at Heinemann for her faith that our proposal had merit, that it would meet a need in the field of professional texts. We earnestly believed that it would and were honored by Heinemann's acceptance. Lois responded quickly—sometimes immediately—to every inquiry. Her feedback was always specific and thoughtful, and her supportive encouragement stoked the fires that helped us persist when the task seemed daunting. We are grateful to Alan Huisman and Vicki Kasabian, also at Heinemann, who worked with us in developing the final manuscript. Their attention to details, thoughtful queries, and suggestions are very much appreciated.

We also wish to thank Bonnie Parsons, principal at Lindbergh Elementary School, for her hospitality. She warmly and enthusiastically welcomed Mary and Rosemary into her building, inviting us to work with teacher committees, teach college classes on-site, and gather data from students and teachers at the school. We spent a great deal of time in Sue Rosche's fifth-grade classroom and Nancy Gantz's first-grade classroom. It was a tremendous opportunity to see master teachers at work while collecting examples for this text. We immediately shared vignettes of life in these classrooms with students in our college classes, providing them with powerful examples of effective teaching.

Jay Basham, another wonderful teacher, invited us into his seventh-grade social studies classroom in Cheektowaga Middle School. He and his students were amazing! The integrated research projects they shared and the PowerPoint presentations we observed were quite impressive.

We'd also like to thank Mary's son Brian Shea, who teaches sixth grade at Wise Middle School. Brian shared information and examples of an end-of-year science project he designed. The project was expanded to the other sixth-grade teams in the building and has been publicly recognized in the community newspaper.

Since the three of us worked separately as well as together, we also have people we'd like to thank separately.

Mary Shea

I am indebted to my dear friend Ardith Cole for her wise responses and suggestions. She's my best sounding board, whether I need professional advice or a friend with whom to talk through a dilemma. Chapter 6 was such a dilemma. It took the longest to complete and was the most difficult. There was so much to discuss, but the focus had to complement the context of this project.

I've included stories from my experiences working with another dear friend, Marcia Cleary. I worked closely with Marcia for many years, sometimes synchronously teaching my own little group and sometimes team-teaching with her. We could and still can finish each other's sentences! Marcia created an inviting environment—one that pulled you into the action in such a way that you didn't want to leave. I know—I was there!

I also thank Nancy Roberts, a first-grade teacher and friend, who shared many of her classroom stories with me, not just for this project but because she loves to talk about her "kids." Nancy's caring spirit and professional knowledge are instantly recognized in a first meeting and just as noticeable when you visit her classroom.

Two other classroom teachers generously shared student work samples with me. Mikal Murray is a very special third-grade teacher at Maplemere Elementary School. She embodies great teaching in action. When I first meet Mikal, as an undergraduate junior participant in my course, I knew she was extraordinary. Melinda Farrar is a first-year, first-grade teacher at Harris Hill Elementary School who invited me into her classroom and took time after school to describe her program and share samples of her students' work. I wish to extend a special thanks to both of these dedicated teachers.

Last but not least, I'd like to thank my family and friends for their patience when my thoughts and time were centered on this project. Their help with the ordinary business of life was greatly appreciated, even though it may not have been soundly stated at the time.

Rosemary Murray
I'd like to give special thanks to my daughter, Lisa Murray-Roselli, for all her professional help and loving support in completing this project.

Rebecca Harlin
I would like to express my appreciation to Dr. Lilia DiBello and her sons, Darin and Dylan, for their participation in and contributions to this project. The projects shared by Karen Crum, Lissette Hernandez, and Amelia Connell, of the St. Thomas Episcopal Parish School in Coral Gables, Florida, helped make this book relevant for teachers. Mr. Steve Schraer's photography captured children from diverse settings. Finally, I am grateful for the support of my husband, Jim, and daughter, Amy.

Introduction

Measuring What's in the Cup

Day-to-day life in the classroom creates much evidence that learning has occurred there. However, we're often too close to the forest to see the trees. We're so focused on narrow, specific lesson outcomes that we fail to notice small nuances of behavior telling us that an "aha" has been achieved. Each interaction—whether between teacher and student, student and student, parent and teacher, or some other combination—has the potential to yield rich information about a learner's growth and achievement. Questions asked, comments made, the manner of personal interactions and reactions, choices of materials and tasks, and gestures (body language) and processes used to complete tasks are but a few of the possible student behaviors ripe for investigative observation. Details, details, details are required in any attempt to understand, with depth and clarity, a learner's present level of achievement.

We should analyze and document both *observed* development and development that's *evidenced* in samples of students' work. In other words, we should start by understanding the contents of a *cup half full*—children's accumulated ounces of development—rather than speculating on *deficits,* or what's missing. Too often, however, the kind of information that can be gathered from daily performances is overlooked. Uncollected for analysis and reflection, it's revisited only as we happen to recall it. Such recall may be sketchy, fragmented, embellished, or simply wrong. More often, the information is completely lost.

Working much as anthropologists in an archeological dig gathering artifacts (the remains of a community that reveal characteristics of its culture), teachers can act scientifically to gather relevant artifacts left from learning episodes. The classroom is rich with artifacts of students' learning. Keeping accurate and complete *field notes* while collecting significant learning artifacts legitimizes a broad assessment and evaluation of students' achievement.

Recognizing Relevant Evidence

In a criminal investigation something seemingly trivial can become crucial evidence if it relates to the questions posed. Criminologists claim that every crime scene holds forensic evidence identifying the perpetrator. A fiber, hair, or drop of blood recovered from the scene and examined by a highly trained professional can become critical evidence. Similarly, forensic evidence is left at every learning scene. It requires a knowledgeable and patient retriever—someone who collects it without contamination, analyzes it objectively in the full light of reason and research, documents it clearly and accurately, and reports conclusions to everyone with a *need to know*—to utilize the evidence to its full potential.

Every gesture, utterance, or performance offers evidence of a child's progress toward developmental standards. With their posture, facial expressions, and gesticulations, learners unconsciously as well as consciously insist that we *read their motions*. Their body language is generally at high pitch and could easily fill volumes. Any parent can tell you all about it. When we say, "Let's talk about it," kids sometimes answer, "But I didn't *say* anything!" "You didn't have to," we tell them, "your *face* said a paragraph." This sensitive barometer is too easily ignored in the rush to teach and assess our way through a curriculum.

Children's words are another indicator of their mood and thinking. Words can be direct, cutting straight to the heart of the matter. They can also demand that we carefully infer between and beyond the lines in order to probe for deeper meaning. Aside from moments of imposed silence, classroom discourse produces a continuous hum, like that in a hive. Children's talk, like adult talk, is all over the place topically; it's social, emotional, even heuristic. Lending a trained ear to this talk allows teachers to capture a great deal of information about their students as individuals and as learners.

Teachers anecdotally note significant thinking, knowing, and problem solving displayed during classroom *performances* that require learners to apply knowledge and skills in situations similar to those they'll encounter outside school. These performances might include taking part in formal and informal discussions, writing personal pieces, participating in problem-solving activities, conducting experiments, playing on a team, working in a group, and giving presentations.

Among a myriad of skills possibly displayed, learners' performances might verify that they

▶ use or attempt to use standard conventions of speech
▶ articulate clearly
▶ express a point of view
▶ persuade others with solid "evidence"
▶ use words that best represent their ideas
▶ listen to another's contribution
▶ extend someone else's comments
▶ encourage others

The evidence, then, is all around us. But a *system* is needed for securing, documenting, retrieving, and analyzing it in the process of building a case for achievement. A plan of attack always makes the task less daunting and the work run more smoothly.

Instituting an Assessment System

This text introduces an *evidence-driven* process for collecting, documenting, analyzing, and reporting what learners can do in a way that meaningfully informs day-to-day instruction. Information gathered during classroom activities reveals learners'

▶ knowledge or lack of it
▶ interest when the activity is presented
▶ motivation to persist with the task
▶ comfort with others and the situation

It also reveals any other influencing variables that must be considered when assessing overall performance.

Plans for a next learning goal are based on this collected information—on what is *proven* to exist. The system is *dynamic*: teachers actively monitor student performance and use what they learn to revise instruction on the run. It's also *generative*: it leads to the refinement and reformulation of instructional objectives as lessons proceed. It encourages learners to construct and reconstruct goals in response to the descriptive, specific, and immediate feedback they're given.

Establishing Essential Assessment Principles

Any system is only as solid as the foundation on which it is built. We've built our assessment system on eight essential principles:

1. *Assessment occurs all day long.* It doesn't just happen during independent work or via a culminating activity. It's continuous—second by second, minute by minute.
2. *Assessment drives instruction.* Teachers use what they discover from monitoring students' learning on the spot to adjust lessons in

progress. They notice who looks confused, whose faces are twisted into question marks. They notice who's bored, whose body language screams, "Not this again!"

3. *Assessment is not subject specific.* Literacy competence is not assessed only during language arts: Can students apply literacy skills in science? In social studies? Children's mathematical competence is not assessed only in math class, it's assessed anywhere these skills are needed, even in the lunch line: Can students determine how much change they should get? Under the broadest umbrella, can they integrate and apply mathematics, literacy skills, and scientific knowledge to solve real problems?

4. *Assessment includes information about the learner's life outside school.* Children display all kinds of competency when interacting with family members and friends in comfortable, relaxed situations. Typically, these tasks relate to life skills or areas of personal interest. A balanced assessment system solicits this information from students, parents, and caregivers.

5. *Assessment engages learners, teachers, and parents collaboratively.* Students are encouraged to take responsibility for their own learning. They set goals and make learning decisions with parents and teachers, who share responsibility for guiding learning. Students examine examples of quality work and assess their own performance against those examples. Students are involved in communicating their status and progress toward learning standards.

6. *Assessment is based on accepted developmental standards.* These standards may be site, district, region, or state based, or any combination of these. What counts is students' achievement of competency defined by established standards. Teaching, assessment, and learning are focused on this goal for *all* learners.

7. *Assessment encourages teachers, learners, parents, and administrators to take ownership of the performance of learners and schools.* Assessment that is only *summative*—conducted at the end or after the fact—perpetuates an attitude of "Oh, well. Some got it; others didn't. Nevertheless, we'll move on to the next topic." Organic assessment calls for action! Everyone involved immediately responds to learners' confusions with fully supported targeted interventions, ensuring that all children are achieving in an *equal-opportunity* classroom.

8. *Assessment focuses on the whole person.* Learners' growth is displayed across physical, social, emotional, and cognitive domains that impact one another. Assessment measures progress in all areas as well as the degree of harmony among them.

Meeting Basic Human Needs

Meeting learners' basic human needs, in and out of school, is a prerequisite for establishing environments in which all growth can flourish. We all have an innate desire to satisfy five needs (Sagor 1993):

1. We need to feel *competent.*
2. We need to feel we *belong.*
3. We need to feel *useful.*
4. We need to feel *potent.*
5. We need to feel *optimistic.*

Imagine very young skiers gliding down a mountain slope, following an instructor like ducklings after their mother. These skiers are *competent* and they know it. All they have to do is look around to realize they are skiing like (and in some cases better than) the bigger people. Without poles, they maintain their balance, turn, and stop as directed. Their perseverance is truly amazing! They pop right up after falling, brush themselves off, and start again.

These tykes also identify themselves as members of the group, moving around on the slopes and in the lodge with an air of *belonging.* Tied closely to the confidence that comes with burgeoning competence, they position themselves as equals in the sport. They are *skiers,* not skiers in training. They also have the social conventions of the group well mastered. When paired in line to share a chair lift with an adult, they engage in conversation about the day, the condition of the slope, what's happening below. They coach and direct stragglers, usually mimicking feedback they've heard from the instructor. The older ones buddy-up with first-timers, extending personal guidance and encouragement. They take this self-appointed role seriously and feel *useful.*

These young skiers also understand that the power to improve lies within them. They know they just have to keep skiing with attention to the forms they've been taught and they'll get better. Understanding the inextricable relationship between effort and success contributes to the sense of *potency* they display.

With the first four needs met, it's no wonder they are *optimistic* about their future as skiers. They already have their sights on downhill races and mogul jumping!

You're probably wondering what these needs have to do with a system for assessing learning in school. *Everything.* When these needs are met, learning in school can be just as successful as learning outside it.

An assessment system that continuously documents what learners *can do* recognizes competence, even in small steps. Repeating *I think you can* makes learners internalize an *I know I can* attitude. Documenting individual accomplishments also allows learners to approach each day with a personal record of competence.

Students regularly deemed competent with shared objectives, goals, and/or learning standards acquire a sense of belonging to the group of successful learners who *can* and *do.* Ongoing assessment maintains a focus on these expected outcomes while recording steps toward them. Teachers' public displays of respect for diverse ways of knowing and showing further increase children's feelings of acceptance by the group; they feel part of a classroom community. Just as tyro skiers are members of the community of skiers, students can belong to the learners club well before they've achieved all the standards.

A variety of activities, tasks, and grouping formats are typically found in learning communities. Everyone's a teacher; everyone's a learner. Children feel useful when they support one another's efforts. Documented markers of their peers' success—ones directly related to assistance, coaching, or credible feedback they've provided—are powerful reinforcements of their usefulness and capacity for caring.

Learners who've discovered that effort determines success are more likely to persist because they know they'll prevail. They see small increments, accrued daily, add up as they're recorded in an assessment system that pays attention to the little things. It's like watching your savings account grow with small additions: the total is growing, and you made it happen! Knowing they hold the key to personal achievement creates a sense of potency that helps learners rebound from failed attempts rather than be discouraged by them.

People who use mistakes as opportunities for learning are usually optimistic. Systems of continuous assessment regard mistakes in the same light. Learners are encouraged to reflect on their performances, identify strengths and needs collaboratively, use the supports provided, and take responsibility for their own success. In this atmosphere, it's natural for learners to be optimistic that the sum of day-to-day progress will be achievement.

Teaching or Testing?

The assessment described in this text looks more like teaching and less like testing because it *is* more like teaching—good teaching. It's *dynamic teaching*, teaching that actively adjusts to meet assessed changes in student performance as learning is mediated. This kind of assessment produces success while gathering evidence of it.

Recognizing Developmental Changes

Assessment isn't just about making the grade, getting it right, or achieving the standards. If that were all that was important, students could master testing techniques and then forget about the information they'd gained and the skills they'd practiced. Assessment is meant to be diagnostic. It's about discovering where you're strong, so-so, confused, and just don't get it. This requires detailed analysis. But if the analysis sits on the shelf instead of provoking development, the process was an exercise in futility.

Assessments should be about determining how well we apply knowledge and skills to real-life tasks the world will expect us to perform. This gives relevance and *authenticity* to the learning *and* the assessment. It also motivates learners to participate.

Assessment Versus Evaluation

Typically, the terms *assessment* and *evaluation* are used in ways that create the misunderstanding that they are synonymous. There is a definite difference. Each identifies a specific procedure.

Assessment is the process of *gathering evidence* of learning. Although the nature and bulk of this evidence varies from situation to situation, the importance of each piece is in its contribution to a distinct, whole picture of the learner's achievement and/or growth (Hanna

and Dettmer 2004). Educators frequently refer to certain planned activities as *assessments* because they intend to gather data about students' learning from them. The semantics involved may seem trivial, but it can be confusing.

At times, teachers are called on to act as *expert witness*, providing testimony of a learner's progress to date. To respond accurately, teachers review the data collected, reflect on it as appropriate, and develop conclusions. They place a value on the data. This may be expressed as a grade, a comment, or a narrative. This process of *placing a tentative value on the data* collected through assessment is called *evaluation* (Hanna and Dettmer 2004). Marie Clay (1987) stresses the importance of day-to-day assessment: "Yet a funny thing happens on the way to those final assessments: day-to-day learning takes place. I am certain that, in education, evaluation needs to pay more attention to the systematic observation of learners who are on their way to those final assessments" (1).

Characteristics of Authentic Assessment

Standardized achievement tests give us a general view of school, district, or state educational effectiveness (Edwards 2002). They are not effective diagnostic tools for individual achievement, since they cannot provide enough items on any discrete concept or skill. That's not their purpose. Standardized achievement tests are designed to test in efficient and cost-effective ways. Test formats and procedures may not always align with the procedures used in the classroom (or in the world) to demonstrate a particular competency. If taken alone, standardized achievement tests give a one-dimensional view of the learner at best. For some, these tests present a misleading indicator of one's present level of achievement.

Authentic means "genuine, real; entitled to acceptance or belief because of agreement with known facts or experience" (*Webster's* 1996, 139). When describing assessment, authentic "is usually intended to suggest that the performances being assessed are important in the real world and that they are highly contextualized" (Kane, Crooks, and Cohen 1999, 7). Thus the term *authentic assessment* identifies the process of gathering data related to students' learning *while* they engage in day-to-day activities (Hanna and Dettmer 2004). These real-life activities occur in students' natural environments both in and out of the classroom. Examples include

► social interchanges
► group discussions
► cooperative work
► student questions
► written and oral responses
► creative work (e.g., art or music)
► recreation (e.g., on the playground)
► activity at home or in the neighborhood
► general interpersonal skills (Spinelli 2002)

In this way, assessment is integrated with curriculum; it's conducted as students engage in classroom activities rather than something constructed apart from them. The instructionally integrative aspect of assessment *for* learning is reiterated throughout this book in order to draw attention to where and how it occurs. Efficient routines, recording tools, and class-room organizational schemes are critical. Otherwise, we *drown in the data!*

Assessment *of Learning and* Assessment *for Learning*

Stiggins (2002) suggests that we must focus more on classroom assessment if we intend to maximize student achievement. Standardized achievement measures provide assessments *of* learning that report *overall* student achievement. That's important to know. Comparing a student's score with an *average* measure of achievement gives an indication of the learner's status among peers or age-mates. It's like weighing a child. With a measure of total pounds, one can determine whether a child's current weight is appropriate for his height and age, assuming the chart reporting appropriate weight is valid. But that single fact doesn't help one make decisions about how to maintain his healthy weight or how to help him gain or lose weight if there's a problem.

On the other hand, authentic classroom measures provide ongoing assessment *for* learning. While once-a-year standardized achievement tests fall short in providing the kind of diagnostic information that teachers need to make instructional decisions, classroom assessments yield information that can be used to refine lesson objectives and instructional practices *on the spot.* Such instructional flexibility leads to increased learning and achievement. Teachers assess *for* learning when they

► have a clear understanding (in advance) of intended learning goals and objectives

► tell students what the learning goals and objectives are, in terms they can understand

► know how to construct and assess learning activities that yield rich assessment data

► incorporate assessment information into descriptive feedback, increasing students' understanding of the learning process as well as their self-confidence, sense of personal control, and willingness to take responsibility for learning

▶ teach diagnostically, adjusting goals, objectives, methods, and/or materials based on findings from ongoing assessment

▶ teach students to assess themselves, initiating a metacognitive process that will become a valuable life skill

▶ develop students' ability to articulate their current level of knowing, their current level of achievement, and their plans for further learning (Stiggins 2002)

In other words, assessment *for* learning is embedded in teachers' professional disposition and practices. It's revealed through behavior that reflects their beliefs and instructional methods.

A meta-analysis of literature on assessment by Black and Wiliam (1998) found that students in classrooms using effective formative assessments had higher achievement scores on summative assessments (e.g., standardized achievement tests). Formative assessments in these studies were typically ongoing and used in the process of teaching and learning, while the summative assessments were measures used to *sum up* what students had learned. Black and Wiliam also found that formative assessment helped low achievers more than other students, thus lessening the gap while raising achievement overall. Students' motivation to persist at learning also increased. Students had a clear vision of what they could do and needed to do and understood how they could close the distance between these two levels of achievement.

These findings deserve considerable attention. With increased pressure for *accountability*, defined as students' successful performance on high-stakes tests, assessment systems *for* learning offer educators a means to meet the challenge—a process that is based on sound teaching practice rather than rote *teaching to the test*. The key is balance.

Assessment That Informs Instruction

Assessment information that sits in a file is of limited value. Standardized, once-a-year measures usually meet this fate. The results from such measures have been used to assess overall program effectiveness within and across sites and they've been used with other formal measures to make decisions about individual students. They rarely, however, help the classroom teacher, resource teacher, administrator, parent, or learner know *precisely* what to do to improve learning. Educators can devise ways to improve scores, but that's not always the same as improving students' learning.

To help learners *catch on and catch up* as expeditiously as possible, the point of cognitive (learning) confusion must be identified, along with the best match of method and materials for teaching and learning with particular students. The process of assessment for learning is cyclical, forming a *closed loop* that turns forward for the most part. However, learning may be *recursive* (one step backward and two steps forward) at times, particularly when the material is difficult; the pace may need to be adjusted. Feedback from the teacher, matched with students' knowledge of their own learning processes, minimizes discouragement and the urge to throw in the towel.

CARP: *The Feedback Loop*

The assessment cycle includes the following steps: collect data, analyze data, report data, and plan instruction based on data findings (Stiggins 2001; see Figure 1-1). Again, these aren't lockstep stages. Recursive movement is highly encouraged. For example, suppose you're analyzing data and realize you don't have enough information to be confident of your diagnosis. Simply collect more information (perhaps using a different type of task that

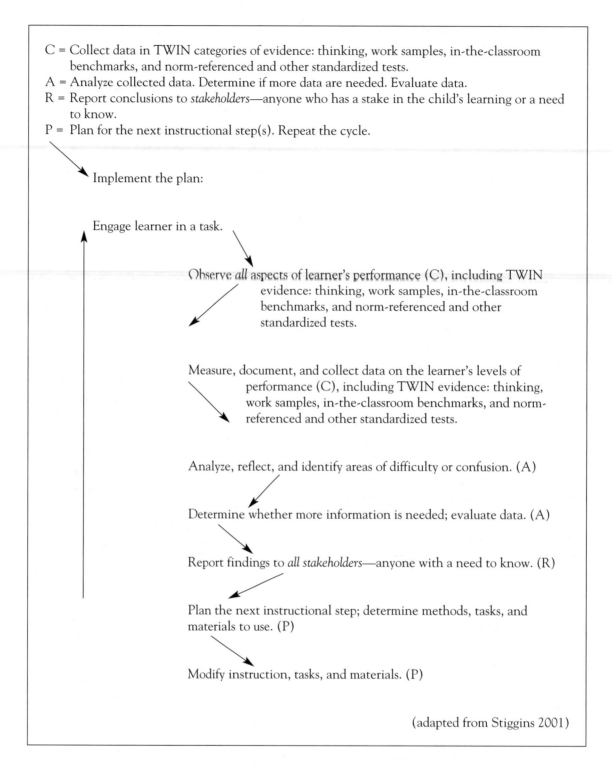

C = Collect data in TWIN categories of evidence: thinking, work samples, in-the-classroom benchmarks, and norm-referenced and other standardized tests.
A = Analyze collected data. Determine if more data are needed. Evaluate data.
R = Report conclusions to *stakeholders*—anyone who has a stake in the child's learning or a need to know.
P = Plan for the next instructional step(s). Repeat the cycle.

Implement the plan:

Engage learner in a task.

Observe *all* aspects of learner's performance (C), including TWIN evidence: thinking, work samples, in-the-classroom benchmarks, and norm-referenced and other standardized tests.

Measure, document, and collect data on the learner's levels of performance (C), including TWIN evidence: thinking, work samples, in-the-classroom benchmarks, and norm-referenced and other standardized tests.

Analyze, reflect, and identify areas of difficulty or confusion. (A)

Determine whether more information is needed; evaluate data. (A)

Report findings to *all stakeholders*—anyone with a need to know. (R)

Plan the next instructional step; determine methods, tasks, and materials to use. (P)

Modify instruction, tasks, and materials. (P)

(adapted from Stiggins 2001)

FIGURE 1–1   The Feedback Loop: CARP

requires the same skills) and then return to analysis.

The feedback loop is a central and critical feature in an assessment *system*, which includes integrated and interdependent elements that cohere to form a complex whole rather than a random collection of assessment pieces (Coladarci 2002). As teachers and learners act on the information gained from assessment, set new instructional and learning goals, work together on these areas, and continuously gather further data on the success of their efforts, learning moves steadily forward. Each assessment piece in the system should be relevant to identified learning goals.

Assessments in the system also reflect multiple formats for assessing students' knowledge, skills, and dispositions. Format types include but are not limited to

▶ selected responses
▶ constructed responses
▶ performance tasks
▶ projects
▶ presentations
▶ personal communication

Certain formats are more effective than others in securing assessment information, depending on the particular learning goals being mastered. Such goals are typically aligned with state learning standards associated with students' knowledge mastery, reasoning proficiency, performance skills, and ability to create products.

Collecting Data in TWIN Categories

Data is collected as students engage in day-to-day learning activities and from products (artifacts) they create based on the learning that has occurred. Data may be collected using a variety of tools, such as anecdotal notes (notes briefly summarizing observed behavior), checklists, scoring rubrics, local (criterion) tests, and running records. Many forms of data, derived from different kinds of tasks revealing similar skills and/or competencies, are collected to provide a full and complete *body of evidence*.

The data collected are organized into four categories: thinking evidence, work samples, in-the-classroom benchmarks, and norm-referenced and other standardized achievement tests (hence the acronym *TWIN*). Each piece of evidence is studied systematically.

Analyzing Data

The teacher spreads out the collected data and evaluates the patterns and details found there. Students are often part of this process, collaborating on the identification of success, sources of confusion, and the best next step. Sometimes, however, the teacher analyzes data independently. This is a thoughtful and reasoned process. Little things—nuances of changed behavior—are not overlooked, for, compiled over time, they form a pattern that documents growth. Teachers use the conclusions to plan the next best steps in the teaching and learning process. Thus, assessments fuel the instructional planning process, streamlining teaching to objectives that are relevant to the learner's place on a continuum of achievement. What's taught is what's needed, and that's not always the next lesson in the teacher's manual.

Reporting Data

Sharing data with others that have a stake in the achievement the data measure invites the airing of multiple points of view. Important others include students, parents, colleagues, administrators, resource personnel, the board of education, and the community. Sharing can be generative, leading to new insights and ideas. The information in the report must be efficiently presented, clear, concise, and error free. Narratives should also be reader friendly, using language that increases understanding rather than jargon that tends to confuse and silence those for whom it is unfamiliar. Reports should flow smoothly to *everyone* involved with the learning and the learner.

Planning How to Use Data

Unused collections of data—piles of *stuff*—and reports gathering dust are monuments to time wasted on meaningless tasks. Teachers and students respond in very natural and predictable ways when faced with data that do not serve an apparent and useful function: they ignore them and choose not to collect them in the future. Therefore, a meaningful plan must be in place *before* teaching and learning interactions begin—a plan that defines what information will be collected, how it will be collected, how it will be analyzed, and how it will be used to help the learner grow. Information gathered from assessments for learning *informs* teachers and students, helping them set purposeful objectives for a best next step in any learning sequence.

Schoolwide Assessment Continuity

Schools have invested large sums of money in standardized achievement tests for assessment *of* learning in order to meet state and federal requirements. Insufficient dollars have been allocated for teacher training in assessment *for* learning. Yet standards of teacher competence developed separately by the National Education Association (NEA), the American Federation of Teachers (AFT), the National Council for the Accreditation of Teacher Education (NCATE), and other professional organizations hold the expectation that teachers will be competent in assessment (Wise 1996). Stiggins (1999b) reports that fifteen states have teacher certification standards that require competence in assessment, ten states explicitly require assessment course work for certification, and the remaining twenty-five states hold no expectation of teacher competence in assessment. For learners' sake, assessment competence should be a universal expectation for teachers to ensure continuity, quality, and equity in instructional programs. State certification requirements should reflect that expectation, as well as require districts to schedule sessions for the continuous upgrading of teachers' assessment skills in their staff development plans. Maybe some dollars need to be reallocated from the testing budget in order to fund training in assessment for learning!

Without teachers' *skillful* application of each component of the local assessment system, student progress could easily be mismeasured. Ongoing instructional decisions would be built on misinformation, causing an array of problems and inhibiting progress (Stiggins 2002). If students' learning is mismeasured,

▶ their *real* needs might go unnoticed;

▶ they'll be inappropriately grouped and receive inappropriate instruction; and

▶ most problematic, they'll discern failure when they didn't fail or success when they didn't actually perform well. (Stiggins 1999a)

Some worry that teachers' assessment of students is too time-consuming, that teachers could spend as much as one-third of their instructional time in assessment-related activities or thinking (Crooks 1988; Stiggins and Conklin 1992). Skillful assessment does take time, but it doesn't take time away from teaching. The assessment system described in this book is a critical component of good teaching; it guides and improves it. However, being able to use assessment for on-target teaching requires more than taking a course and passing an exam. Teachers must understand basic tenets related to student assessment if they are to avoid the pitfalls of mismeasurement.

The assessment principles described in the introduction are a beginning, and additional principles are offered throughout the remaining chapters. Among many points that must be considered in the context of schoolwide assessment, teachers need to know the following:

▶ Different *stakeholders* (i.e., students, parents, administrators, community) need different information about student achievement. They also need the information in different forms.

▶ Different forms of achievement must be assessed with different methods. Teachers must know how to select the most appropriate assessment method, how to apply that method, and how to analyze the results accurately.

▶ Bias can creep into assessment. Teachers need to be able to recognize bias and ensure that it does not distort the assessment data. (Stiggins 1999b)

Stiggins (1999b) suggests a strategy for developing schoolwide professional expertise on assessment for learning. His plan includes three elements, in the following proportions:

▶ workshops that build interest and knowledge (10 percent)

▶ team meetings in which professionals share what they've learned about students' learning and the assessment process (25 percent)

▶ individual study, practice in the classroom, and reflection on *what works* in *each particular* classroom (65 percent)

Each facet in this plan for professional development has strengths and limitations. Blending them in the prescribed proportions increases the chances that individual classroom and schoolwide assessment competence will grow steadily and exponentially.

Workshops and Staff Development

Outside experts help professionals create a research-based, pedagogically sound local culture of assessment for learning. As a culture, each locally designed assessment system will have its own characteristic rituals and traditions while adhering to overarching principles of effective instruction. One-shot visiting expert presentations are typically ineffective when they lack planned follow-through. To avoid such pontificate-and-run staff development, experts can be retained as consultants, offering periodic maintenance and/or debriefing sessions as teachers put practices in place. Sometimes, particular teachers are designated as *turnkey* trainers. They receive more intensive training (e.g., at professional conferences) and then present this information to their colleagues, acting as mentors and leaders.

Learning Teams

Within the school, teams of teachers work together to put the assessment system in place and use it effectively. Colleagues consult and support one another. Since collective intelligence is always more insightful than individual intelligence, teamwork helps teachers work through anomalies (e.g., a student's uncharacteristic misunderstanding) that at first seem mystifying.

A team can critically discuss topics, journal articles, and issues related to assessment, broadening everyone's knowledge and taking each individual to new levels of expertise.

Individual Study

Teachers spend time in solitary study of assessment as a process, using current professional resources. They also closely examine assessment data gathered on individual learners in their class. Integrated conclusions based on this reflection prepare teachers to articulate reason-based ideas and ask the right kinds of questions.

Are They Learning?

Mary Shea remembers the way she used to prepare for a final exam in history:

I literally filled my mind to overflowing with facts, dates, and names of important people in the days before the test, which covered a semester's worth of work. Although I performed well, I hadn't learned much, since most of the information flowed quickly out again once the test was over. My mind was a temporary holding pen for information until I could walk away from the assessment and the course. I hadn't become interested in the topics, nor did I appreciate their significance to my current experience. My performance on the test after memorizing information *looked like* learning, but it was *veneer* learning. It looked good when it was new. However, it quickly began to flake off, leaving gaping spaces.

Several years later, I had a history teacher who sparked curiosity about historical figures and events by sharing *gossipy* details. I was hearing, in Paul Harvey's words, "the rest of the story." I completed required and even suggested readings for this class and looked forward to lectures and class discussions. More important, I learned that history is a *story* about people and societies. From then to now, I have enjoyed reading biographies as well as historical fiction. I began to *learn* and *appreciate* history in that class and continue to do so.

This is *real* learning—learning that includes personally constructed knowledge and a positive disposition toward the subject.

Real learning causes *change*. This may be reflected in internalized knowledge or skills as well as in a newly developed (or enhanced) positive attitude toward the topic. Change like this doesn't easily evaporate. It may become dormant without use but can be awakened when stimulated. Real learning is about becoming—it's about the "changes or moves that people make from what they are to what they come to be" (Goodman, Goodman, and Hood 1989, 3). The journey of becoming is one that the learner willfully pursues (Kohl 1994).

Students are in control of real learning. They choose to learn or not to learn based on their disposition toward the topic and/or the environment. Students can be coerced to perform well on a test, but *real* learning is a personal choice. "Learning to not-learn is an intellectual and social challenge; sometimes you have to work very hard at it. It consists of an active, often ingenious, willful rejection of even the most compassionate and well-designed teaching" (Kohl 1994, 2).

How can we determine if students' learning is real?

Tests sample knowing from a body of information on a topic and hardly, if at all, measure attitudes and motivation related to that topic. Tests typically sample students' ability to mirror test makers' inferences and conclusions. Tests are quick and convenient but not thorough and sensitive to *individual ways of knowing and showing*. The danger is that they create a veneer.

Student performance data from the classroom compiled over time by way of an array of situations and tasks present a clearer picture of real learning. When classroom focus is on real learning, assessment data reveal where children fall along several developmental continuums. The data also uncover learners' idiosyncratic approaches to learning, interests, and personalities. With such *actionable intelligence* (usable information), teachers can differentiate instruction, materials, and response tasks appropriately, ensuring equal-opportunity learning for all children.

What Assessment Data Should We Collect?

An open mind is critical when designing the evaluation portion of a lesson plan. We cannot set out with an objective for every bit of assessment data the lesson could generate. Often, students' "aha"s come unexpectedly. Something from a previous lesson may have just made sense to them, or they may have caught a spark of interest or enthusiasm. Such signs of learning *must* be noted. Some teachers insist that you can't evaluate that which was not first established as an objective! That's what they were taught. But why would you ever overlook evidence of learning milestones that you didn't plan for? Does a detective overlook unexpected clues or leads? Does a parent overlook new behavior or skills demonstrated by a child because they weren't anticipated? Each encounter with the learner offers rich data about her level of learning. The key is to recognize what is significant evidence, however small, and then to have an efficient method for collecting and storing the data.

This process of gathering bits of information that answer the question *Are they really learning?* is assessment (Burns, Roe, and Ross 1999; Cooper 1997; Hancock, Turbill, and Cambourne 1994). It takes place during teaching and learning rather than after it. The purpose of assessment should be the ongoing improvement of instruction for *all* students rather than merely an accounting of where they fall on a comparative scale of perfor-

mances (Assessment Reform Group 1999; Shepard 2000). Effective assessment emphasizes progress rather than merely success or failure in reaching a milestone (Stiggins 2001). Effective documentation of progress (however small the steps forward) requires a persistent focus on students as they go about learning. Teachers, parents, and learners themselves are in the best position to engage in this kind of prolonged observation that leads to a collection of complex, varied data.

Although ways of generating assessment data differ in process, purpose, and product, both quantitative and qualitative approaches can be used efficiently. Quantitative approaches (e.g., tests) have traditionally been rated as more objective, reliable, and valid. However, qualitative approaches (e.g., interviews and observations) also provide trustworthy data when used in connection with well-designed methods of collecting, analyzing, and interpreting the information (Middle States Commission on Higher Education 2002). With each bit of evidence that appears to be significant, the teacher and/or learner asks, "Why am I doing (gathering) this?"

How Should We Collect and Evaluate It?

When the response to *Why am I doing this?* passes the litmus test of our beliefs, we move on to consider the most appropriate procedure for data collecting and representation (Pikulski 1994). Such reflection and decision making in individual classrooms is essential for genuine assessment that leads to an accurate evaluation of individual student learning and efficient plans for further instruction. Those directly involved in the moment-to-moment assessment for learning, particularly teachers and students, are the most important instruments in a process that considers multiple evidences of learning (Johnston 1992b; Paris et al. 1992; Winograd, Paris, and Bridge 1991). Decisions should flow from basic questions.

Atkins, Black, and Coffey (2001) outline three questions that learners ask as they continuously assess their own progress with support from teachers and others:

▶ *Where am I trying to go?* The target goals must be clear and perceived as worthwhile and attainable.

▶ *Where am I now?* Students analyze their work, comparing it with defined criteria and high-quality examples. They determine the progress they've made and the journey still ahead. They also identify the conditions under which they learn best (Chappuis and Stiggins 2002).

▶ *How do I close the gap* (between where I'm trying to go and where I am now)? Students establish a workable plan for the next learning step. The action plan focuses on instructional changes, sources for help, and materials to be used.

When the information collected in this question-and-answer process is accurate, complete, and varied, sound decision making is more likely to occur—decision making that leads to notable achievement over time.

Multiple pieces of data, collected over time and via different types of tasks that address similar knowledge, skills, or dispositions, offer *triangulated* evidence of growth. This means that an evaluation of learning is based on multiple (at least three) pieces of assessment data (Eisner 1998; Jimerson and Kaufman 2003). Eisner outlines eight criteria for appropriate assessment of real learning (ongoing development of skills and knowledge that have relevance in learners' lives):

1. Tasks used to assess students' knowing should parallel those they will encounter in the world outside schools. Skills needed for success outside school should not be so different from those needed for success in school.
2. Tasks used for assessment should reveal what and how students think as they solve problems rather than simply focus on the solutions they reach.

3. Assessment tasks should complement the pedagogical theory from which they are derived. Valencia, Heibert, and Afflerbach (1994) point out that assessment and evaluation systems used in classrooms should lead to optimal learning for all; inform instruction; and be accurate, valid, reliable, rigorous, and perceived as trustworthy.
4. Assessment tasks don't have to be solo performances. Other working formats (e.g., dyads, triads, small groups) provide information on students' ability to contribute to a team effort as well as their growing sense of responsibility for team success.
5. Assessment tasks should allow for a number of acceptable responses. Learners are encouraged to think divergently—creatively, logically, out of the box—rather than converge on a singular correct answer. Such creative thinking reflects students' development as synthesizers of information and their ability to construct more complex wholes from seemingly disparate bits of information.
6. Assessment tasks should have curricular relevance. Asa Hilliard (1989) notes that assessments should have *content validity* and *instructional utility*. They should provide information that can be used to modify, refine, or expand instruction, helping students close the developmental gap between their targets and where they are.
7. Assessment tasks should require students to demonstrate an understanding of wholes rather than merely discrete elements. For example, successful literacy performances would reflect growth in reading continuous text with deep understanding, not merely fluency with isolated subskills.
8. Assessment tasks should allow learners a choice of formats for representing their knowing and progress. Development is reflected in an array of performance formats that match students' interest and strengths.

Meeting these principles for effectively collecting data, making decisions, and documenting achievement is a daunting but conquerable challenge. Instructional plans must ensure that there will be appropriate data to collect. Teachers and students must be prepared to gather this data systematically, organize it efficiently, and analyze it collaboratively in the process of evaluating overall learning and development and making instructional decisions.

How Should We Organize and Preserve All This Data?

In *A House Is a House for Me*, Mary Ann Hoberman (1982) creatively identifies the houses of creatures around us: "A web is a house for a spider" (3); "A dock or a slip is a house for a ship" (15); "A husk is a house for a corn ear" (17); "And pens can be houses for ink" (31). Following this line of thinking, a portfolio is a house for evidence—a repository for students' thinking, expressions of knowing, projects, and benchmarks that reflect ongoing development and learning. This includes data related to cognitive areas and also to affective areas that may otherwise go unnoticed (Valencia, Heibert, and Afflerbach 1994). In the same way that an organized house makes day-to-day living more comfortable, an organized portfolio facilitates assessment and evaluation. Having a system for ordering *stuff* in this portfolio house is essential or learners and teachers will drown in frustration.

Using Portfolios

A group of teachers in one elementary school, with the support and assistance of their principal, had their students use portfolios to set goals, monitor progress toward those goals, and determine what they must do to improve. The portfolios helped their students analyze work deeply for strengths and weaknesses rather than merely for surface correctness (Farr and Tone 1998).

This team wanted to fine-tune their portfolio use in order to be confident that students' portfolios

▶ included a systematic, purposeful, and meaningful collection of student work

▶ allowed students of all ages to select appropriate pieces for the portfolio and give reasons for those selections

▶ included input from anyone who had a stake in the student's achievement: the learner, the teacher, parent(s) or guardian(s), and administrators

▶ included day-to-day information on students' learning

▶ reflected an ongoing collection of relevant data that described students' efforts, progress, and learning over time

▶ include work accomplished using a variety of media (DeFina 1992)

The classrooms in this school used two kinds of portfolios; each served a distinct function in the total assessment process. One was a *showcase portfolio*, which went home with students at the end of the school year. The other was a *passport portfolio*, which followed the learner into the next year's classroom.

Showcase Portfolios

A showcase portfolio is mainly student controlled. While teachers establish appropriate criteria, provide models of exemplary work, and support learners' efforts to improve, students are expected to take responsibility for their own learning (DeFina 1992). Such meaningful involvement throughout the assessment process builds students' commitment to self-directed, lifelong learning (Johnston 1992a).

Students in our example school selected work that showed something significant about their progress. Samples could come from any area of the curriculum, special classes, or work done outside school. Students prepared a reflection sheet telling why they had included each portfolio submission. Sometimes these reflections were more significant than the work samples, because of the insights they revealed about learners' metacognitive processes (DeFina 1992). Students expressed what they understood about themselves as learners. They stated their personal reactions to what they were learning, how they were learning, and why they were learning. A context of shared responsibility developed—a context in which the students could make decisions about their learning (Valencia, Heibert, and Afflerbach 1994).

Most classrooms in this school used individual hanging folders, kept in a wire rack with wheels, for their showcase portfolios. This portfolio cache moved easily around the room and was readily available for showing off to visitors. Routinely, teachers had conferences with students to review what they'd placed in their showcase portfolios and to discuss their overall learning during that period of time. They used questions like these to focus their discussion:

▶ What change in your learning does this work show?
▶ Why do you think this change occurred?
▶ What further changes will you be working on?
▶ How do you plan to make those changes?
▶ What was hardest for you during this period of time?
▶ What was easiest for you during this period of time? (Johnston 1992a)

Through analysis and negotiation, the teacher and learner considered which, if any, pieces of evidence should be moved to the passport portfolio.

Passport Portfolios

The passport portfolios followed students from grade to grade, introducing them to their new teachers and describing developmental milestones they'd reached. The milestones were related to a learning continuum identified at the district or state level and based on accepted theory related to children's cognitive, social, and emotional growth. They were housed in a more secure location (a file cabinet) but were not *classified* material (for teachers' eyes only).

The teacher scheduled one-on-one passport portfolio conferences at least four times a year. At the conference, the teacher acted as a coach, playing a critical role in developing students' skill in assessing their own strengths, needs, interests, and overall performances (Farr and Tone 1998). Students and the teacher considered

▶ what had been collected
▶ whether the student had additional evidence ready to be included
▶ areas that needed evidence to support achievement
▶ goals or next steps for further learning

Additional analysis and reflection determined a focus for ongoing instruction and learning, making connections between evidenced achievement and appropriate next learning steps in the classroom—and in the world.

This ongoing cycle—collect work, write a reflection, analyze data, select significant evidence, and make connections with learning goals—is an essential part of effective portfolio assessment in any arena (Epstein 2003).

A Universal Classroom Model

Although relatively new to the classroom, portfolios have been used for a long time to showcase work in other fields. Some benefits are obvious while others become apparent as coach and student come to understand each other and the learning that has occurred. As one third grader said, "Your portfolio shows you how much you have improved. You can compare your papers and see what has improved" (Clemmons et al. 1993, 14).

Effectively conducted portfolio assessment

▶ stimulates reflection on performances
▶ increases learners' motivation to reach goals
▶ helps learners take control and accept responsibility for learning
▶ creates a climate of trust in which teacher and learners assess work together

▶ emphasizes the principle of learning as a continuous process

▶ involves others in the learning community in the process

▶ promotes learners' self-esteem

▶ emphasizes the *process* of learning as well as products (Clemmons et al. 1993)

To ensure that the process yields actionable results, teachers need to have well-defined routines and procedures in place and follow them. They need to systematically and categorically organize data in ways that allow patterns to be revealed.

Categories for Organizing Information in a Passport Portfolio

Useful portfolios contain several compartments, organizing work for clearer analysis (DeFina 1992). In regard to our metaphor, this means a passport portfolio house has *rooms* that serve different purposes. One holds evidence or data that reflect students' thinking. In another, students organize work samples that show growth. A room for in-the-classroom-benchmarks highlights achievement on long-term curricular topics: unit tests, projects, or major presentations of work; they are often culminating events in a unit of study. A fourth room displays data from norm-referenced and other standardized achievement tests. The evidence within these rooms must be arranged and well labeled or it will be mislaid, disregarded, or lost.

Thinking Evidence

Thinking evidence is accumulated bits of information that are windows into learners' minds, revealing thinking, wondering, and connections under construction. The evidence is representational. Although it seems like a crazy quilt at first, patterns slowly emerge as teachers and students consistently collect, organize, and reflect on data. Missing pieces or sparse areas become obvious, helping teachers and students refine learning goals and set new ones. Henson and Gilles (2003) propose that along with documenting stu-

dents' thinking related to curricular topics, we need to determine what they believe about themselves as learners, their level of trust for teachers and school, and their comfort with risk taking.

Where do we find evidence of thinking? Sometimes in students' direct expressions of what's on their minds. At other times, their thinking may be inferred from their conversations, behavior, body language, or drawings. Different tools and different purposes are needed to capture data accurately and efficiently. For example, teachers can

▶ take anecdotal notes on learning "aha"s

▶ make careful note of areas covered in conferences

▶ support or reference checklists with evidence from students' oral or written performances

▶ have cooperative group members complete *exit reporting sheets* outlining the thinking behind their conclusions

Figure 2–1 is a reporting sheet in which fifth graders Kelly, Brad, Nick, and Heather outlined the conclusions drawn by their literature study group. They inferred character traits for White Fang and expressed their surprise that White Fang's mother forgot him. Figure 2–2 shows a teacher's anecdotal notes on Donald, a hearing-impaired first grader who did not always use his hearing aids at home. Initially, his participation in group and individual activities was sporadic and inconsistent. Over time he demonstrated an interest in specific activities and materials. Figure 2–3 is a checklist used by a sixth-grade science teacher to note students' application of established discourse criteria during group and class discussions. Criteria changed as the teacher emphasized other discourse skills. The teacher explained to students the expectations and complimented them when they demonstrated these skills.

Thinking evidence is discussed in more detail in Chapter 3, which includes additional

---

Literature Study Group

Date: 4/2

Book: *White Fang*

Names: Kelley, Brad, Nick, Heather

Recorder: Heather

Summary of Group's Discussion:

We were surprised that White Fang's mother forgot him. They ate together, slept together and even fought together. BUT she forgot him.

We told Nick who the gods were. He was confused. We were trying to figure out what kind of a wolf White Fang is. We think he's a good citizen but he's a bully too. But, he's respectful and follows the laws too. The part we liked was when White Fang's mother didn't know him. That made the book interesting because we wonder why the writer did this.

Self Check: Did you...?
✓ read journals
✓ summarize
✓ question, predict, respond
✓ clarify, make connections to real life, to other books

FIGURE 2–1   A Group's Discussion Summary

examples. However, different and perhaps even richer displays of thinking are happening in your classroom every day. Identify and record them. Capture the moments!

Work Samples

Work samples are concrete *artifacts* of students' involvement in short-term, day-to-day learning activities. They include, but are not limited to, journal entries, writing pieces (from drafts to published works), drawings, and graphic organizers. Obviously many work samples have a dual value in that they also yield evidence of learners' thinking.

Figure 2–4 is first grader Sarah's journal entry responding to *Just a Mess*, by Mercer Mayer, which her teacher had read aloud. She included an analysis of the author's craft: "I like how he wanted to draw the pictures and thought about the words." She also made a personal connection: "I don't know a kid like Critter." The lines she drew after each type of response appropriately mark changes in paragraphs. Chapter 4 explores work sam-

2/1 Donald's beginning to interact w/ peers more spontaneously. He talked at his table about his weekend—going to a movie he liked

2/14 Donald excitedly contributed comments in our discussion of *Barn Dance*. He pointed out what he liked about the illustrations.

3/16 Donald identified endings s, ing, ed in words in today's news. He explained why s and ed were added.

3/26 Donald decided which group suggestions to use and revised his story. He made additions to it and said, "Now, it tells more."

4/4 Donald read 2 complete books during SSR. He was really on task! At sharing time he said he knew they'd be good because Billy said so.

4/12 Donald's running record showed increased self-correction for meaning — improved retelling too

FIGURE 2–2 Anecdotal Notes on Donald

ples as artifacts of students' learning in more detail and includes a variety of examples.

In-the-Classroom Benchmarks

In-the-classroom benchmarks measures assess learning across broader areas, like a unit of study. Publishers' or teacher-created tests are often used, but long-term projects can also assess achievement of unit goals and objectives when the criteria and expectations are rigorous and clearly defined. These projects can be done individually, with a partner, or

15

Discussion Checklist

Period 1
Dates 3/21 – 3/25

Name	Asked thinking questions	Gave support for ideas, conclusions, inferences	Extended and/or respectfully questioned responses of others	Thoughtful, creative interpretations	Co-operates with others	Respects opinions of others	Comments
Rebecca	✓✓✓✓		✓ Theory Debate		✓✓✓	✓ Debate	Outstanding in debate
Mark	✓ magma?	✓✓✓	✓✓	✓ magma convection	✓✓✓✓	✓✓✓✓	
Rudy		✓✓	✓	✓ Improving	✓✓✓		
Megan	✓✓	Presentation		✓✓✓✓			
Michelle	✓ Discussion leader				✓ Discussion Group	✓	Positive group discussions
Connor			✓ Theory Debate			✓ Debate	Outstanding in debate
Lucas	Plate Density?	✓		✓✓		✓	
Nicole	·		✓✓✓		✓	✓✓✓	Has stopped inturpting people
Brittany	✓✓✓	✓ Presentation		✓✓✓		✓	

Samantha	✓	✓	✓ Theory Debate	✓✓		✓ Debate	Outstanding in debate
Kelly	✓ Discussion leader	✓ Presentation		✓		✓✓✓	
John		✓✓	✓		✓ Improving	✓✓✓ Improving	Behavior Mods are helping somewhat
Robert	✓		✓			✓✓	Listening Improving
Nicholas		✓	✓ Quicksand			✓	
Bradley	✓ Growing Earth?		✓✓			✓✓✓	Starting to think much deeper
Jeremiah		✓		✓ Boiling Water		✓	
Alicia		✓ Presentation		✓✓	✓ Discussion Group	✓	Positive group discussions
Judd	✓				✓✓✓✓✓	✓✓✓✓✓	Listening Improving
Thomas	✓✓		✓ Theory Debate	✓		✓ Debate	Outstanding in debate
Kurt	✓	✓	✓	✓ Wagon	✓	✓	
Joseph	✓ Earth's Interior?		✓✓			✓	Asking deeper questions
Scott			✓ Helped Aaron		✓ Improving	✓✓✓	
Aaron	✓	✓ Essay Similar	✓	✓	✓	✓	
Desiree	✓ Discussion leader	✓				✓	

FIGURE 2–3 Discussion Checklist

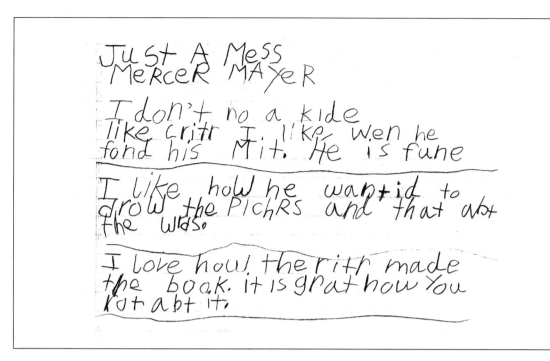

Just a Mess
MeRceR MAyeR

I don't no a kide
like critr I like wen he
fohd his Mit. He is fune

I like how he wantid to
drow the PichRs and that abt
the wlds.

I love how the rith made
the book. it is grat how you
rot abt it.

FIGURE 2–4 Sarah's Journal Response to *Just a Mess*

in groups. However, unless there is individual accountability for group members, problems quickly arise that erode the validity of scores for less engaged students. Rubrics, carefully designed to make criteria clear, can be used by the teacher, the students, and peers to eval-

A Student's Benchmark Presentation of Learning for
a Unit on the Rainforest

uate unit projects and/or presentations. The teacher can summarize resulting rankings for a final score.

Figure 2–5 is a student's proposal for a culminating project in a sixth-grade science class. Figure 2–6 is a page from the log for a group project. Figure 2–7 shows a graded rubric for a final project. Chapter 5 discusses in-the-classroom benchmarks in detail and includes additional examples. When the goal is to find a way for all students to demonstrate successfully what they've learned in a unit, culminating products—or any form of *final* assessment—must offer choice. Traditional one-size-fits-all final assessments pinch some and sag on others (Tomlinson 2001).

Norm-Referenced and Other Standardized Achievement Measures

Norm-referenced and other standardized achievement tests include both state and national measures used, sometimes by mandate, at the local level. Districts often contract with companies to machine-score

SCIENCE PROJECT PROPOSAL
DUE: APRIL 7

Name: _Connor_

Period: _2_

Please check one:

Model	___
Invention	___
Experiment	✓
Research Report	___

G O O D!
great!
OK for project
board.
_BB_

Catchy Title: _A Bright Idea; Solar Power;_

Brief explanation of what you plan to do:

I plan to make a car and include a solar panel. Then Test the design and solar panel with different types of light over a certain distance. Then record the results and calculate miles per hour. I will record my results on graphs. So on the most part I will calculate which type of light works best for the solar panel.

FIGURE 2–5   Student Proposal

national tests (like the Iowa Test of Basic Skills, for example). However, the essays on standardized achievement tests with constructed responses might be scored locally by trained raters. Student achievement on these measures is reported in raw scores, percentiles, stanines, scaled scores, or performance levels, depending on the type of test used.

Chapter 6 discusses norm-referenced and other standardized achievement tests in detail. The tests differ in some ways, but they're all *standardized achievement* measures, and in many states, very high stakes are attached to them. Across the country, test failure bodes serious consequences for teachers and learners.

Science Project Log Record

Project Title: One small step for man, one giant leap for mankind.
Name: Ana
Date Begun: 3/15   Date Finished: 5/24

DATE	WHERE	WHO	B/F TIMES	TOTAL TIME	COMPONENT WORKED ON
3/15/03	Library	Ana Martin	1:00 p.m to 1:30pm	30 min.	Internet Research
3/26/03 3/27/03	Uncle's House + Home	Lisa Zelazny + Ana martin	8:30 A.M to 9:00AM + 8:00 to 8:30pm	1 hour	Internet and telephone research for Extra Credit
3/29/03	Library	Ana Martin	2:15 to 3:15 p.m.	1 hour	Internet Research
3/29/03	Library	Ana Martin	3:15 pm to 3:45pm	30 min.	Gathering Resources (Book + Movies)
4/6/03	Home	Ana Martin	4:30 p.m. to 5:30 p.m	1 hour	Extra Credit Interview Questions
4/10/03	U.S. Post Office	Lisa Zelazny	12:00 p.m 12:05p.m	5 min.	Mail Extra Credit letter.
4/17/03	Computer at mom's work	Ana Martin	12:30 p.m to 12:45 p.m.	15 min.	Internet Research for model + Extra Credit
4/19/03	Paul's Teachers Pet	Lisa Z. + Ana M.	4:30 p.m. to 5:30pm	1 hour	Plan and Purchasing of materials
4/25/03	Uncle's House	Ana M. + Lisa Z.	1:45 p.m to 3:15 p.m.	1 hour + 30 min.	Internet research for lunar maps

FIGURE 2–6   Page from Science Log

Science Project Rubric

Project Title: __The Moon__

Name: __Ana__

Science Period: __4__

50/50
100%

POSSIBLE POINTS	POINTS RECEIVED	EXPERIMENTAL DESIGN
20-11		All required elements of the valid experimental design were followed.
10-1		Some required elements were missing from your valid experimental design.

POSSIBLE POINTS	POINTS RECEIVED	INVENTION
20-11		All required elements of the invention design were followed.
10-1		Some required elements were missing from your invention design.

POSSIBLE POINTS	POINTS RECEIVED	MODEL
20-11	20	All required elements of the model design were followed.
10-1		Some required elements were missing from your model design.

POSSIBLE POINTS	POINTS RECEIVED	RESEARCH REPORT
20-11		All required elements of the research report design were followed.
10-1		Some required elements were missing from your research report.

Excellent work Ana!
It's quite clear that you put in
a lot of hard work

FIGURE 2-7   Rubric

POSSIBLE POINTS	POINTS RECEIVED	PRESENTATION
15-13	15	Exemplary, confident presentation; proper and effective use of scientific vocabulary and terminology; complete understanding of topic.
12-10		Well-organized, clear presentation; appropriate use of scientific vocabulary and terminology; knowledge of topic.
9-7		Presentation acceptable; adequate use of scientific terms; acceptable understanding of topic.
6-4		Presentation lacks clarity and organization; little use of scientific terms and vocabulary; poor understanding of topic.
3-1		Poor presentation; cannot explain topic; scientific terminology lacking or confused; lacks understanding of topic.

POSSIBLE POINTS	POINTS RECEIVED	EXHIBIT
15-13	15	Highly appealing exhibit layout that is self-explanatory, and successfully incorporates a good sensory approach; creative and effective use of material.
12-10		Layout logical, concise, and easy to follow; materials used in exhibit appropriate and effective.
9-7		Acceptable layout of exhibit; materials used appropriately.
6-4		Organization of layout could be improved; better materials could have been chosen.
3-1		Layout lacks organization and is difficult to understand; poor and ineffective use of materials.

15-10	15	EXTRA CREDIT INTERVIEW

Averaged into 4th marking Period

Point Breakdown:

A= 46-50   B= 41-45   C= 36-40   D= 31-35

FIGURE 2–7   Continued

Evidence of Thinking

Only if we understand can we care. Only if we care will we help. Only if we help shall all be saved.

—JANE GOODALL

Effective teachers, in the manner of anthropologist and animal researcher Jane Goodall, carefully observe students in order to understand their behavior, patterns, interests, motivations, and changes. In other words, they are active *kid watchers* (Goodman 1986). Goodall's words could be adapted by teachers to say, *Only if we understand can we care. Only if we care can we teach effectively. Only if we teach effectively shall all learn to their fullest potential.* The first step, understanding, can be achieved only with focused observation and ongoing interactions characterized by genuine dialogue and critical listening.

Like the anthropologist, the effective teacher watches from afar and takes copious notes on what she observes. In quiet moments, these notes are examined for "aha"s—patterns that are obvious among lots of data but not as clear during the moments they're unfolding, when one can't see the forest for the trees. Once accepted into the subjects' community and recognized as a trusted member, the teacher can interact with them and observe their responses. It takes time, attention, efficient organization, and patience.

As children go about daily routines in the classroom, their behavior and responses reveal changes in their emotional, social, and cognitive development (Anthony et al. 1991). The teacher as anthropologist is persistent

in following hunches based on accumulated observed behavior. A combination of professional training and opportunity leads to effective assessment for informed instructional practice.

What Constitutes Evidence of Thinking?

Thinking is a covert mental activity that is revealed only when it's openly demonstrated. *Evidence* of that thinking can be gathered as learners reveal what is going on in their minds—expressing thoughts intentionally or unintentionally, explicitly or implicitly, orally or in writing. To assess learners' emotional, social, and cognitive development, we look for indications of changes in knowledge of self, others, and the world. Any significant evidence of creative thinking, problem solving, logical reasoning, or interesting musing should be noted, for it will most likely relate to general standards of developmental growth or specific (state or specialty organization) learning standards.

Thinking Made Visible

In a fourth-grade classroom, the teacher used paper dolls as a concrete way to explain character traits. She had the children cut out a paper-doll foldout to represent a story character. They decorated the front and back of the folded doll to reflect the character's physical traits as described in the text. Then they opened the doll up. On the inside they listed an inferred character trait and how they knew the character had that trait. *Well, he said thus and so. She did this, then that. The other characters said such and such about him.* The class concluded that authors give us clues about what people are like on the inside through the characters' words and deeds as well as through what others say about them. Matching these clues with our life experiences, we know what kind of person the character probably is.

Our students' thinking *is* on the inside, but it's revealed through words and actions, just as the characters in a novel reveal who they are. Students' words (oral and written) and behavior reflect the thinking behind them. Skilled teachers recognize what these words and actions imply, analyze the implications, and use what they learn to inform further assessments and teaching.

Body language—gestures, facial expressions—are a subtle indication of people's thoughts. We recognize when students have a question—they're confused and don't know what to ask or how to ask it; their contorted faces cry out, "I just don't get it!" The opposite—when their faces say, "By George, I think I've got it!"—is a teacher's greatest joy. It's just as important to read the words, actions, or body language that says, "I'm sad, I'm mad, I'm bored, I'm nervous, I'm excited." Reading people is critical to good teaching.

Gathering Thinking Evidence

Collecting evidence of students' thinking must be compatible with the flow of good teaching rather than disrupt it. Teachers can make brief notations during natural breaks in the lesson (Anthony et al. 1991): when children are reading silently, working independently at learning centers, having discussions, playing, socializing, or working on a group project. Stiggins (1999a) suggests that a seamless way to integrate assessment and instruction into classroom life is to involve students in the process. Learners need to understand—and take part in determining—*what* data are relevant and *how* they will be gathered.

Conversations

In the classroom discussions in which learners are expected to ground their ideas (Calkins 2001), rich evidence of thinking becomes available. Learners explain *on what grounds* they drew conclusions. Supporting one's ideas and opinions becomes a *habit of mind*—a natural part of informal as well as academic discourse. This combination of ideas and the basis for them is a window into children's thinking and experiences. Every learner's perceptions create a unique and logical reality worthy of respect. During genuine discussions, teachers document children's thinking as revealed in their comments and responses. Conversations, potentially rich with assessment data, can be between the teacher and student(s) (conferences, group discussions, informal talk) or between students (study groups, project groups, informal talk).

Multipurpose data-collecting tools streamline assessment. Figure 3–1 is an example of a form for collecting thinking evidence during discussions. Of course, appropriate conversational procedures and behavior must be collaboratively developed, modeled, and practiced before students are held accountable for using them. This checklist is very flexible, because you can change the skills and criteria and they are not content specific. Each week you can introduce new skills and rotate previous ones in order to keep the form current. If you want to make a supporting comment, circle the appropriate checkmark and key it to a numbered footnote. This checklist can also be applied to writing, since these same skills are applicable to written expression (documenting evidence from work samples is discussed in Chapter 4).

Daily Anecdotal Notes

Effective anecdotal documentation consists of *brief* notes taken throughout the day in both curricular and social situations. The key to capturing this data is to have a system, a readily available and consistent procedure that is

The following verbs can be used to articulate the behaviors that are the focus at any particular moment. The categories on the chart change as different conversational and/or discourse skills are emphasized. Notes can easily be made when a student's response represents a type not currently listed on the form.

retell	refine	review	analyze
identify	interpret	enjoy	request
compare	describe	define	predict
paraphrase	inquire	speculate	reflect
entertain	create	remember	contrast
persuade	summarize	specify	explore
elaborate	share	clarify	synthesize
explain	inform	evaluate	justify

Discussion Checklist for week of _____

Name	Justified predictions in content reading	Could retell informational text w/MI and signif. details	Could persuade others to agree with interpretation	Able to clarify 'tough text' for self and others	Elaborated with information from other sources (synthesis)	Comments
Tom	⊘ ✓	✓		⊘		1, 6
Maria		⊘	✓		⊘	2, 5
Jake	✓	⊘ ✓				3
Melissa	✓ ✓		⊘ ✓	⊘	✓	4, 7
Anna		✓ ✓		⊘		8
Wayne	⊘		✓		⊘	9, 11
Brandon		⊘				10,
Adam	⊘		⊘		✓	12, 14
Liz		⊘		✓ ✓		13

Comments:
1. Supported predictions based on subheadings and bold typed words.
2. Great main idea. Statement in own words — good paraphrasing
3. Much improved — solid summary w/ key concepts.
4. Could talk a tiger out of his stripes! Made good, strong points
5. Expanded on what Seth said about Supreme Court w/ new info.
6. Broke down paragraph and paraphrased to make it clear
7. . . . . . .
8. . . . . . .

FIGURE 3–1 Discussion Checklist

not easily lost or misplaced. It also has to work for you. No single system will be right for everyone. If yours doesn't fit, you'll abandon it like a stripped mine.

Self-stick address labels work well for one fifth-grade teacher. She keeps a sheet of them on a clipboard, dates six of them a day, and enters a student's name on each. This directs her concentration and keeps her from getting overwhelmed. She lets students know whom she'll be watching: "Today, I'm watching Julie, Tim, Bob, Daphne, Gloria, and Peter to see good things they're doing and what they've learned." Of course, if someone else has a great insight or does something of particular significance—a *road-to-Damascus event* (being struck with sudden understanding, undergoing a transformation)—she records that as well. Often she'll comment out loud when writing a note, and students are free to pick up the clipboard and read the labels. At the end of the day, she removes the labels containing comments (see Figure 3–2) and sticks them onto a sheet of paper in each student's folder, creating sequentially dated anecdotal notes for each child. Sectioning off the collecting sheets in students' folders (e.g., social skills, reading, writing, math, content areas, special classes) and placing the notes in the appropriate sections allow her to organize them by learning contexts (see Figure 3–3).

As she moves around the room during writers workshop and interacts with students,

fifth-grade teacher Sue Rosche records notes on five-by-eight-inch index cards attached to a ring (see Figure 3–4); she has one card for each student. The data collected reveal writers' struggles as well as their blossoming skills. They also become the grist for planning mini-lessons that capture *teachable moments*. Sue also uses the inside cover of students' writing folders. After reviewing a folder, she jots the date and her reactions, leaving students with an ongoing record of reminders, suggestions, and praise (see Figure 3–5).

Anecdotal notes can also be spoken into a small tape recorder and transcribed at a later time. Be sure to record the date with each entry.

Parents as Co-observers

While respecting children's uniqueness as individuals, teachers must frequently view students' behavior with a wide-angle lens, in the broader context of developmental benchmarks and in relationship to learning standards with expected performance levels. Parents, on the other hand, primarily view their children with a close-up lens, appreciating their personal characteristics and accomplishments. When combined, the wide- and close-angle views create a detailed image of the learner.

Parents can be very effective as data gatherers, recording snapshots of their children's thinking as they witness it at home. In the form shown in Figure 3–6, Madeline's mother provides a great deal of insight into Madeline's learning behavior at home.

Student Records of Thinking Evidence

Students can also contribute records of evidence of their thinking. For example, a group meeting independently can tape its conversation. The group leader identifies the group members, their purpose, and the date before the discussion begins. Later, the teacher listens to the recording, makes anecdotal notes on the children's thinking and learning, and plans for follow-up instruction.

Giving students individual opportunities to record their thoughts on a curricular topic

10/28 Sam
Defended strong opinions about branches of government and their work.

10/28 Emma
Used expression with Readers' Theater script to portray character's mood.

10/28 Julia
Came up with creative alternative way to solve math problem!

10/28 Ryan

10/28 Jack
Asked insightful questions to probe Tom's comments.

10/28 Jamie
Clearly explained what she didn't get in math journal.

FIGURE 3–2   Anecdotal Notes

1st Quarter Grade 5 Year 03-04

Anecdotal Notes for Dylan

Reading

9/8 Dylan
Effectively led discussion group—shared interesting character traits w/evidence

Writing

9/15 Dylan
Using more strategies to self correct spelling errors. Tried-write 3 times

9/19 Dylan
Struggled with ending in research report worked w/ John and likes suggestions

Math

9/10 Dylan
Explained how you can figure which sale is really a better deal—% discount AND fine print

Science

9/23 Dylan
Science log had clear, detailed drawing of experiment w/labels
Conclusions strongly supported

9/30 Dylan
Shared what he learned from show on Discovery Channel—very detailed

Social Studies

9/26 Dylan
Likes working w/maps can use legend. Helped others caculate distance w/ scale

Other

9/23 Dylan
Cheered team to keep trying in PE. They strategized and won the game!

FIGURE 3–3 Collection of Anecdotal Notes for Dylan

and their progress in learning about it or on their interests, complaints, or goals produces very interesting results. Children's comments are typically straight from the heart and right on target. Brendan prepared for a fall conference by identifying his strengths and setting immediate goals (see Figure 3–7). His teacher, Sue Rosche, also prepared goals that she felt were appropriate for Brendan at that time (see Figure 3–8). In their discussion, they compared notes, negotiated, and prioritized. Because of the thinking he had done beforehand, Brendan was invested in the outcome and more motivated to improve.

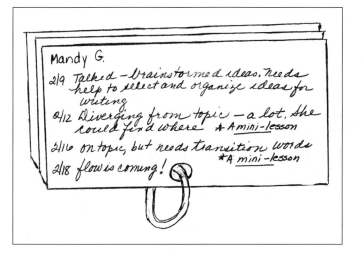

FIGURE 3–4   Anecdotal Notes on Index Cards

Written Reflections

Children's written reflections also provide thinking evidence. These reflections can be completed on a teacher-designed or commercial form that directs the response. Alternatively, journals are also an excellent repository for reflections on content topics, literature, or personal issues.

Sue Rosche often uses a 3-2-1 procedure after her lessons. Students briefly write down the following:

▶ three new things they've learned

▶ two things they're confused about or two questions they have

▶ one thing they want to know more about

Figure 3–9 shows Erica's 3-2-1 thinking after a social studies lesson. Sue's notations correct, suggest, and question.

Open-ended prompts or sentence starters can also be used to elicit student thinking about a lesson. Here are some examples:

▶ My goal for tomorrow is _____.

▶ I was surprised that _____.

▶ I was pleased that _____.

▶ I still don't understand _____.

▶ I liked _____ the most [least] about this lesson because _____.

10-20 You're off to a great start! I particularly enjoyed reading your literature response. You used good details.

11-12 Did you finish The Lemonade Trick? If so, fill in a date. If you decided not to finish this book, put an 'X' in the second column.

I enjoyed your response dated 11-3. I hope my notes help. Remember to see me for the two comments I made.

1-21 Wow! I enjoyed reading your next. I hope my notes help.

2-4 I hope you are working on your reflection + illustration. I'll assign a new Book Club genre but finish your reflection first.

3-15 I'm glad you're starting your next Book Club.

5-28 Your literature responses have improved this year, don't you think? I enjoyed reading your responses for this trimester. Enjoy your summer reading, Olivia.

(Remember to read Trumpet of The Swan with Mom!)

FIGURE 3–5   Conference Notes on Student's Writing Folder

▶ The most difficult part of the lesson was _____.

▶ The thing I learned today that I didn't know before was _____.

Exit reporting sheets let group members reflect on their discussion (see Figure 3–10). When a group is working on its own, these individually recorded reflections on the

---

Assessment Program
Parent Observation Guide
Grade 1 - Fall

Dear Parents/Guardians,

    It is almost time for us to meet for our student/parent/teacher conferences. I am sending you a copy of an observation guideline so that you can have time to consider and complete it. Your comments are very valuable and will be used as a guideline at our conference. **Please bring it with you at your scheduled conference time.**

    Your child will join the conference and I look forward to our meeting.

                           Sincerely,

MY CHILD AS A LEARNER   Child's Name *Madeline*

1.   What do you see as your child's strengths as a learner?

We think that Madeline is creative — she is a good problem solver. Madeline has always been a very good listener and she enjoys learning new things.

2.   Please share areas where your child needs extra help.

reading — confidence — coping w/out "perfection" — trusting her own abilities in all academic areas

FIGURE 3–6   Parent Observation Form

group's activity, productivity, and conclusions provide data that would have been lost otherwise. They sometimes yield multiple perspectives on the same event.

    Learning activities can also produce thinking evidence. Sue Rosche has a word wall in her fifth-grade classroom that changes as new units of study are explored. She uses these words in an activity called *word splash*. She gives teams a random set of four or five words from the wall and asks students to arrange them in a reasoned configuration that indicates connections to a theme. Figure 3–11 shows the connections Alex's group has made.

Conferences

Scheduled and impromptu teacher–student (or student–student) conferences yield important evidence of student thinking. These con-

3. How do you view your child as a reader/writer?

We are happy to see Madeline starting to see herself as a reader/writer. She has been very interested at home ~ reading to the family and writing notes to us 😊

a. When you are reading/writing with your child, and he/she does not know a word, does your child try to figure it out for himself or does he/she keep going?

She is attempting to sound words out and she will say blank — she also uses picture clues quite a bit ~ she still needs much encouragement

b. Please describe your child's attitude toward reading/writing.

Madeline is starting to show great interest in reading and writing. She reads to all of us and she initiates it! She writes notes to us and leaves them all around the house ~ she also takes our "breakfast orders" in the morning (weekends)

4. How does your child use math at home (shopping, travel, cooking)?

We do a lot of baking & shopping Madeline has always been interested in money. Madeline has also begun to be more interested in adding numbers together —

She reads in her room every night but also loves to be read to... and always has!

5. Please list any areas of concern that you would like to share at conferences.

— reading, memory skills (seems selective)

FIGURE 3–6 Continued

ferences can be related to curricular areas (a writing conference, a reading conference) or held specifically for assessment (a portfolio conference). Cooper (1997) offers the following guidelines for effective conferences that are win-win experiences in which both teacher and learner gain information that helps them understand and improve ongoing teaching and learning:

▶ Establish and follow clear purposes and procedures.

▶ Keep conferences brief and focused.

▶ Follow up on students' responses, probing for further information and clarification. Act like a good interviewer.

▶ Create a positive, interactive atmosphere.

Assessment Program
Grade 5 Fall Student Observation Guide
THE LEARNER

Name: Brendan   Date: 10-20

1. My strengths as a learner:	2. Areas where I need to improve:
•Homework	•getting my desk cleaner ★
★remembering my supplies	•social studies ★
•Math	•bringing all my work home
•making good choices	•
•doing my work	
•Listening	
•reading	
★getting things out	

3. What do you choose to do in school when your work is finished?
I used to not do anything, but now I'm seeing if I did all of the questions.

4. How do you organize your materials and work area?
I used to just toss stuff in my desk but now I'm putting books in my binder.

5. How do you take responsibility for getting your work completed on time? I used to forget my supplies that needs to come home. But now I'm not haveing that problem.

6. Reflect on your behavior and attitude in class.
My behavior isn't bad. My attitude is normaly always happy.

FIGURE 3–7 Brendan's Fall Observation Guide

Fall Conference Goals 2003

Brendan

- Always use your *best* **listening** skills.
- Improve your **literature responses.**
- We'll take a look at your **note-taking skills.**
- We'll look at your **writing samples** (add details, revise, edit, paragraph).
- Spend one hour each night (Monday–Thursday) on **homework.** Fill any remaining time with **silent reading.**
- Be certain that all **homework** is turned in on time. When we **organize** at the end of the day, be sure you have everything you need.

FIGURE 3–8 Teacher's Fall Conference Goals for Brendan

▶ Carry them out as real dialogue; avoid the QRE model (teacher question, student response, teacher evaluation).

▶ Collaboratively establish goals for further teaching and learning.

▶ Record key points.

One of the best sources for conference note-taking forms is *Assessing Literacy with the Learning Record* (Barr et al. 1999). This book presents a clear rationale for the assessment process it describes, sets out step-by-step directions, provides reproducible forms for recording observations and for summative semester reporting, and includes examples of completed forms. (There is a companion volume for grades 6–12.) However, hardly anything comes packaged just as we'd like; any resource can be modified to meet your specific instructional needs, and being able to do so is an essential teaching talent. It's like fixing up or customizing that "charming" house after you've bought it!

Checklists: Inventories of Target Skills and Strategies

Since children's academic and personal growth is uneven and idiosyncratic—in a fluid stage of acquisition (Perrone 1991)—many kinds of checklists are needed to document it accurately. *Continuous* checklists cover broad areas and are used *over time and across grades* to accumulate data on long-term learning goals directed toward district and state standards. Other checklists are narrow and address quarterly learning goals or specific goals and skills (these are also usually directed toward district and state standards). Both types can bring a learner's social, emotional,

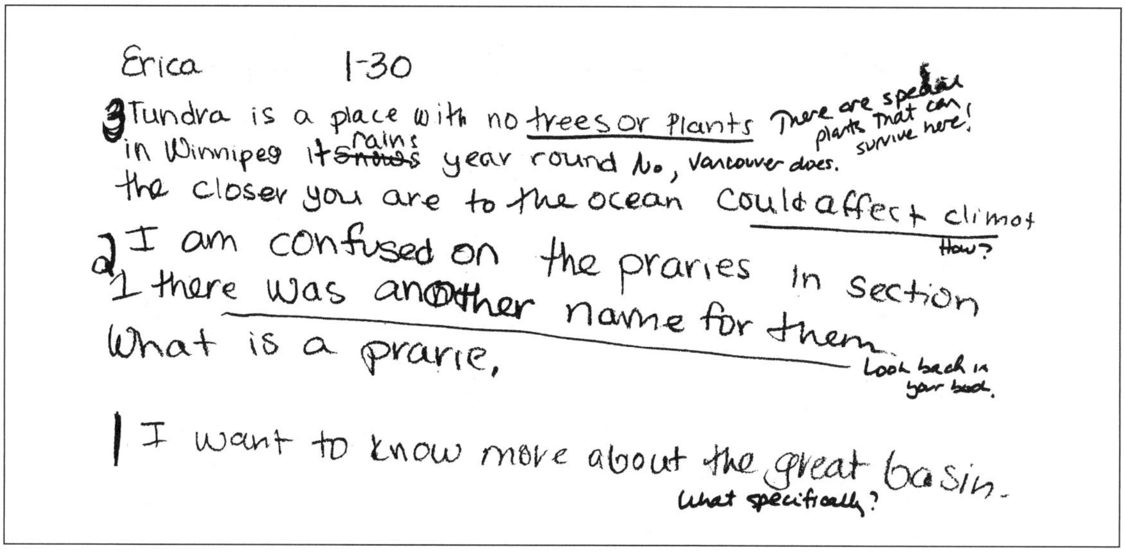
Erica 1-30
3 Tundra is a place with no trees or Plants [There are special plants that can survive here!]
in Winnipeg it ~~snows~~ rains year round [No, Vancouver does.]
the closer you are to the ocean could affect climot [How?]
2 I am confused on the praries in section 1 there was another name for them
What is a prarie, [Look back in your book.]
1 I want to know more about the great basin. [What specifically?]

FIGURE 3–9 Erica's 3-2-1 Response

Name Maggie   Date 5-29
Book Top Secret
My Role This Week vocabulary enricher

Literature Circle Sharing Day Exit Slip

Reflection on Group Functioning:

What is one thing that went well in your group today?

everybody was talking much more then usale.

What is one thing that needs work in your group?

making sure we have enough time left for each other.

Reflection on Your Learning:

Think of <u>two</u> things you learned from your peer teachers today. Be specific so I can get a sense of what was discussed and what you were thinking:

Ex. The Vocabulary Enricher taught me about the word flagrant. I guessed that the word means "confusing" which wasn't accurate. Something that is flagrant is something that is obvious or conspicuous. I am beginning to understand this word better but then when it came to creating our own sentences, I noticed that all of us did sentences about a flagrant error. I raised the question of whether flagrant could used to describe other things, but none of us could come up with anything so we got out the dictionary. It gave examples of flagrant violations and flagrant abuse. It seems to me that flagrant is used with things that are bad.

I think that we were having an accutal disscussion

FIGURE 3–10   Maggie's Literature Circle Exit Slip

and/or cognitive development into focus by associating pieces of data with specific criteria. A checklist logically and systematically stores documented demonstrations of students' learning behavior, whatever the source.

Providing a *crosswalk* within a checklist enhances its usefulness. A crosswalk documents, skill by skill, which district and state learning standards are addressed and assessed in the classroom, and how. For the most part specialty organization standards (like those promulgated by the National Council of Teachers of Mathematics and the International Reading Association) are subsumed in the district and state standards. However, a column can be added in any crosswalk for these content-specific standards. Figure 3–12 is a segment of a grade 6 social studies check-

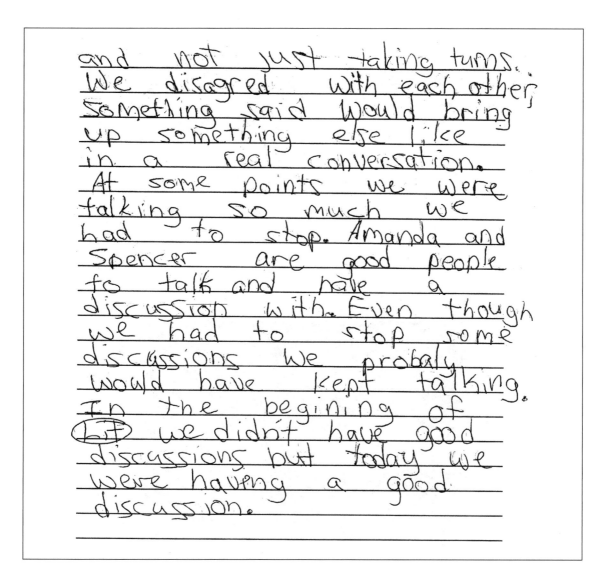

and not just taking turns. We disagred with each other, something said would bring up something else like in a real conversation. At some points we were talking so much we had to stop. Amanda and Spencer are good people to talk and have a discussion with. Even though we had to stop some discussions we probaly would have kept talking. In the begining of (It) we didn't have good discussions but today we were having a good discussion.

FIGURE 3–10 Continued

list with a crosswalk to district, state, and National Council for the Social Studies (NCSS) standards. Figure 3–13 is a segment of a grade 3 comprehension checklist that includes a record of materials and activities involved in the demonstrations as well as a crosswalk to standards. Checklists can easily serve multiple purposes when they're thoughtfully constructed.

Creating sections on a checklist for subskills related to a complex target skill (see Figure 3–14) focuses attention on the acquisition of each facet or subskill and helps you get to the bottom of confusions or quickly identify aspects that still need to be taught and

practiced. Figure 3–15 shows how tasks requiring competence in the same skill in alternate contexts provide *triangulated* evidence regarding specific learning standards or goals.

Multiple Successful Performances

Since only fully acquired skills can be generalized to broader contexts and real-life situations, it's important to understand whether or not the learner has reached this level. Accumulation is key on all checklists. Once just isn't enough! Several significant demonstrations of individual skills verify that the demonstrations weren't aberrations but were knowledgeable executions of the particular

Students are asked to consider a given number of key vocabulary terms from a unit of study. They are to organize a display of word connections and be prepared to explain the rationale for these. This can be done verbally, manipulating words from the classroom word wall as in the picture, or in writing as demonstrated in the journal entry.

Example:

Group is asked to display connections between the following words.

history — colony — government — civilization

history

colony — government — civilization

This student explained that as we study the history of a group of people, we note how those people formed a group or colony. Next, they typically developed a government that provided laws and order for their coexistence. With a relatively stable and peaceful community, groups built a civilization over time.

FIGURE 3–11 Explanation of Word Splash and Photograph of Student Showing Splash Connections

skill or behavior. Here's a simple way to indicate this on a checklist (see Figure 3–16): At the first demonstration of the skill, enter a diagonal slash on the recording line and note the date underneath. (Include evidence—a work sample or anecdotal note—as support.) When the same skill is fully demonstrated again, place a second, reverse diagonal line across the first to form an X. Again, record a date and include evidence in the student's portfolio. Record a third demonstration with a line through the middle of the X (forming an asterisk), record the date, and include the evidence. When the asterisk is fully formed (three entries), the skill or behavior is considered reasonably *acquired*. Continued practice and monitoring ensures that acquired skills and strategies are *mastered*.

Leaving empty lines on a checklist indicate that skills or strategies have not yet been

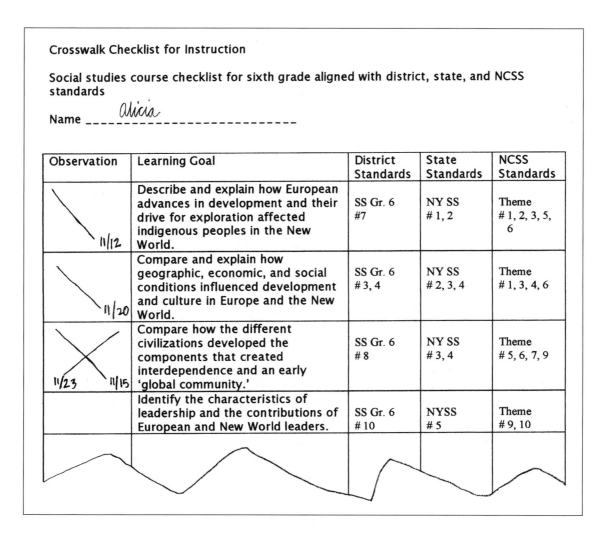

Crosswalk Checklist for Instruction

Social studies course checklist for sixth grade aligned with district, state, and NCSS standards

Name _____ Alicia _____

Observation	Learning Goal	District Standards	State Standards	NCSS Standards
11/12	Describe and explain how European advances in development and their drive for exploration affected indigenous peoples in the New World.	SS Gr. 6 #7	NY SS #1, 2	Theme #1, 2, 3, 5, 6
11/20	Compare and explain how geographic, economic, and social conditions influenced development and culture in Europe and the New World.	SS Gr. 6 #3, 4	NY SS #2, 3, 4	Theme #1, 3, 4, 6
11/23 11/15	Compare how the different civilizations developed the components that created interdependence and an early 'global community.'	SS Gr. 6 #8	NY SS #3, 4	Theme #5, 6, 7, 9
	Identify the characteristics of leadership and the contributions of European and New World leaders.	SS Gr. 6 #10	NYSS #5	Theme #9, 10

FIGURE 3–12   Crosswalk Checklist for Instruction

demonstrated is better than writing *no*. Negatives are unnecessary and demoralizing. Blank lines are the fuel for goal-setting conversations that focus on the cup being half full and end with *How can we add more?*

When a checklist moves with a student to the next grade, the new teacher can see at a glance those areas that need reinforcement and those that need to be introduced. Noting when skills were acquired in previous academic years is important too. Are the skills newly acquired or has the student been using them for a while? Customizing instruction toward maintenance, reinforcement, or skill introduction based on this easily accessed information lets teachers reach all learners.

Organizing and Storing Data Efficiently

Thinking evidence is housed neatly in its own section of the portfolio. The table of contents may vary, but it typically includes anecdotal notes, conference forms, checklists, and written reflections. A summary page describes achievement at designated benchmarks (e.g., reporting periods) and notes goals, which have been set collaboratively. Each summary is dated. *Assessing Literacy with the Learning Record* (Barr et al. 1999) is a wonderful resource for this summary page, or you can use the one there as a model for defining your own.

Grade 3 Reading Comprehension Checklist

Observation	Learning Goal	Materials /Activities Used	District Standards	State Standards
X — 12/5 11/10 10/5	Uses title, tables of contents, chapter headings, a glossary, or an index to locate information in a text.	• Guided Reading w/ literature • Class discussions • Reading Series • Textbooks • Research project • Library	ELA Gr. 3 #9	NY ELA # 1
X 12/10 10/20	Shows understanding by recalling major points, revising predictions, distinguishing the main idea and supporting details, and locating significant information in the text.	• Oral retelling • Class/group discussions • KWL charts • Story mapping, graphic organizers • Reading Series • Guided Reading w/ literature • Journal writing	ELA Gr. 3 # 4, 6, 8	NY ELA # 1, 3

FIGURE 3–13 Grade 3 Reading Comprehension Checklist

Dual Purposes: Doesn't That Go Somewhere Else?

The lines between the portfolio TWIN categories, as they do in life, sometimes get blurry. And the categories include gray areas. Some data seem to fit in more than one room. What do you do then? Simply decide where you want to store it. What makes sense for you, for your school? Of course, cross-references are always helpful.

Checklists are an easy way to document data collected from thinking evidence, work samples, and in-the-classroom benchmarks,

so they cross over most frequently. But they are not the only data-collecting tool that does. As we saw earlier, journal entries are work samples that demonstrate thinking.

Running records are also an example of crossover data. They provide an in-the-classroom benchmark measure while capturing rich evidence of children's thinking. Figure 3–17 is Nancy Gantz's running record taken with Maddy. The form also documents thinking evidence: Maddy's repetition to correct what didn't make sense to her, her question about a word, and her ability to retell

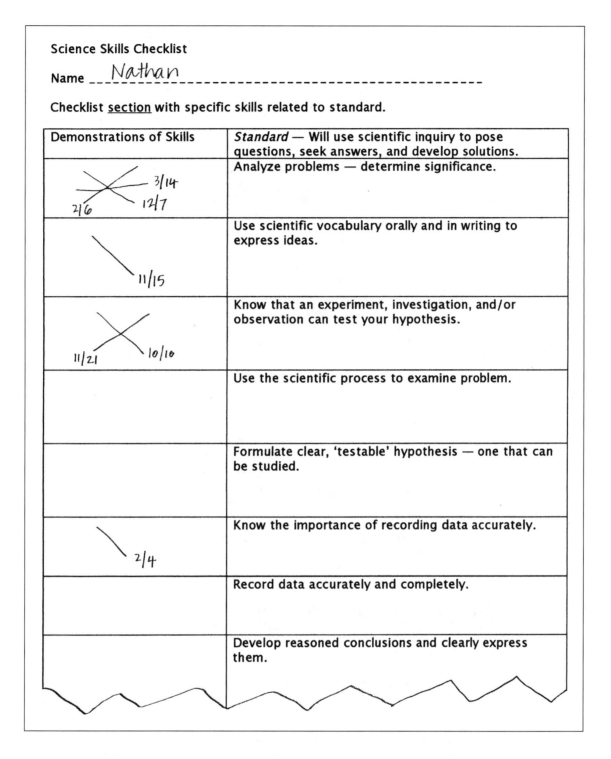

Science Skills Checklist

Name ___Nathan_____

Checklist <u>section</u> with specific skills related to standard.

Demonstrations of Skills	*Standard* — Will use scientific inquiry to pose questions, seek answers, and develop solutions.
3/14 12/7 2/6 (X mark)	Analyze problems — determine significance.
11/15 (line)	Use scientific vocabulary orally and in writing to express ideas.
11/21 10/16 (X mark)	Know that an experiment, investigation, and/or observation can test your hypothesis.
	Use the scientific process to examine problem.
	Formulate clear, 'testable' hypothesis — one that can be studied.
2/4 (line)	Know the importance of recording data accurately.
	Record data accurately and completely.
	Develop reasoned conclusions and clearly express them.

FIGURE 3–14   Science Skills Checklist

with a personal evaluation. The running record would be placed in the in-the-classroom benchmark section, while these details about the performance would be noted anecdotally or on a checklist in the thinking evidence section.

Any time children read orally, even when we're not taking a running record, we have an incredible opportunity to note anecdotal information on the performance. And quite often we get snippets of insight into their mental processing. Here's an example, from a

Triangulated Demonstrations of a Skill: The learner performs the skill (or variations of it) in different contexts with different kinds of tasks.

Students' Name _ _ _Daniel_ _ _ _ _ _ _ _ _ _ _

Learning Standard

The learner understands one-to-one correspondence of objects to numeral and number name that represent the amount.

Observance of Skill	Demonstration
9/18 ✕ 10/2 9/10	Keeps track while orally counting a set of at least 10 manipulatives in math lessons.
10/5	Counts with one-to-one correspondence to find 10 blocks of the same size in the play area.
	Accurately 'reads' numeral associated with picture sets of objects (1–10) in a counting book.
	Represents sets of objects (1–10) with the appropriate numeral when illustrating pages in class-adapted book or LEA chart.
	Can accurately count and name the number of days (1–10) between two dates on the calendar.
	Can accurately represent the number of items counted on a graph with shaded blocks and numeric labels.

FIGURE 3–15   Triangulated Demonstrations of a Skill

Recording Significant Demonstrations of Skills

• First, leave a line item blank when there is not yet evidence of the skill.

_ _ _ _ _ _ _ _ Makes reasonable predictions before reading.

• Second, record a diagonal line with the date under the space once the skill is significantly demonstrated. This may be more than a single demonstration.

_ _ _/_ _ _ _ Makes reasonable predictions before reading.
11/5

• Continue to record additional lines (e.g., another diagonal and a vertical). Note dates when additional lines were added, forming a sequential record as the skill is consistently demonstrated in different contexts. There should be a minimum of three lines to indicate that the skill has been reasonably acquired.

_ _✕_ _ _ Makes reasonable predictions before reading.
11/5 4/12 3/18

FIGURE 3–16   Recording Significant Demonstration Skills

video of a first grader reading an informational text about butterflies. The reader was working hard at performing *and* processing. Throughout the reading, there was appropriate emphasis on phrases and words. The reader was making it sound like talking. However, his skill integration was shaky. As he paid more attention to processing, his expression became more monotonous. His interjected thoughts at these moments made it clear that he was mentally filing the ideas. For example, when reading about the steps in the butterfly's metamorphosis, his sidebar comments were "Hmmm"; "OK"; "I didn't

---

Running Record/Reading Conference for Early or Transitional Readers

Student _____ Grade __1__ Date __2/5__

Teacher __Mrs. Gantz__ Recorder __Mrs. Gantz__

Text __Spot__ (Fiction) Non-Fiction

Calculations

Error Rate ——— = 1: __9.8__

Accuracy __90__%

S/C Rate ——— = 1: __6__

Fountas & Pinnell Level __E__

Independent (Instructional) Frustrational

Error Rate

Running Words Errors

Self-Correction Rate

Errors+SC SC

Conversions

Independent	Instructional	Frustrational
1:200 = 99.5	1:17 = 94	1:9 = 89
1:100 = 99	1:14 = 93	1:8 = 87.5
1:50 = 98	1:12.5 = 92	1:7 = 85.5
1:35 = 97	1:11.75 = 91	1:6 = 83
1:25 = 96	(1:10 = 90)	1:5 = 80
1:20 = 95		1:4 = 75
		1:3 = 66
		1:2 = 50

Error Rate = % Accuracy

Familiarity of Text

___Previously Read (silently)

___Modeled (parent, teacher, buddy)

___Student Selected

✓ Teacher Selected

Attitude

Confident

Risk Taker

(Lacks Confidence)

Dependent

Expression

Very expressive

(Some expression)

No expression

Cueing Systems Used

(Semantic)

Graphophonic

Syntactic

She named all the (?) ✗ *Great job!*

Retell

Main Idea	(Yes)	(Prompted)	No
Details/Facts	(Yes)	(Prompted)	No
Characters	(Yes)	(Prompted)	No
Setting	Yes	Prompted	No
Problem	Yes	Prompted	No
Solution	Yes	Prompted	No
Plot	Yes	Prompted	No
Sequencing	Yes	Prompted	No

Response

✓ Made no response willingly

✓ Explained why he/she liked or disliked the text *It was funny when he had spots!*

___Related the text to life experiences or other literature

___Analyzed, predicted, inferred, or concluded something about the text

Instructional Goals/Comments:

Maddy did a nice job of reading. Errors did not interfere with comprehension. She used beginning sounds and picture clues. Encourage her to use the blank strategy and continue to work on dev. phonics skills. Finger pointing will also help her keep her place.

over →

FIGURE 3–17 Maddy's Running Record

(continues)

	E	SC	**Behaviors**
✓			_____ **Attended to Print**
✓ ✓ ✓ ✓ · to you to T down	1		_____ **Finger Pointed**
			_____ **1:1 Word Matched**
✓ ✓ tail toes	1		_____ **Voice Pointed**
			_____ **Made Long Pauses**
✓ ✓ ✓ even ✓ ✓ nose ? except nose	1		_____ **Read Fluently**
✓ ✓ ✓ ✓ ✓ N 7 ·· p - ✓			_____ **Phrased Reading**
			_____ **Created Text**
✓ ✓ ✓ ✓ ✓ ✓ ·✓			_____ **Omitted Words**
· ✓ ✓ ✓ · f · four ✓ few	1		_____ **Inserted Words**
the is sc		1	_____ **Read for Meaning**
here and			_____ **Chose Appropriate Text**
✓ ✓ ✓ ·· many ✓ ✓ measles	1		

Strategies Used

✓	Looked/Asked for help
✓	Used Picture Clues
✓	Recognized high frequency words
✓	Used beginning sounds
___	Used beginning and ending sounds
___	Sounded out whole word
___	Checked back for previous clues
___	Repeated words/phrases
___	Used "blank" strategy
✓	Reread to solve problems
✓	Self corrected errors
___	Used punctuation
___	Recognized story pattern
___	Relied on story memory

Other_____

E: 5   SC: 1

FIGURE 3–17   Continued

know that"; and "Wow. Now he's done. I saw that kind of butterfly." (More fluent readers express this self-talk as fully formed queries.)

On the tape that accompanies his book, Peter Johnston (1992a) provides a wonderful example (number 10) of a child's thinking while reading. The child is reading a passage about beavers. After reading the segment explaining that the beaver has to cut down trees on the land and move them to the deep water where he's building his lodge, the reader poses a question to himself and perhaps to

Peter Johnston as well: "Now, how is it going to get a big tree to its home?"

Peter responds, "A good question. I don't know. Does it tell us?"

The child indicates that it doesn't and goes on: "I mean a tree is a gazillion times bigger than it, so?"

Peter supports the child's puzzlement ("You have to wonder") and directs the child's focus back to the text, encouraging him to continue reading to find out how the beaver accomplishes this feat.

Teachers love this passage. They never fail to break out in smiles and laughter when they hear it. It so obviously resonates with their experiences. Interactions during such reading events help teachers understand much more than learners' current skill level. The additional discovery of unique qualities in children's approaches to learning allows teachers to customize materials, time, instruction, and learning activities.

Considerations for Diverse Populations

Learners are diverse in ability, interests, personality, background, and cultural, ethnic, and religious identity. These factors create differences in beliefs, values, orientation toward school, and speech patterns. Each area of divergence influences how a child learns and performs (Burns, Roe, and Ross 1999). Understanding the learners who create a classroom's diversity is critical to be able to teach successfully. Teachers who care find varied ways to construct an accurate understanding of each learner in the class. They also ensure that all children are able to participate fully in classroom activities and are supported in doing so.

All learners deserve to be recognized for the achievements they've made, be involved in planning the next step, be clearly presented with what is expected of them, and be fully supported as they work toward goals. Fulfilling this mandate requires attention to

individual needs. Every child in the classroom is *special* and has unique needs. Some need a lot of support. Some need unusual kinds of support. Some appear self-sufficient but need to be appropriately challenged in their areas of talent.

Consultants and resource teachers who work with remedial, special education, gifted, or ESL students can provide expert insight on individual children's behavior and learning demonstrations. This discussion expands the classroom teacher's knowledge of the child's special needs. Conversely, it offers the consulting teacher a glimpse of the child's performance when working with peers in small and large groups. Resource teachers and classroom teachers can pool their assessment data, as well as clarify the significance of particular items.

Summing Up

The classroom is rich with thinking evidence. But sometimes it's hard to see the big picture. It's like looking up close at something as big as an elephant from several angles. Unless descriptions from each angle are compiled, a full and accurate image is not achieved. Teachers, using a trained eye, recognize thinking even in the smallest amount. They also know how to dust for prints—to make difficult-to-notice learning evidence visible. However, competent assessment isn't an automatic reflex. Teachers need training that helps them detect learning evidence around them, productively listen to other views, and construct a clear picture of learners in their class.

Deciding *what* thinking evidence to collect and *how* to collect it stimulates grand schoolwide or districtwide conversations. Respectful debate that leads to consensus ensures that the system used in a school or district is consistent. It might also guarantee the system's longevity, with everyone on board and rowing the boat!

◀ c h a p t e r 4 ▶

Work Samples

Students are at the center of what we do, but just next to the center lies student work.

—KATE NOLAN

Artifacts such as tools, cooking and eating implements, letters, artwork, and innumerable other objects, when collected and analyzed by anthropologists, allow the examination of a culture. Classroom artifacts—student work samples—must be similarly gathered and analyzed. Analyses of these work samples, combined with our assembled evidence of thinking, are part of a triangulating process proving that learning has occurred.

Analyses of classroom work samples yield both interpreted and tangible evidence of learning. Teachers must interpret the work samples in order to identify the underlying thinking processes children used to complete the work. Additionally, the samples themselves are tangible evidence of students' current level of performance in meeting daily lesson objectives that have been aligned with local and state standards. Nolan (2000) says that "rich, complex work samples show us how students are thinking, the fullness of their factual knowledge, the connections they are making" (1).

What Is Student Work?

Student work is simply the output that results from the myriad tasks students engage in during the school day: guided practice, group work, center work, independent projects. Some of these tasks are completed within a

lesson or during a single day, while others may take several days or even weeks. The resulting products are used both to measure short-term objectives and to demonstrate students' progress toward overall goals and standards. However, not every work sample can or should be housed in the portfolio.

A student work sample worthy of being archived as an artifact of learning is one that shows a *significant* milestone in the learner's development. Significance is not determined by size but by what it represents. A worthy artifact might show

▶ breakthroughs or "aha"s—skills or strategies that were used but confused are now performed well

▶ solid demonstration of a target goal

▶ unique insights

▶ creative thinking

▶ problem solving

▶ connections made to self, to other texts, to the world

Recognizing key pieces of work-sample evidence requires a comprehensive understanding of the learner, daily learning objectives, and target goals and standards. But this knowledge is not enough. Teachers need to be vigilant. They need to find the evidence in the details—to separate the wheat from the chaff. For example, teacher Sue Rosche found evidence of Kayla's ability to behave metacognitively in her 3-2-1 response (three things I learned, two questions I have, one thing I want to know more about) to a lesson on the geography of the United States and Canada (see Figure 4–1). An activity like this does not generate the same kind of student work as a *benchmark* measure produced during a culminating activity for a unit of study. But such pebbles and stones of evidence reveal that learners have reached periodic benchmarks or stepping-stones on the way to target outcomes, goals, or standards.

Benchmarks as Stepping-Stones

A *benchmark* is an established point of reference against which learners can be measured. Children's current performance in any developmental area can be compared with examples or anchor responses that represent "known standards or credible developmental norms" (Wiggins 1998, 246). Day after day, students take step after step toward a larger goal while focusing on immediate learning objectives. Benchmark checkpoints along the way allow them to take stock of how they're doing, celebrate accomplishments, regroup when necessary, and press confidently ahead when ready. Benchmarks are identified at the local and/or state levels in specific subject areas.

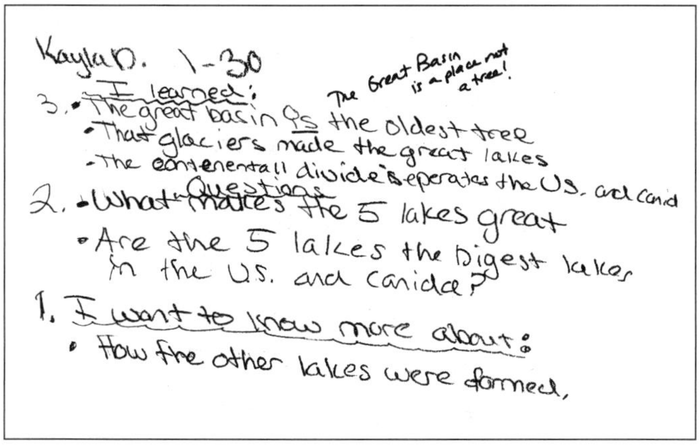
Kayla D. 1-30
The Great Basin is a place not a tree!
3. I learned:
• The great basin is the oldest tree
• That glaciers made the great lakes
• The continental divide seperates the US. and Cand
2. Questions
• What makes the 5 lakes great
• Are the 5 lakes the bigest lakes in the U.S. and Canida?
1. I want to know more about:
• How the other lakes were formed,

FIGURE 4–1 Kayla's 3-2-1 Response

In a Wisconsin school district, for example, a grade 7 social studies benchmark states: "Students will apply attributes of the ten universal cultural characteristics to various societies and construct interdisciplinary connections to various cultures" (United School District of De Pere, Wisconsin 2004). This local benchmark aligns with and is a step toward Wisconsin state standard E.8.9, "Give examples of the cultural contributions of racial and ethnic groups in Wisconsin, the United States, and the world" (Wisconsin Department of Public Instruction 1998).

In real-world learning, we can easily identify benchmark points in our journey toward larger goals. Here's a cooking analogy: Perfecting an exotic bruschetta to use as an hors d'oeuvre is a first step in serving an elaborate meal. The preparation of each succeeding dish compares with students' day-by-day activities focused on target outcomes. The benchmark performance is a dining experience that rivals one in a four-star restaurant. That means serving an excellent meal is not enough. We have to set a table worthy of the feast, select an appropriate wine, and create an ambiance that stimulates enjoyable repartee among the guests. In other words, we integrate several objectives across the culinary arts in completing this benchmark activity. And this single fine-dining experience is itself a stepping-stone to the long-term target of becoming a gourmet restaurateur.

Work Samples Versus In-the-Classroom Benchmarks

It's important to draw a distinction between in-the-classroom benchmarks, typically in the form of culminating unit projects, presentations, or tests, and classroom work samples. Simply put, work samples result from work focused on short-term objectives, while in-the-classroom benchmarks are broader measures of larger, more integrated, long-term goals. A student's research project presented to the class after a unit spanning several weeks is an in-the-classroom benchmark, a project for a long-term, cross-curricular goal.

For instance, after Sue Rosche's class spent several weeks studying pre–World War II United States, student pairs researched a topic from the unit in detail. Over four weeks, students worked in school and at home, consulting various sources and taking notes. Sue taught minilessons on research and presentation techniques, scheduled time in the library and computer room, worked with individual students, gave feedback, and provided assistance. Then each pair made an oral report to the class that centered on a PowerPoint presentation. Their classmates used a rubric to evaluate the presentations. Peer reviewers were required to justify the scores they assigned. After all presentations were made, students completed a unit test that provided an additional benchmark for measuring individual progress. This maxi–research project and the unit test were in-the-classroom benchmarks for that unit of study.

However, research projects can span only a few days and have more immediate, shorter-term objectives. In Jay Basham's seventh-grade social studies class, students completed a Web-based, mini–research project in less than a week that integrated short-term objectives in language arts and social studies. (Jay worked with the seventh-grade English teacher, and both graded several components of students' work based on course-specific objectives.) As part of African American history month, student partners researched a famous African American, identified significant events in that person's life, and prepared a PowerPoint presentation for the class. Jay and his language arts colleague evaluated students' notes, rough drafts, final copies, and PowerPoint presentations. Peers and teachers provided oral feedback. (The complete assignment and evaluation rubric is shown in Appendix 4–1 at the end of this chapter.) Since there were fewer objectives and less time was allotted for this project than for most major projects, the products were categorized as work samples. The project did, however, *contribute* to students'

attainment of benchmark unit goals and larger state outcomes and learning standards.

Planning for Work Samples as Worthy Artifacts

Designing short-term tasks and evaluating the work samples that result require a specific set of criteria and specified learning standards that are clearly communicated to students, parents, and the school community ahead of time. By systematically collecting and evaluating work samples, teachers are able to detect changes in students' learning that reflect attainment of specified standards. Everything students do reveals something about them— their personalities, thoughts, background knowledge, feelings, aspirations, and level of achievement.

Short-term guided or independent practice reinforces what has been taught and, one hopes, learned. However, these lessons and tasks are not randomly selected; they're tied to larger outcomes or learning standards. Thoughtfully designed classroom tasks ensure that we'll collect worthwhile evidence—grains in a body of evidence documenting students' progress toward learning standards. Each task is relevant to a meaningful, immediate, short-term objective while also logically constructed to lead toward long-term outcomes or learning standards. In his Assessment Bill of Rights, Wiggins (1993) says that all students are entitled to "worthwhile (engaging, educative, and 'authentic') intellectual problems that are validated against worthy 'real-world' intellectual problems, roles, and situations" (28). According to Nolan (2000), "Learning standards remain lifeless, as non-operational statements in heavy binders, unless we articulate them clearly across the learning community and bring them to life with daily connections to the work students are doing in the classroom" (2).

What Are Learning Standards?

Standards allow performers (learners) to understand each accomplishment in relationship to larger goals. With the target in focus, they continuously monitor progress, aim for the next level, and expect to reach it (Wiggins 1991, 20).

Not all standards are created equal. Some are absolute standards; others are educational standards. "A true or *absolute* standard points to and describes a *specific and desirable level or degree of exemplary performance*—a worthwhile target irrespective of whether most people can or cannot meet it at the moment" (Wiggins 1998, 104). Absolute standards are very different from *educational standards*, which define the level students ought to attain if they persist. Both types of standards imply attention to the kind of excellence demonstrated in quality performances. However, absolute standards reach far beyond the norm to the performance of experts, while educational standards focus on performance quality expected at an exit or graduation point. We frequently do not meet the absolute standard, but we know what it looks like, and we can judge our efforts in relation to that standard (Wiggins 1991, 20).

Classroom instruction is designed around objectives and evaluated by rubrics that focus on students' *developmental* steps toward outcome learning (educational standards). For example, an exit learning (educational) standard in mathematics, although rigorous, would not represent a performance worthy of a Nobel prize for mathematics. Achieving a Nobel prize signifies that one has reached the absolute standard in a respective field. Educational expectations for performance are norm based—they reflect performance accepted as developmentally normal at given points. Students can exceed norms and expectations at interval levels on the way. Educational learning standards—graduation-worthy outcomes—are not the absolute standard for performance in any discipline. There's more learning to be done to become an expert.

Wiggins (1998) outlines three types of learning standards that should be considered when planning lessons in any area:

► *content standards*, which define what students should know and be able to do

► *performance standards*, which specify how well students must do their work

► *task* (work design) *standards*, which delineate worthy and rigorous work—tasks students should be able to complete successfully (106)

Confusion arises because people often use the word *standard* inconsistently. Too often, learning standards vary depending on who defines them. The standards referred to by state education departments are typically developmental standards. The standards of the national professional organizations are often more global but also more vague. For example, the National Council for the Social Studies (1999) provides ten themes that serve as organizing "statements of what should occur programmatically in the formal schooling process." The first theme is culture: "Social studies programs should include experiences that provide for the study of culture and cultural diversity." This goal differs somewhat in its translation from state to state.

The NCSS culture standard correlates with the New York State Education Department's Social Studies Standard 2: "Students will use a variety of intellectual skills to demonstrate their understanding of major ideas, eras, themes, developments, and turning points in world history and examine the broad sweep of history from a variety of perspectives." To provide a better understanding of expectations for this standard, the NYSED explains, "The study of world history requires an understanding of world cultures and civilizations, including an analysis of important ideas, social and cultural values, beliefs and traditions" (NYSED 1996, 8). The NYSED has also established developmentally appropriate performance expectations at the elementary, intermediate, and secondary level. At the elementary level, these expectations are partially met if students successfully "read historical narratives, myths, legends, biographies, and autobiographies to learn about how historical figures lived, their motivations, hopes, fears, strengths, and weaknesses" (8). Students at the intermediate level must "know the social and economic characteristics, such as customs, traditions, child-rearing practices, ways of making a living, education and socialization practices, gender roles, foods and religious and spiritual beliefs that distinguish different cultures and civilizations" (10). Finally, in order to graduate, students must "analyze the roles and contributions of individuals and groups in and to social, political, economic, cultural, and religious practices and activities" (12). Clearly, performance expectations are developmentally appropriate as students work toward the exit outcome for this state learning standard.

In order to facilitate students' achievement of Wisconsin state learning standards, a school district in Wisconsin has identified grade-level benchmarks in each curricular area. For example, a grade 8 social studies benchmark states, "Students will evaluate the importance of various social changes and reforms such as the women's movement, industrialization, racial injustice, and class distinction" (United School District of De Pere, Wisconsin 2004). This is aligned with several grade 8 social studies standards, one of which requires students to "describe the ways in which local, regional, and ethnic cultures may influence the everyday lives of people" (Wisconsin Department of Public Instruction 1998).

To further complicate matters, people are liable to refer to standards in a number of ways during the same conversation. According to Kohn (1999), "Sometimes they're referring to standards as guidelines for teaching with an intention to change the nature of instruction" (13). As an example, Kohn points out that standards drafted by the National Council of Teachers of Mathematics in 1989 sought to create a "horizontal shift from isolated facts and memorized procedures toward conceptual understanding and problem solving" (13). On the other hand, *raising standards* calls for a "vertical shift, declaring that students ought

to know more, do more, and perform better" (14). It's important to understand local and state terms specific to the schools we work in as we plan instruction, assess students' learning, and document achievement toward standards.

Growing Toward Standards

Structuring day-to-day meaningful work toward achieving standards requires little steps with short-term objectives that lead to long-term goals. In designing work-sample tasks that lead toward learning standards, we need to provide multiple, varied opportunities for projects, performances, and brief responses. Tasks such as oral reports, miniproductions, and constructed responses put student work on display and allow teachers to assess work in the regular rhythm of the classroom. Lesson by lesson, day by day, we're focused on target competencies while celebrating every inch moved toward them.

When planning a lesson or a unit, we begin with an organizing concept. This provides the framework or focus and outlines parameters for the content to be taught. Lesson objectives specify what students are to learn as well as performance and task expectations. Lesson objectives are developed with the intention of moving students closer to meeting specific learning standards. But which standards should lessons address? Should they focus on national standards, state standards, local standards, grade-level standards, or textbook standards? Many school districts mandate that local or state standards be specifically identified for each lesson or unit.

After we have identified the organizing concept and standard(s) to be addressed, we are challenged with the task of designing work that enables students to progress toward the standard(s) in a meaningful way. We need to design work that is *authentic* and *useful* as well as *meaningful* to the students. These tasks can range from a brief daily entry in a learning log to a literature circle response to a major culminating project.

Healthy Growth, Useful Goals: Authentic and Productive Work

Authentic work is productive work. It has a purpose that is real and relevant. It is recognized as useful—to the student, to the teacher, to the school, and perhaps even to the community. For example, as a culminating activity after a unit on ecology, a fourth-grade class participated in Earth Day by cleaning up recyclable items on the shoreline of Lake Erie. This is not *busywork*, designed to keep students quiet and occupied; it is real, important, and interesting work that promotes real learning. Ideally, all work tasks should be designed with a purpose—with the journey toward meaningful learning standards in mind. The selection of instructional approach is also critical. It must match students' needs and modes of learning.

Children are intrinsically curious and eager to learn—and not just in school. They are naturally this way twenty-four, seven, as they say. Therefore, worthy artifacts of learning or work samples can also come from outside school. To get them, we need to enlist the help of parents or significant caregivers in each child's life. Parents and caregivers can engage children heuristically, challenge them, and build on their inherent motivation to learn. Children's boundless curiosity is evident from birth; it does not suddenly appear when they enter school.

Recently, a grandmother showed us a copy of an email from her daughter-in-law. It contained a dialogue between the daughter-in-law and her three-and-a-half-year-old son, Wilder, about the ocean and volcanoes (see Figure 4–2). The week before, Wilder had watched a movie at the American Museum

---

WILDER: Mommy, what's on the bottom of the ocean?
ME: Well, at the very very very bottom of the deepest part of the ocean is land.
WILDER: And that's where the underwater volcanoes are.
ME: Oh, is that right?
WILDER: Many animals live there. (*Hands spread open*) But how do they live there, how?
ME: I don't know.
(*Short pause.*)
WILDER: Scientists are shocked by this.

Michael, my dad, and I break into laughter.

WILDER: The water is so boiling hot, it would turn a lobster red. It could even cook a human! It could cook, you, me, and daddy!
ME: Wow, I wouldn't want to be cooked.
WILDER: How come?
ME: Because then I would be dead and the sharks would come eat me.
WILDER: Oh, no, it's too deep for the sharks to go there. And too hot. Nothing should be able to live there, but they do.
ME: Like what, what lives there?
WILDER: Tube worms, shrimp, bacteria. . . .
ME: Oh. . . .
WILDER: The shrimp scrape the bacteria off their shells and eat them. But what do the bacteria eat?
ME: I don't know.
WILDER: Nothing should be able to live there, but they do. And scientists are thrilled by this.

FIGURE 4–2 Wilder's Conversation with His Mother

of Natural History in New York about underwater volcanoes. Wilder's conversation with his mom shows us the natural curiosity and enthusiasm of a three-year-old. But an essential component of this scenario is Mom and the mother-child interaction. It is through sharing our insights and our thoughts with another—a peer, a parent, or a teacher—that learning takes place. Documenting these Kodak moments adds so much to our understanding of learners.

In Sue Rosche's classroom one morning, we experienced authentic student learning that was enhanced and articulated through peer interaction and Sue's strong and skillful scaffolding. Sue was using a "stand as you believe" strategy to review for a social studies quiz. In this strategy, the teacher makes a statement related to a unit of study; gives students time to refer to their notes, the textbook, and any other resources in the room; and then asks them to stand in a line at a spot that represents how they feel about the statement, in a continuum that goes from *strongly agree* to *strongly disagree*.

Sue's first statement was: *If there were no laws or no government, people would behave reasonably*. The children thought for a moment and began to move toward spots along the continuum. They didn't check their notes, perhaps feeling that to do so would be a sign of not knowing. However, when Sue and their peers called on them to defend their stand, they realized they needed facts and went back to their books and binders for more information. Some then changed their positions; others held firm. Many of the children possessed the self-confidence to defend their positions and not be intimidated if the majority of the class took an opposite stance.

As the children responded, Sue jotted down anecdotal notes (see Figure 4–3) related to their responses: Had the child used notes to support his or her opinion? Did he or she seem to understand the somewhat abstract concepts related to the functioning of government? We silently cheered as these novices listened to one another and used their work

on the unit to take a stand, verify their opinions, and even change their stances. The validity of the strategy became even more evident when we reviewed their written responses, in essays titled "Why I'm Proud of the American Constitution" (one example is shown in Figure 4–4).

Authentic tasks like this help students attain educational standards. They encourage students to use what they have learned to analyze, interpret, synthesize, and evaluate, not just reproduce knowledge. They motivate them to explore certain topics in depth and become experts. As experts, they have the self-efficacy, knowledge, and skills needed to articulate their ideas to others (Newmann 2000, 2).

Work Samples That Reveal Understanding—and Wisdom

Wiggins (1998) questions whether we *understand* understanding—whether we can accurately define what this complex process entails. Gardner (1981) defines *understanding* as "a sufficient grasp of concepts, principles, or skills so that one can bring them to bear on new problems and situations, deciding in which ways one's present competencies can suffice and in which ways one may require new skills or knowledge" (181).

We also need the wisdom to know what we don't yet understand. Wisdom goes beyond understanding. Sternberg (2003) tells us:

It's possible to create work tasks that yield evidence of students' creative, analytical, and practical thinking. More challenging, however, is designing work tasks that reach beyond just thinking and all the way to thinking *wisely*. When schools teach for wisdom, students learn that it's not just what you know, but how you use what you know that's at issue. Whether you use your knowing for good ends or bad is very important. Wisdom, the opposite of foolishness, is the use of successful intelligence and experience toward the attainment of a common good. (7)

Review for Ch. 1 test — There were 3 other parts

Rosche 2003-2004	#1	#2	#4	#5	#6a	#7-10			
ⓇAdams, Brendan		✓	✓+	+	−	−	trbl giving rationale #7-10 - didn't remember ques.		
ⓇAllen, Karl			+	+	−	−			
Amoia, Santino		✓		+	+	✓	difficult		
Baker, Erica		✓	✓	+	+	+			
ⓇBarton, Andrew		✓	−	+	+	++			
ⓇBlatz, Anna		✓	+	−	+	+			
ⓇBoyle, Christopher			✓+	+	+	+			
D'Angelo, Kayla		+	−	+	+	−			
Fisher, Nicholas	✓		+	+	+				
Grandits, Ryan		✓	✓	+	−	✓			
ⓇKeller, Alex		✓+	+(++)	+	+	+			
ⓇLobaugh, Stacy		✓++	+	+	+	−			
ⓇLongwith, Rachel	++		✓+	+	+	+			
Mooney, Amanda	✓	✓+	✓	−	−	✓			
Oexle, Katharine			✓	+	+	✓			
Pellien, Shannon	✓	✓	−	→+	+	✓			
ⓇReigstad, Leif			+	→+	+	+			
Sprigg, Christopher	✓	✓	−	+	−	✓			
Trafalski, Olivia		✓	+	+	−	+			
Vaccaro, Shannon			−	+	+	✓			
VanDyne, Dylan			+	+	−	−			
Weick, Marissa		✓	✓	+	+	✓			
Yoder, Tiffany			−	−	+	+			
Zaccagnino, Isabella			✓+	+	+	✓			

• Choose key children to record data

• Use C for children who remain at Confused position

• Be sure everyone shares Rationale over time — indicate w/ Ⓡ

#2 difficult for most

(diagonal notes:)
more PE as go higher
lubricant, shakes friction
friction = resistance force
weak = more
energy - store PE, chemaveness
work meets in Joules
focus: who's chg notes

✓ = chg notes

++ = gave good rationale
+ = correct
− = incorrect

( ) = trbl expressing self
Ⓡ = asked for rationale

FIGURE 4–3 Sue Rosche's Anecdotal Notes

Andy   11/10

Socail Studies   essay

Why I'm proud of the American Constitution

I'm proud of the American Constitut Constitution. I couldn't imagine being told what to do by a King, Queen, or Dictator.

I'm glad that the framers made the bill of rights. I like the fact that my family dosent have to provide a home for for a solgers. I would be scared if there was a job man or woman with a gun lurking around my house at night

I'm glad that we har have a the three branches of government, Legislative, Executive, and Judial The reason I glad that we have the legislative branch, is because, there tto would be alot of robberies and murders I if there was no laws. I think it is would would be scary. You could wake

FIGURE 4–4   Andy's Essay

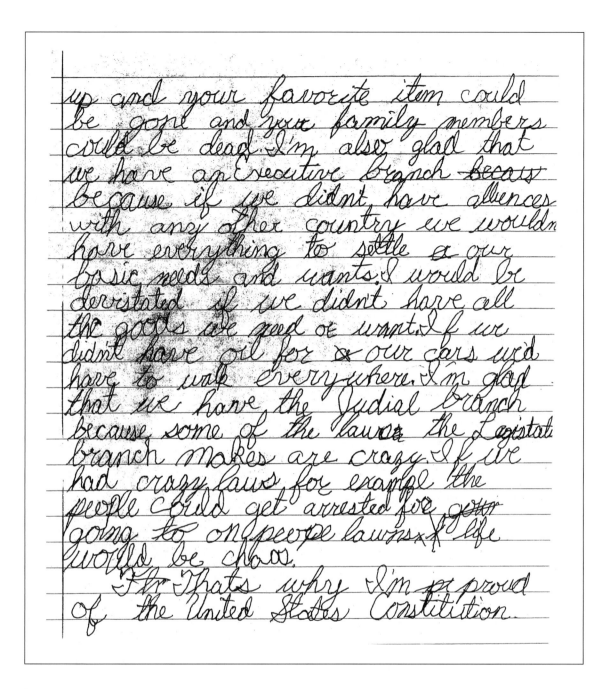

FIGURE 4–4 Continued

Monitoring the Pulse of Learning: Collecting Daily Data

Day-after-day work samples create clear longitudinal (i.e., accumulated over time) evidence of individual student learning. Wiggins (1993) believes that all students are entitled to "ample opportunities to produce work that they can be proud of . . . [and] thus ample opportunity in the curriculum and instruction to monitor, self-assess, and self-correct their work" (28). What appear to be simple steps become, when compiled, a road to achieving standards. Recognizing small bits of daily evidence is critical. Collecting them before they're lost is just as important. Each instance must be archived and its relevance to specific learning standards identified if we are to see the big picture of students' achievement.

An enormous amount of evidence is available in our classrooms every day. We take anecdotal notes as we observe students working. We assess learning products, big and small. We gather significant work samples or worthy artifacts for student portfolios. Methods for efficiently gathering, categorizing, and using this data to document students' learning is a challenge. The task becomes less daunting if we have a system, a guide, a procedure:

▶ Identify assignments in each content area that are directly aligned with the standards.

▶ Collect these assignments and file them in individual student folders according to content areas.

▶ Based on results of early-in-the-year assessments, save individual student work that supports those assessments or demonstrates growth in a particular area.

▶ Save a variety of work samples. These will demonstrate students' strengths, interests, and needs. Some children excel in visual or spatial work such as drawing maps or creating graphs, while others demonstrate learning through verbal skills such as writing a poem or an essay.

The portfolios described in this text provide a storage place for work-sample evidence and a process for using this evidence to understand, wisely, students' growth toward learning standards.

Work Samples Aligned to Standards: An Array of Possibilities

Individual samples of student work are as various and individual as the students who produce them. However, some common sources can be found in almost every classroom, from kindergarten onward.

Journals

Journal entries come in every imaginable size and shape and provide us with a wealth of information about our students. The example in Figure 4–5 was the result of a prompt: *Select a classmate and have a discussion with her/him to discover how you are alike. Write about these similarities. Don't forget to provide evidence and examples.* In the example, Shannon does a fine job comparing herself with her friend Matt.

In another class, students completed an entry on their feelings about the last day of school. For many of them it was also their last day in the school they had attended since kindergarten; they were moving on to middle school. Isabella describes receiving an award in Figure 4–6.

Authentic voice and enthusiasm dominate the journal entry of a student who wrote about how he *loves* roller-blading and offered almost poetic reasons for this passion (see Figure 4–7).

Mini–research Projects

Mini–research projects can serve a number of purposes, but for the most part they are completed in less than a week. They can be worked on individually, in pairs, or in small groups and often culminate in a presentation to an audience of peers and/or adults as a means of *publishing* the work. In contemporary classrooms, they may be web based or at least supported through use of the Internet.

As a regular part of unit reviews, Jay Basham's seventh-grade social studies students, in pairs, prepare PowerPoint presentations related to topics they've studied. One requirement is that presenters include review questions the audience (the class) will answer after the presentation. Figure 4–8 shows questions prepared to accompany a presentation on the War of 1812.

A student in Brian Shea's class capitalized on his artistic and creative strengths and skills. As part of his final project, he created and illustrated a model of a solar-powered car (see Figure 4–9). Included in his research were

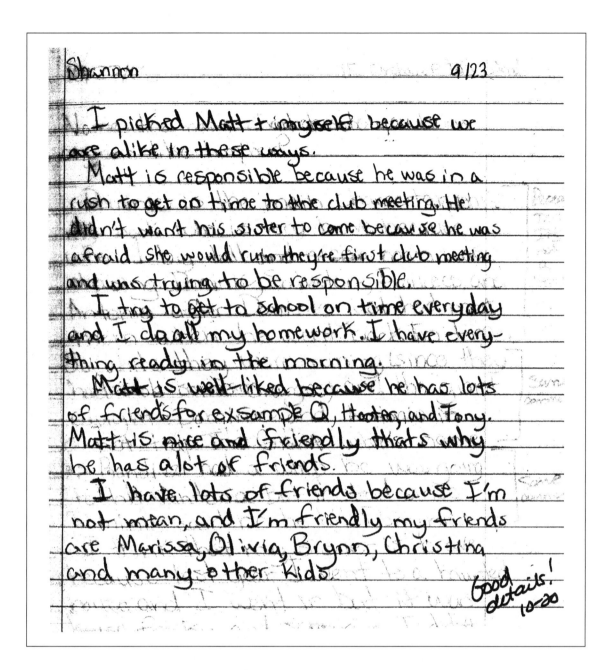

Shannon   9/23

1. I picked Matt + myself because we are alike in these ways.

Matt is responsible because he was in a rush to get on time to the club meeting. He didn't want his sister to come because he was afraid she would ruin they're first club meeting and was trying to be responsible.

I try to get to school on time everyday and I do all my homework. I have everything ready in the morning.

Matt is well-liked because he has lots of friends for exsample Q, Hooter, and Tony. Matt is nice and friendly thats why he has a lot of friends.

I have lots of friends because I'm not mean, and I'm friendly my friends are Marissa, Olivia, Brynn, Christina and many other kids.

Good details! 10-20

FIGURE 4–5   Shannon's Journal Entry

graphs and charts comparing speeds (miles per hour) possible in sunlight versus floodlight.

Work Samples Accumulated on Larger Projects

Sandy Terrance and her third graders embarked on a yearlong exploration of world geography and cultures in social studies. On the last day of school the children proudly presented their finished and bound books, the culmination of day-to-day work, to an audience of their parents, their peers, the school principal, and a variety of other members of the school community. The final product was an in-the-classroom benchmark. However, each entry represented students' independent practice that extended over several days and followed a specific lesson. Figure

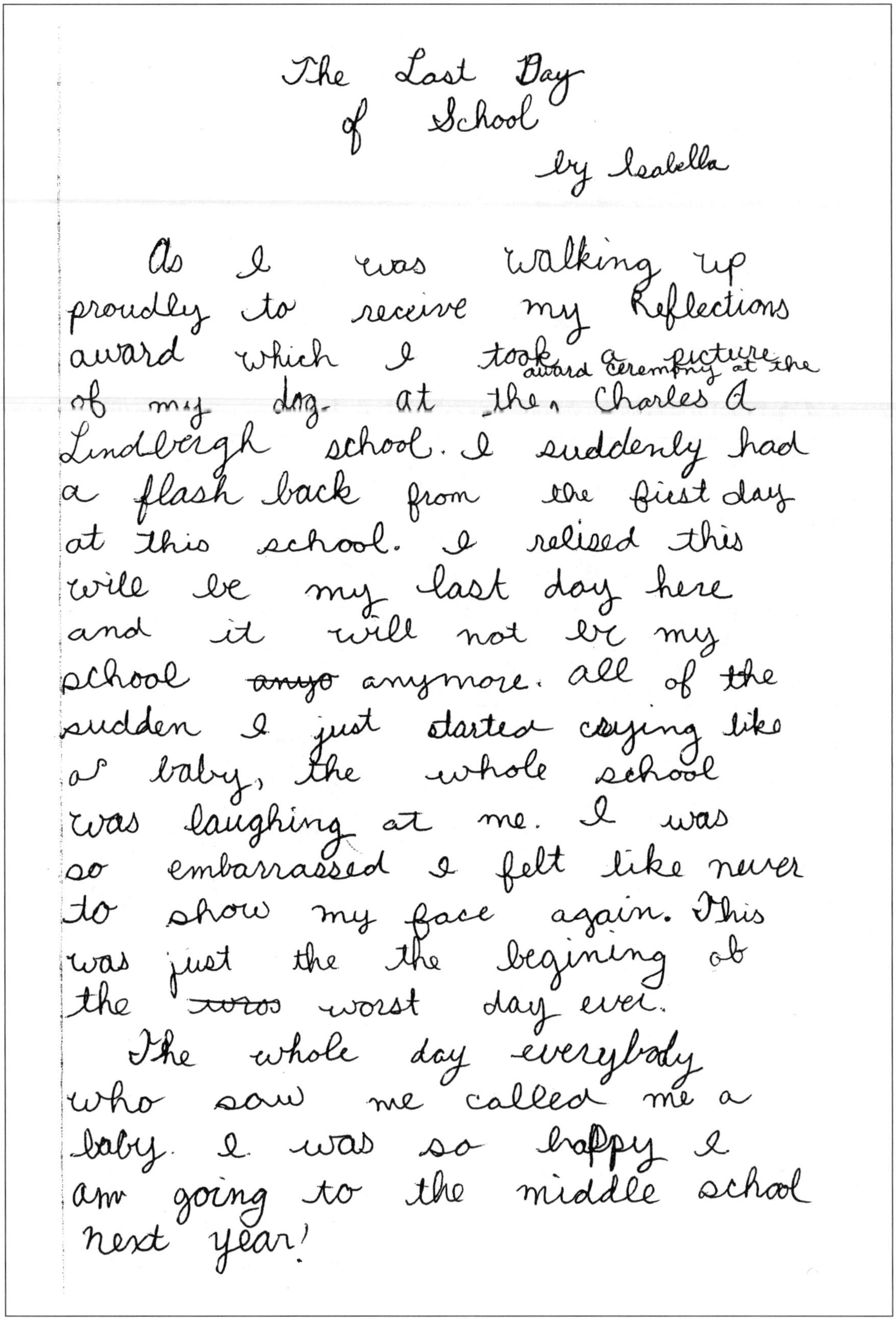

The Last Day
of School
by Isabella

As I was walking up proudly to receive my Reflections award which I took picture award ceremony at the of my dog. at the, Charles A Lindbergh school. I suddenly had a flash back from the first day at this school. I relised this will be my last day here and it will not be my school anyo anymore. All of the sudden I just started crying like a baby, the whole school was laughing at me. I was so embarrassed I felt like never to show my face again. This was just the the begining ob the worst worst day ever.

The whole day everybody who saw me called me a baby. I was so happy I am going to the middle school next year!

FIGURE 4–6 Isabella's Journal Entry

idea	details
I "love" Roller Blading	- Roller Blading is my favorite sport because it's easy to go off ramps you'd feel the wind in your face
	- I have a ramp at home and I love the ramp because Roller Blades are less weight than a bike or a skateboard and you go higher in the air but I'm not at that level of Roller bading
	- It's also fun b/c you can also go faster on Roller Blades because they don't way much

FIGURE 4–7   Journal Entry About Roller-Blading

The War of 1812
The Treaty of Ghent officially ended the War of 1812.
No one actually won the War of 1812.

Now here's a few questions that I am going to ask you:

1. What did the British set up in the US ports during the war to block ships from entering and to stop trade?
2. What are the two sides that fought in the War of 1812?
3. What are the British telling the Indians to do, and what are they giving them?
4. Did the British agree or disagree with shipping rights?

FIGURE 4–8   Questions About the War of 181

4–10 is one such sample: a student's diagram of the lines of latitude and longitude.

Students studying the grassland animals of Africa were asked to create a "Who Am I?" page for a book about them. Sarah's work is shown in Figure 4–11.

Student Writing

Students in one elementary school are asked to complete a student observation guide at two intervals during the school year. Dylan's observation of his progress (see Figure 4–12) shows a child who is learning to reflect honestly on his strengths and needs in attaining his goals. Max, a second grader, gives us a very enthusiastic response about his reading: "I have never read so good in my life. It's fun when I could look at restaurant signs that I went to long ago and I could just explain the restaurant, now I can tell it by name." (See Figure 4–13.)

At another school, Austin, in a journal entry, reflected on his progress—and lack of it: "I learned that if I state a problem I can solve it. I noticed that my writing has gotten better over the year . . . I also noticed that my revision got better over the year and that my editing got worse." (See Figure 4–14.)

Work Samples Showing Strengths, Interests, and Needs

Students in a first-grade classroom were asked to make a map of one of their favorite places. Aric's map of the Newport (Kentucky) Aquarium (see Figure 4–15) introduces us to a young man who excels in visual representation. His attention to detail suggests that his trip to this aquarium was a great adventure for him and a real learning experience.

Fifth graders were asked to write an "exit visa" after a math session. In this document they were to reflect on the lesson, tell what surprised them, and set a goal for the next day. These visas gave the teacher vital information to use in planning upcoming lessons. A number of students' responses are included in Figure 4–16.

In Chapter 3 we talked about Sue Rosche's word splash activity as one that yields thinking evidence. This strategy can also be used as an organizational foundation for brief essays. In Figure 4–17, Brendan uses the words *work, force, resistance, effort, potential energy,* and *kinetic energy* to create a brief summary of what he has learned about energy.

These examples are artifact *treasures.* They provide evidence of student learning, they give us a picture of the whole child, and they help us know where to go next to best enable each student to learn.

Reporting, Scoring, or Both: Looking for Evidence of Understanding

Reporting here refers to using students' work as a basis for reporting progress to and with students—interacting with them and posing questions that uncover understanding or misunderstanding. "Given these insights [teachers] can decide what would help the student move closer to the target. This analysis leads teachers to a deeper understanding of the link between their instruction and their students' learning" (Langer, Colton, and Goff 2003, 4). Through this dialogue teachers and learners begin to envision what the next step should be.

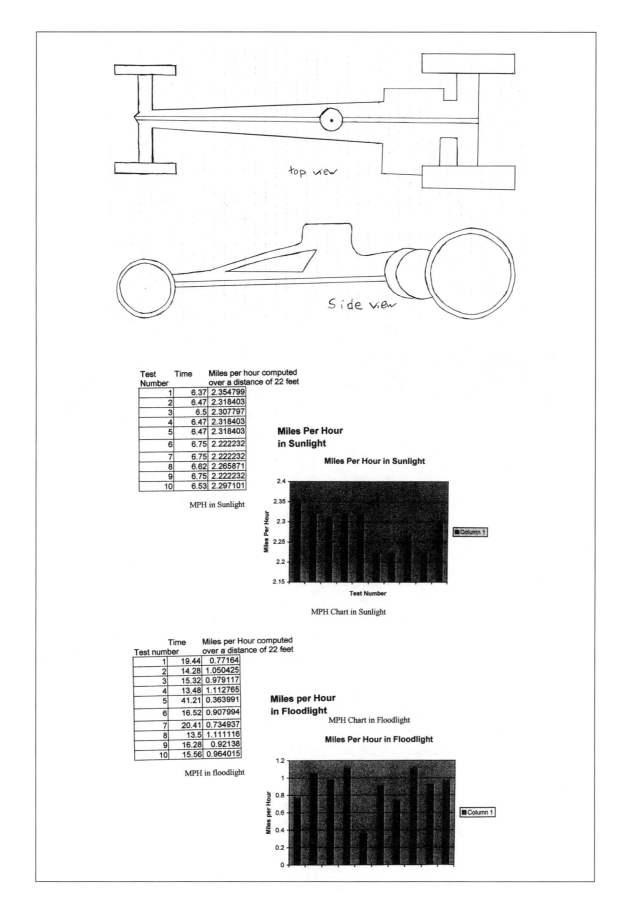

top view

Side view

Test Number	Time	Miles per hour computed over a distance of 22 feet
1	6.37	2.354799
2	6.47	2.318403
3	6.5	2.307797
4	6.47	2.318403
5	6.47	2.318403
6	6.75	2.222232
7	6.75	2.222232
8	6.62	2.265871
9	6.75	2.222232
10	6.53	2.297101

MPH in Sunlight

Miles Per Hour in Sunlight

MPH Chart in Sunlight

Test number	Time	Miles per Hour computed over a distance of 22 feet
1	19.44	0.77164
2	14.28	1.050425
3	15.32	0.979117
4	13.48	1.112765
5	41.21	0.363991
6	16.52	0.907994
7	20.41	0.734937
8	13.5	1.111116
9	16.28	0.92138
10	15.56	0.964015

MPH in floodlight

Miles per Hour in Floodlight

MPH Chart in Floodlight

Miles Per Hour in Floodlight

FIGURE 4–9   Connor's Illustration of a Solar-Powered Car

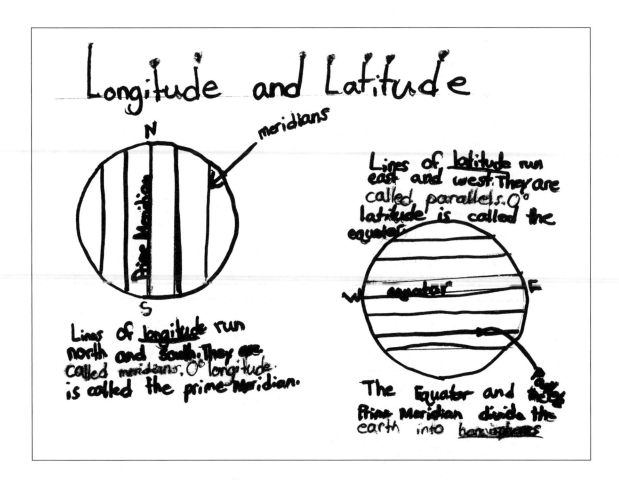

FIGURE 4–10 Student Diagram of Latitude and Longitude

The feedback shared in these conversations is central to students' success. Wiggins (1993) feels that students are entitled to *genuine* feedback, characterized by *usable* information that outlines their strengths and weaknesses. It's an accurate assessment of their long-term progress toward a set of exit standards framed in terms of essential tasks.

Students receive oral feedback for much of the work they complete in school. However, sometimes work samples are graded. When they are, our scoring or grading policies should give students incentives and opportunities to improve their performance and identify real progress toward exit and real-world standards.

Often such scoring involves a rubric. The construction and use of rubrics is discussed in Chapter 5. However, for our purposes here,

Figure 4–18 is an example of a journal entry, and Figure 4–19 is the rubric that was used to score it. Figure 4–20 is another example of a rubric that can be used to grade daily work.

Using the definitions of *understanding* previously discussed, we can begin to look for evidence of real understanding in day-to-day work samples. Can students, with clarity and insight, explain what they've learned, what it means, where it connects with other learning, and why it's important? This evidence is provided in several ways. Each of the following demonstrations of understanding, which are taken from Grant Wiggins' *Educative Assessment* (1998), is unique. Together, like multiple views of an elephant, they lead to fully developed concepts.

Primarily, understanding is being able to qualify opinions, see the big picture, and

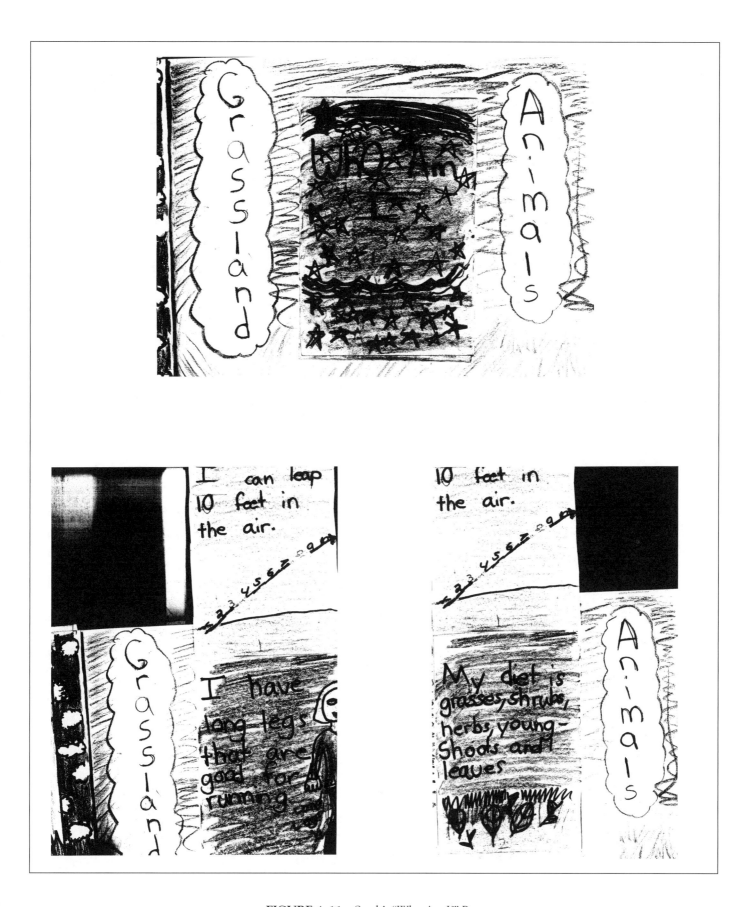

FIGURE 4–11   Sarah's "Who Am I?" Page

Assessment Program
Grade 5 Spring Student Observation Guide
THE LEARNER

Student Name: Dylan   Date: 3|29

1.   What have I done to attain the goals that I set for myself in the fall?

(A) I have learned most of my facts up to 14. I've been →

(By doing count on me)

(D) rememembering (every) thing for a while.

2.   What have I done to become more independent as a learner at home and at school? I've been looking at my DAB to remember things and to put them in my book bag.

3.   What would I like to improve on before I enter Middle School?
Writing cersife, Reading faster, asking questions more saftens, and remembering my homwork.

#1 (B) I've been studieing my studie skill by looking at things with my mom And she'll ask me some questions.

(C) I havent been doing to good at practicing spelling.

(E) So far i've had 3 or 4 diffrent types of books.

(F) I havent done to many literature responses.

(G) I only have three or four writing peaces.

FIGURE 4–12   Dylan's Self-Reflection

60

Assessment Program
Grade 2 Spring Student Observation Guide
THE LEARNER

Student Name: Max   Date: 4-29

1. What have you learned to do really well in second grade?

I have never read so good in my life. It's fun when I could look at restraunt signs that I whent to long ago and I could just explain the restraunt now I can tell it by name.

2. How do you think you can improve your daily work?

I will write neat all the time. Then people will be able to read my work like now.

FIGURE 4–13 Max's Self-Reflection

justify a position with specific evidence. Shannon, a fifth grader, shows that she is beginning to see the big picture as she tells about Latin American countries that need to diversify their resources in order to strengthen their economies (see Figure 4–21). After reading a book about Hawaii, Olivia was amazed about what she had learned. When she began reading the book, she thought Hawaii was a lot like New York State. The fact that it was not, along with many other features about Hawaii, amazed her. (See Figure 4–22.)

Understanding is also revealed in students' ability to use and apply knowledge effectively in diverse, real-world contexts. When students really understand, they view genuine feedback as constructive. They value and appreciate how it can help them. In both Sue Rosche's and Jay Basham's classes, the students were effectively able to present the knowledge they had gained from their research projects. As other class members provided feedback, presenters possessed the self-confidence and sophistication to listen attentively, ask their own questions, and clarify misunderstandings when necessary.

Understanding also involves the ability to extend knowledge in novel and effective

Austin

I learned that if I state a problem I can solve it. I noticed that my writing has gotten better over the year. My goals have helped me and I think that I shall still use them. I also noticed that my revision got better over the year and that my editing got worse.

FIGURE 4–14 Austin's Journal Entry

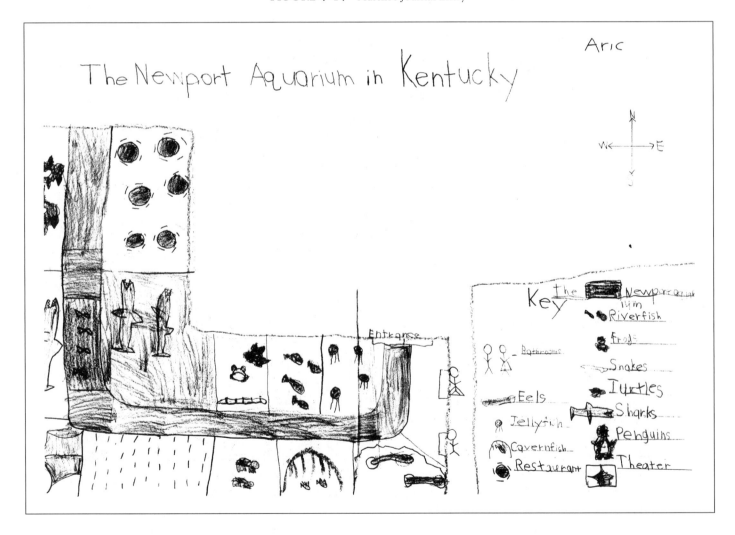

FIGURE 4–15 Aric's Map of an Aquarium

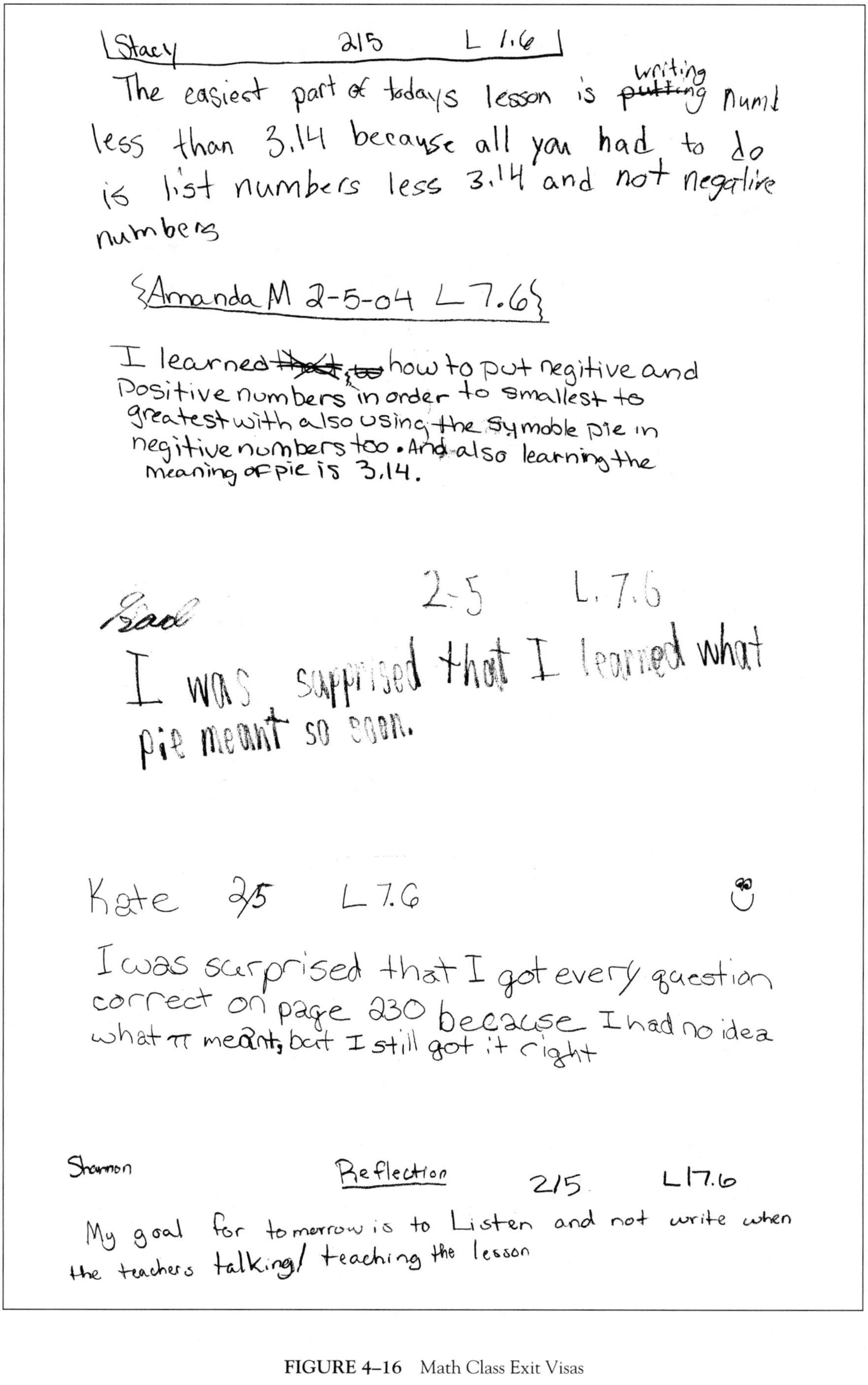

Stacy   215   L 1.6

The easiest part of todays lesson is ~~putting~~ writing numb
less than 3.14 because all you had to do
is list numbers less 3.14 and not negative
numbers

{Amanda M 2-5-04 L 7.6}

I learned ~~that too~~ how to put negitive and
positive numbers in order to smallest to
greatest with also using the symoble pie in
negitive numbers too. And also learning the
meaning of pie is 3.14.

Sad   2-5   L. 7.6

I was supprised that I learned what
pie meant so soon.

Kate   2/5   L 7.6

I was scarprised that I got every question
correct on page 230 because I had no idea
what π meant, but I still got it right

Shannon   Reflection   2/5.   L 7.6

My goal for tomorrow is to Listen and not write when
the teachers talking/ teaching the lesson

FIGURE 4–16   Math Class Exit Visas

Work and force goes together because force means a push or pull. If that's not being doen work isn't being doen. Resistance force and effort force goes together because the effort and resistance forces are faceing eachother so friction can be done. Potential energy goes with kinetic energy because kinetic energy means to move in any direction. Potential energy means to stop at one point.

FIGURE 4–17 Word Splash Activity

ways. A couple of participants in a literature circle debriefing added interesting and novel ideas to the discussion (see Figure 4–23). Anna felt she had a friendly debate about one question and reported a groupmate's idea that not everyone was depressed during the Great Depression.

In addition, understanding is revealed in students' critical thinking as they explore multiple points of view and analyze the worth of ideas. In quite a remarkable literature circle response as the *connector*, Erica compared an event in the story the students had read with a local news story about a racial incident involving police brutality (see Figure 4–24).

Also important is the idea that understanding undergirds the empathy that students develop—their ability to walk in someone else's shoes. To do this, students must decide what is really plausible, sensible, or meaningful in the ideas or actions of others. Kayla displayed empathy as she compared herself with Carlie, a character in her book. She said, "Carlie is a mean, snobbish, selfish kind of girl! I like this character because at the end of the book she changes and I think that takes a lot of practice! I would know. I was just like her last year!" (See Figure 4–25.)

Another essential aspect of understanding is self-knowledge—the ability to know our own intellectual prejudices as well as how they influence our thinking and acceptance of new ideas. Students demonstrate self-knowledge when they recognize personal prejudices, question their convictions, assess their own work, and defend personal views without being defensive. Erica's response to *The Journal of C J Jackson* (see Figure 4–26) is an example. She clearly states how she felt about the book and the genre before she read it. But in the end she said, "I realized that books about the depression that are in journal form aren't that bad!"

And sometimes we find a piece of student work that stands by itself for creativity, excellence in writing, and the strength of its voice. A story titled "The Mysterious Well," written by a fifth grader, was such a piece (see Figure 4–27 for an excerpt from this story).

Considerations for Diverse Populations

As with the thinking evidence described in Chapter 3, work-sample evidence represents process and performance under classroom conditions. The conditions and populations found in contemporary classrooms are increasingly diverse. Students demonstrate a wide range of ability and interests and come from a variety of cultural and ethnic backgrounds. We truly believe that all children can learn and are entitled to an environment that encourages learning and enables them to suc-

ceed. Work samples collected daily give both the student and the teacher multiple opportunities to assess, evaluate, and plan. This process ensures that no single day and no single grade counts more than any other. Regularly collected work samples demonstrate what can be accomplished over time with necessary adaptations and scaffolding. It enables us to

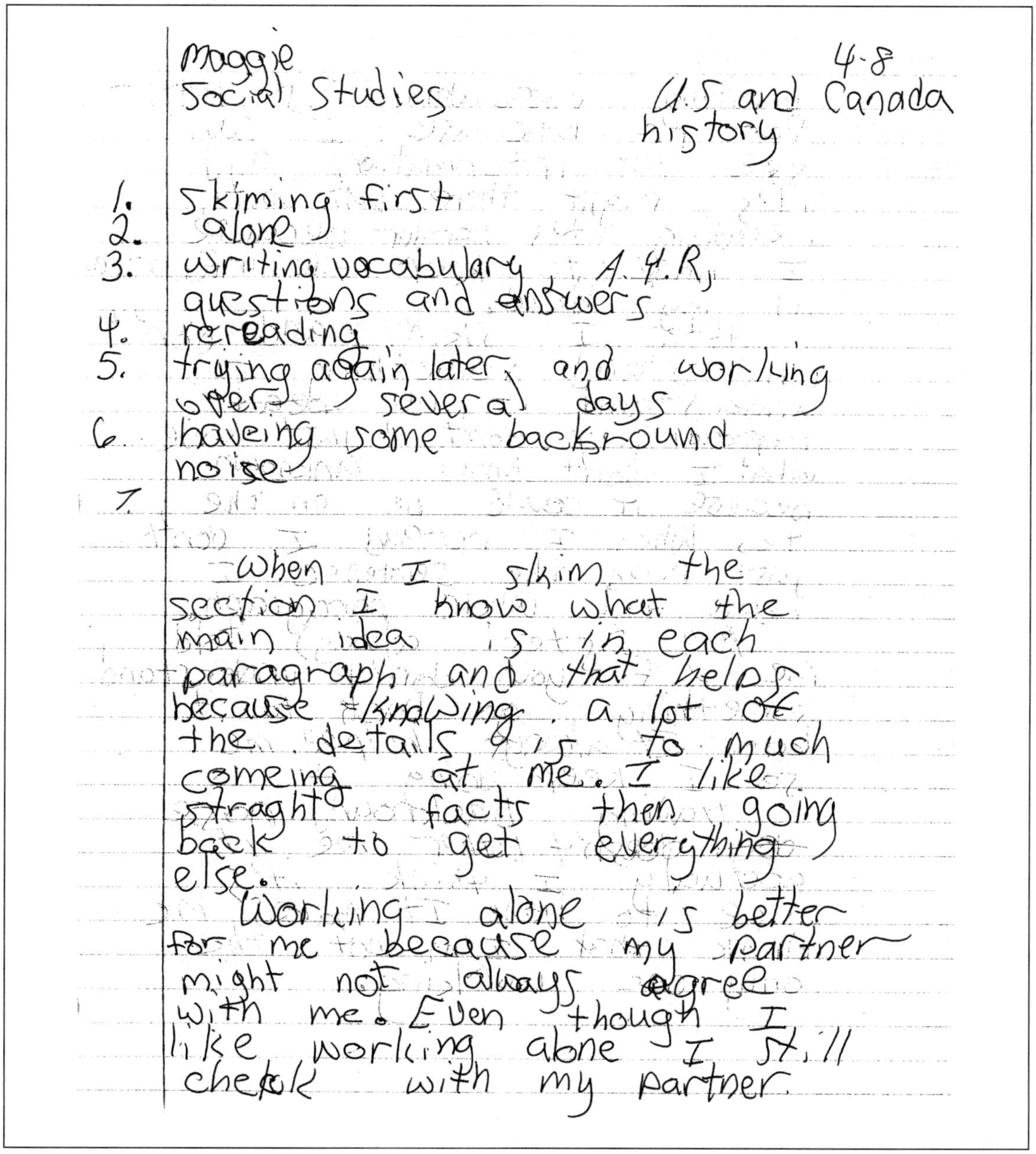

> Maggie
> Social Studies   4·8
>   U.S and Canada
>   history
>
> 1. Skiming first
> 2. alone
> 3. writing vocabulary , A.Y.R,
>   questions and answers
> 4. rereading
> 5. trying again later, and working
>   over several days
> 6. haveing some background
>   noise
> 7.
>
> When I skim the section I know what the main idea is in each paragraph and that helps because knowing a lot of the details is to much comeing at me. I like straght facts then going back to get everything else. Working alone is better for me because my partner might not always agree with me. Even though I like working alone I still chefck with my partner.

FIGURE 4–18 Journal Entry

(continues)

writing vocabulary is better for me because I can see the information and it's right there but with reading it's harder because I have to keep the information in my head.

After I skim and don't understand something I understand it by ~~dead~~ rereading. I don't just leave what I don't know unknown because it could be on the tes. When I reread I don't just read the sentence I read the whole paragraph.

My sister always told me if you don't understand something go back to it later. It always helped me so I keep doing it.

Having backround noise ~~even~~ doesn't bother me it accualy I think it's nice to have. It makes me think that I'm not the only one working.

FIGURE 4–18 Continued

Scoring Rubric for Journal Entries

Criteria	Exemplary 4	Accomplished 3	Developing 2	Beginning 1	Score
Purpose	Strong voice and tone that clearly addresses the purpose for writing.	Appropriate voice and tone. The purpose is largely clear.	Attempts to use personal voice and tone. Somewhat addresses the intended purpose.	Demonstrates limited awareness of use of voice and tone. Limited evidence of intended purpose.	
Understanding	Many interesting, specific facts and ideas are included.	Many facts and ideas are included.	Some facts and ideas are included.	Few facts and ideas are included.	
Conventions	All grammar and spelling is correct.	Only one or two grammar and spelling errors.	A few grammar and spelling errors.	Many grammar and spelling errors.	

Social Studies Learning Log
Scoring Rubric

Name: Maggie
Date: 4 – 8 – 03

Purpose   3   Accomplished

Understanding   4   Exemplary

Conventions   2   Developing

FIGURE 4–19   Rubric Used to Score Journal Entry

study a *videotape* of a child, which captures images over time, rather than a *snapshot* of the child, which captures a single image.

Sensitive to the individual needs of individual students, we plan instruction based on ongoing assessment. It readily becomes clear to even the most novice teacher that one size does not fit all. We need to be sensitive to the diversity of the students in our classrooms and adapt instruction accordingly. All students in a class can progress toward the same goal and the same standard. However, the route and the time required may differ. We can structure and adapt tasks so that all students can meet the same objectives. One student in Brian Shea's science class demonstrated his knowledge of solar energy through a drawing and diagrams, while another interviewed an astronaut and wrote a report. Clearly, two different approaches accomplished the same goal.

Assigning students to work in pairs, trios, or small groups is very beneficial to children who have a range of abilities. English language learners benefit greatly from working in collaboration with one or more students. Language develops through practice and interaction with others. Tasks accomplished collaboratively promote greater understanding for the participants. Literature circles are often organized so that each group contains students of a variety of reading levels. More able students can be paired with less able students to fulfill a literature circle role.

One adaptation that helps less able students is to provide them with the material in advance—perhaps an audiotape of a reading selection. Also, instructional material related to many topics can be found at several reading levels and in many formats. It is important to provide a variety of resources, both print and nonprint, to ensure that all students will have the opportunity to experience success.

Extra hands in the classroom help provide a stimulating learning environment in which

---

Scoring Criteria for Student Work

Accuracy

Score	Criteria
4	all concepts used and explained with high degree of accuracy
3	shows good grasp of most information; only slight inaccuracies
2	shows evidence of understanding but some inaccuracies
1	terminology used but considerable confusion of meaning
0	incomplete, nonsense statements

Depth

Score	Criteria
4	elaborate, connective, and/or expansive thinking shown
3	thorough treatment of entire assignment
2	minimal coverage of all aspects of assignment
1	surface treatment of parts of assignment
0	doesn't begin to address the assignment

Creativity

Score	Criteria
4	clever, inventive response to assignment
3	pervasive use of own imagination
2	moderate demonstration of own language and ideas
1	glimmers of original ideas shown but not elaborated
0	relies on examples and language used in class

(adapted from Hein and Price 1994)

FIGURE 4–20   Another Rubric Example

all students can learn. Many schools have programs whereby parents and grandparents are welcome in the classroom to work with children. Preservice teachers can also be extremely helpful to children who need extra or special support. Preservice teachers consistently tell us how much they learn about teaching and about children when they are given this opportunity.

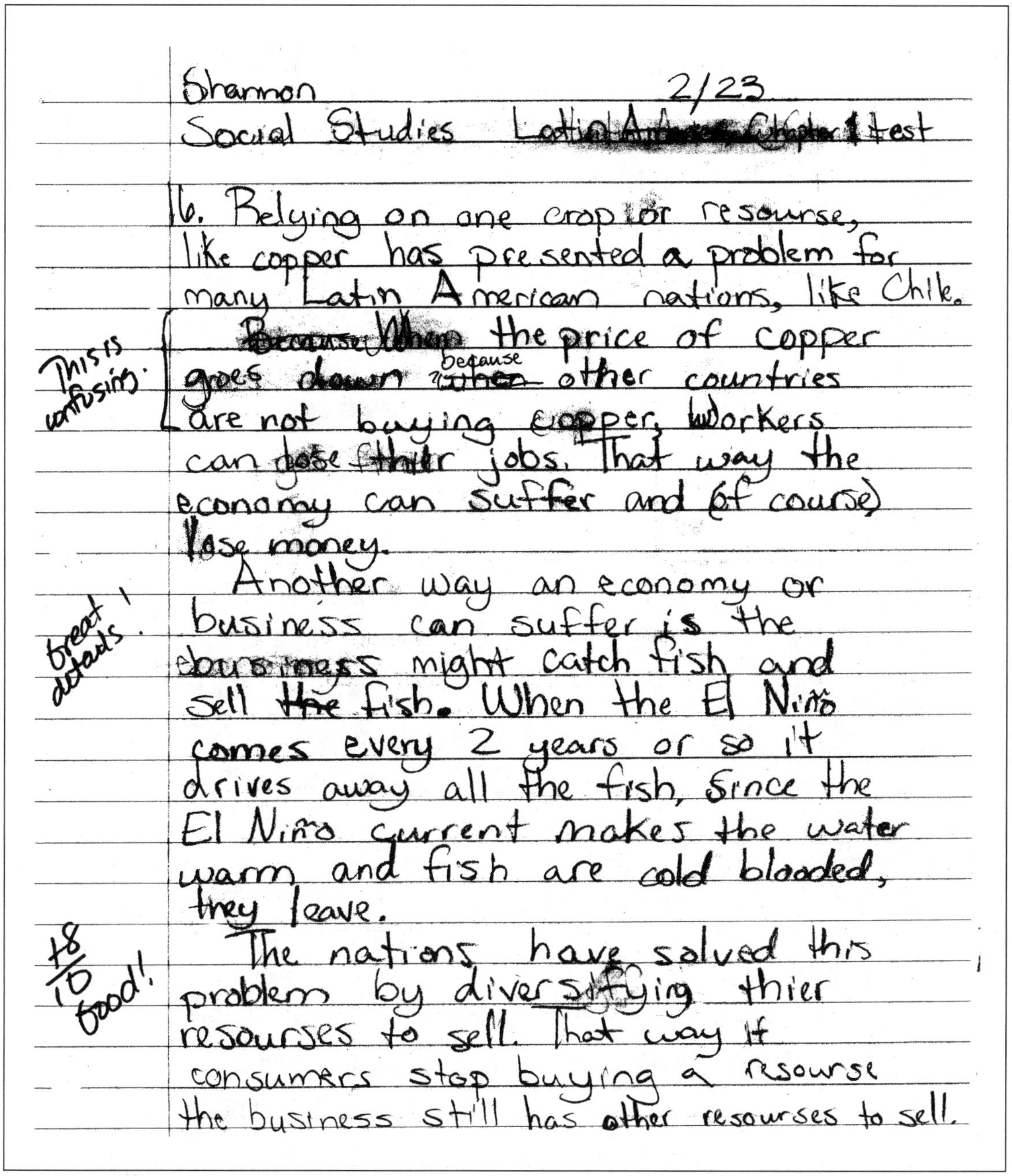

Shannon   2/23
Social Studies   ~~Latin America Chapter 1~~ test

16. Relying on one crop or resourse,
like copper has presented a problem for
many Latin American nations, like Chile.
This is confusing. ~~Because When~~ the price of copper
goes ~~down when~~ because other countries
are not buying ~~copper,~~ Workers
can ~~lose thier~~ jobs. That way the
economy can suffer and (of course)
lose money.
great details! Another way an economy or
business can suffer is the
~~business~~ might catch fish and
sell ~~the~~ fish. When the El Niño
comes every 2 years or so it
drives away all the fish, since the
El Niño current makes the water
warm and fish are cold blooded,
they leave.
+8/10 good! The nations have solved this
problem by diversifying thier
resourses to sell. That way if
consumers stop buying a resourse
the business still has other resourses to sell.

FIGURE 4–21   Shannon's Social Studies Response

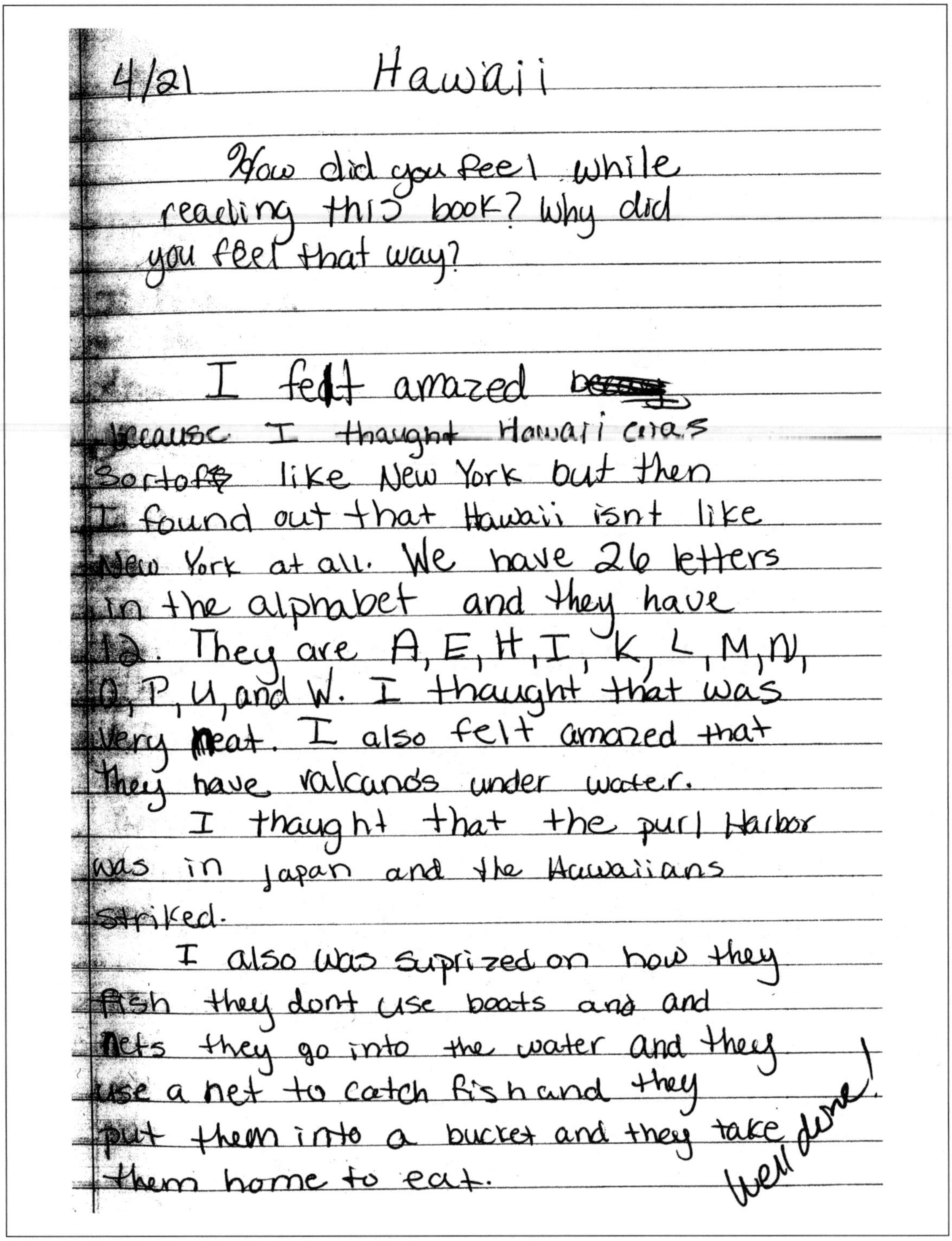

4/21   Hawaii

How did you feel while reading this book? Why did you feel that way?

I felt amazed ~~because~~ because I ~~thought~~ Hawaii was sortof like New York but then I found out that Hawaii isnt like New York at all. We have 26 letters in the alphabet and they have 12. They are A, E, H, I, K, L, M, N, O, P, U, and W. I thought that was very neat. I also felt amazed that they have valcanos under water.

I thought that the purl Harbor was in Japan and the Hawaiians striked.

I also was suprized on how they fish they dont use boats and and nets they go into the water and they use a net to catch fish and they put them into a bucket and they take them home to eat.

well done!

FIGURE 4–22   Olivia's Literature Response

Literature Circle Debriefing

Name _Anna_   Date _3-15_

1. How much did you participate in the discussion today? Comment.

    (about the right amount)   too much   not at all   too little

    I think I participated enough because I
    always did my share and encouraged others to join in.

2. What was an important contribution you made to the discussion?

    i.e. During the Dissution leader question
    I had a friendly debate.

3. What was an important idea expressed by someone else in the group during the discussion (Identify the person and tell what s/he said.)

    Left That not everyone was depressed
    during the great depression.

•Use (but do not limit yourself to) this list of strategies to help you answer questions 4 & 5:

    participating   staying on topic
    contributing appropriate information   encouraging others to contribute
    listening carefully   making good eye contact
    being considerate of others' opinions asking for clarification
    summarizing   using appropriate voice levels

4. What group strategies did **your group** use well?

    Participating, listening carfully and being
    sensitive were some of the things our group did well.

5. What strategies did **you** struggle with?

    I struggled with the volume of my
    voice. I was to quiet.

6. What are your suggestions/comments/goals for your next literature circle discussion?

    My goal for the next Literature
    Cirdle is too for all of us to speak
    up. I also think everyone should
    share about the same amount.

FIGURE 4–23   Anna's Literature Circle Debriefing

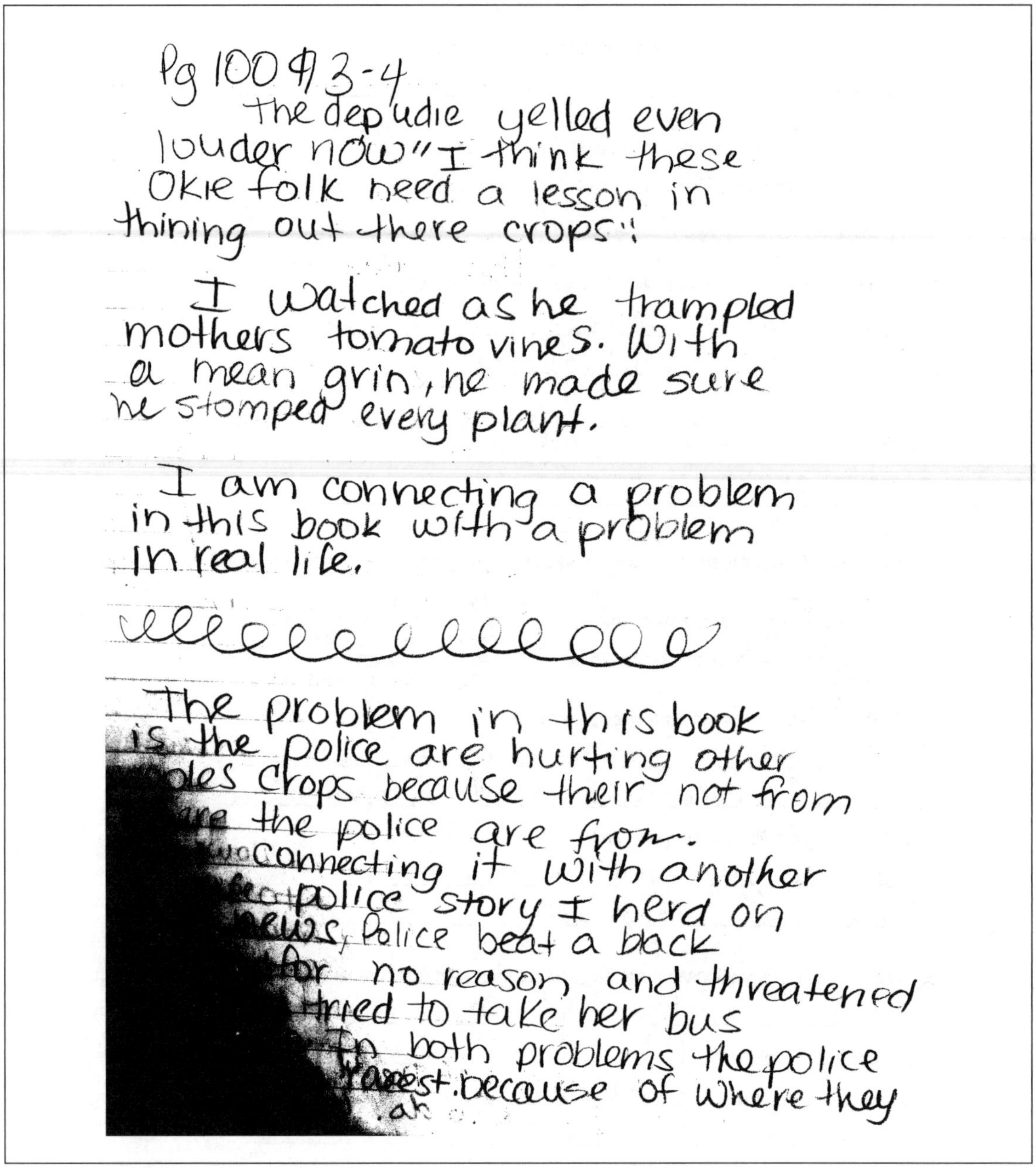

Pg 100 ¶ 3-4
The dep'udie yelled even
louder now "I think these
Okie folk need a lesson in
thining out there crops"

I watched as he trampled
mothers tomato vines. With
a mean grin, he made sure
he stomped every plant.

I am connecting a problem
in this book with a problem
in real life.

llllll lllll

The problem in this book
is the police are hurting other
oles crops because their not from
are the police are from.
Connecting it with another
police story I herd on
news, police beat a black
for no reason and threatened
tried to take her bus
In both problems the police
arrest because of where they
ah

FIGURE 4–24   Erica's Literature Response

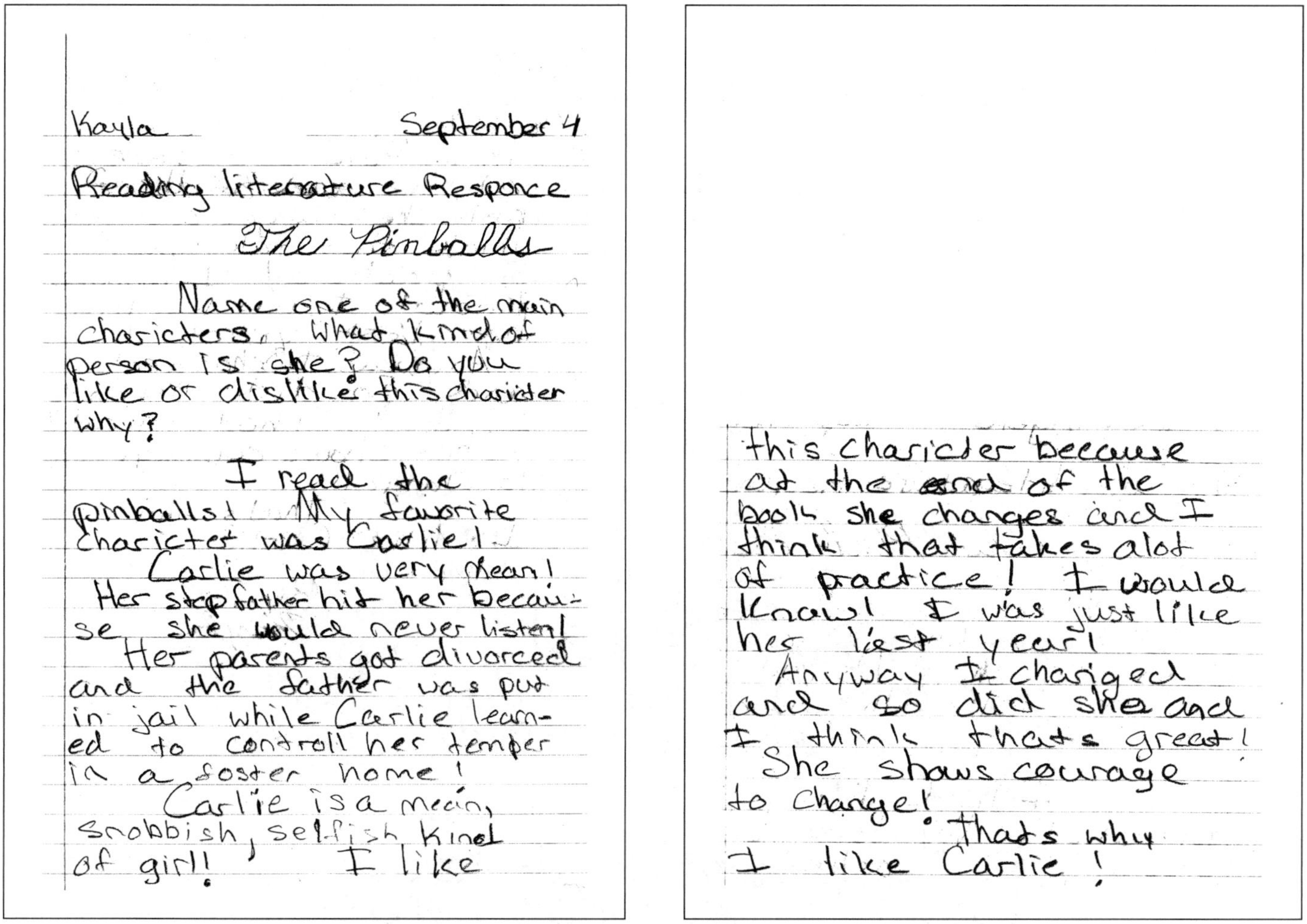

Kayla   September 4

Reading literature Responce

The Pinballs

Name one of the main
charicters. What kind of
person is she? Do you
like or dislike this charicter
why?

I read the
pinballs! My favorite
charicter was Carlie!
Carlie was very mean!
Her step father hit her because she would never listen!
Her parents got divorced
and the father was put
in jail while Carlie learned to controll her temper
in a foster home!
Carlie is a mean,
snobbish, selfish kind
of girl! I like

this charicter because
at the end of the
book she changes and I
think that takes alot
of practice! I would
know! I was just like
her last year!
Anyway I changed
and so did she and
I think thats great!
She shows courage
to change!
Thats why
I like Carlie!

FIGURE 4–25   Kayla's Literature Response

73

The Journal of CJ Jackson 3-29

Is this book like any other book that you've read? If so how are they alike?

I have never read a book like this about the great depression. I never was really interested. Even if I was interested in the great depression I would have ofs never ~~choose~~ chosen this book because I never really liked how books were written in journal form.

I realized that books about the depression that are in journal form arnt that bad!

you prepared well for (it) (except for one incomplete role) and you shared well in your group, too!

FIGURE 4–26   Erica's Literature Response

The Mysterious Well
by Leif

Meet Bob Peters. He was a simple country boy, with nothing much to fear or dislike. Until now.

Ever since those creepy neighbors moved in next door, some strange sounds have been occurring. The strangest thing about them is that they brought their own well with them! The noises were so bad one day, that the howling and screeching caused father to "go teach them something they'll never forget." He always says that when he gets annoyed with something.

As father approached the doorstep, an eerie howl apparently came from the house.

But the howl wasn't coming from the house. It was coming from the equally eerie well next eerie house.

Don't expect father to notice that, though. He isn't exactly the most observant in the family.

As I was saying, the eerie howls were coming from the well. Father rang the doorbell, which was triggered by a long, frayed rope leading to a rusted, oversized bell.

FIGURE 4–27 Excerpt from "The Mysterious Well"

Famous African Americans Biography Prewriting Worksheet

Task: In order to complete this assignment and receive an acceptable grade your group will complete the following tasks:

a) **Research:** Conduct research based on a Famous African American. You will randomly draw a card to find out who your group will conduct research on and then answer the Biography Core Questions on.

b) **Compose:** Write a biography based on your research as well as your answers to the biography core questions. Remember as with an writing assignment, you must have what three components:

1) _____

2) _____

3) _____

c) **Create:** Create a Power Point presentation, which will be presented to the class along with your oral presentation about your person. Your presentation should contain clear images of your subject, at least 2 as well as information about your subject. ****<u>You will print only ONE PAGE</u> of your PowerPoint for display purposes, <u>it must be a page with both an image as well as information</u>.**

d) **Present:** Orally present your PowerPoint Presentation to the class. Remember all group members must present equally. All group members will be graded down if one person fails to present.

Getting Started

Names of <u>all</u> group members: _____

Due Date: _____ Presentation Dates: _____

Subject Name: _____

Biography Core Questions: Utilize the Internet as well as the books provided to complete this section.

1) Date of birth? _____

2) How old is the person or was the person when they died? _____

3) Where was this person born? _____

4) Is the person still alive? _____ If not when did they die? _____

5) If the person is alive, where do they live? _____

* If the person is dead, where and how did they die? _____

_____

_____

_____

APPENDIX 4–1 Mini-Research Project on African American History

Team Members 1. _____ 2._____

Famous African American : _____

Social Studies and ELA Project

Mr. Basham and Mr. Linsey

African American Biography Project
__Assessment Rubric__

Criteria		Excellent	Competent	Limited
Biography Core Questions (10 Points)		Student answers all questions with complete historical accuracy.	Student answers all questions with some historical accuracy.	Student answers all questions with little historical accuracy.
Biography Graphic Organizer (10 Points)		Student uses many concrete details about the subject's appearance, behavior, and background.	Student uses some concrete details about the subject's appearance, behavior, and background.	Student does not use concrete details and the subject is incomplete.
Biography First Draft (10 Points)		Student completes a first draft including all required information.	Student completes a first draft including some required information.	Student completes a first draft including little required information.
Biography Final Draft (30 Points)		Biography is organized, logical, has no or few errors in spelling, grammar, usage, or agreement.	Biography is organized, logical, has some errors in spelling, grammar, usage, or agreement.	Biography is organized, logical, has many errors in spelling, grammar, usage, or agreement.
Power-Point Presentation (25 Points)		Student clearly communicates what the person has done for society in a minimum of five slides.	Student communicates what the person has done for society in a minimum of five slides.	Student poorly communicates what the person has done for society in a minimum of five slides.
Oral Presentation (15 Points)		Excellent volume, projection, and eye contact during the presentation.	Adequate volume, projection, and eye contact during the presentation.	Poor volume, projection, and eye contact during the presentation.

6) What did this person do for a living? _____

_____

7) What made this person such an important part of our history, what did they do that made them famous?

_____

_____

_____

_____

8) List five facts (<u>other than the ones listed above</u>) about this individual or their life:

a) _____

b) _____

c) _____

d) _____

e) _____

9) After conducting research on this person, what three questions would you ask them if given the opportunity?

a) _____

b) _____

c) _____

10) Identify two character traits to describe your person and then explain why you chose each by giving specific examples of things your subject has done.

Character Trait: **Why chosen and specific examples:**

a) _____

_____

_____

b) _____

_____

_____

** You should now use the information you gathered in the Biography Core Section to write your biography.

*** REMEMBER: You must have a **draft** and your **final copy must be typed.**

HINTS: Before writing the biography

a) Perfect paragraphs have _____ sentences.   b) Each biography consists of what three parts:

APPENDIX 4–1   Continued

DRAFT: Graphic Organizer for your biography.

Introduction: 3-5 sentences that identify the topic and two of the most important facts about it.

Body: Should be 7-12 sentences which present the relevant facts about the life of the topic.

APPENDIX 4–1 Continued

Body Continued

_____

Conclusion: The Conclusion should be 3-5 sentences that reinforce the introduction and the most important facts from the biography. It should tell us about the subjects most important contribution to society.

_____

APPENDIX 4–1   Continued

In-the-Classroom Benchmarks

When our children are born, we eagerly await the firsts—their first time eating solid food, sitting up, crawling, walking, and, of course, talking. We pore over books on infant development to determine the next normal milestone. Every visit to the pediatrician is a search for reassurance that they are developing and growing as they should.

Teachers, like new parents, are concerned about their students' development. In our classrooms, we are constantly watching and rating our students' performance in each of the content areas. While we may have a general feel for how our students meet our expectations, we may not have a systematic way of collecting this information. There is no baby book to consult. Since there is a range of development at each grade level, our longitudinal assessment needs to include benchmarks—developmental indicators—to guide our interpretation of the data and observations we gather. Benchmarks help anchor the data collection and subsequent instructional decisions.

In-the-classroom benchmarks reflect what students learn and do under normal day-to-day conditions; thus, these measures are authentic assessments. They enable teachers to continue to collect essential information about students' level of performance in relation to instructional goals. While work samples are taken from daily or short-term work,

in-the-classroom benchmarks include student work from culminating activities, completed units, and long-term projects based on the content standards. Criterion-referenced tests (CRTs), such as running records and the Concepts About Print test, which are designed to show developmental progress, are also classroom benchmarks. These data help teachers focus instruction, group students, and use their time effectively. They are clear indications to teachers, students, and parents of progress over time.

Criterion-Referenced Measures

One useful tool to gauge students' performance is the criterion-referenced test (CRT) or task, which can be commercially published or teacher created. The norm-referenced or standardized achievement test compares a student's performance with that of others but is not designed to determine how well your instructional goals are being met (Stiggins 2001). A CRT is related to an instructional or curriculum objective, which in turn is based on a district and/or state standard; it identifies a concept, skill, or item of knowledge to look for, measure, and compare with an expected performance level (Gillet and Temple 2000). The norm-referenced test relies on a multiple-choice format; the CRT is a performance measure. For special-needs and English language learners, a CRT is usually a fairer assessment, since students are assessed under normal classroom conditions on what they have learned recently. While standardized achievement tests are administered at prescribed times of the school year and the results are made available at a later date, teachers can administer CRTs whenever there is the need to collect information. In addition, CRTs enable teachers to assess the same objective at regular intervals to ensure students are improving or maintaining performance levels.

Concepts About Print Test

Children entering school vary in their understanding of written language and how books work. One way to discover what they do know is to use an appropriate benchmark measure designed for emergent learners, like the Concepts About Print (CAP) test, developed by Marie Clay (1995). Similar to the growth charts in a pediatrician's office, the CAP is a benchmark of normal progress in emergent literacy. This commercially published tool uses a child's storybook and a set of specific questions designed to allow the child to demonstrate understanding of book orientation, print direction, and letter-word concepts. For example, the teacher asks, "Where should I start?" The child then points to the place on the page—we hope the upper left of a line of print—where he thinks the teacher will begin to read. Thus the child has the opportunity to show what he understands, rather than try to explain this abstract knowledge.

Teachers can administer the Concepts About Print test to a child in about ten minutes, so a whole class can be assessed within two weeks. Most teachers administer it two or three times a year in order to monitor changes in children's growing knowledge and experiences as literate behavior is modeled during daily shared reading and writing. The test has been translated into several languages, including Spanish, Portuguese, and Hebrew (Clay 1989). Spanish versions of the stories "Sand" ("Arena") and "Stones" ("Peidras"), along with instructions, have been published in the United States (Escamilla et al. 1996). There is also a Braille version (Tompkins and McGee 1986).

Kindergarten teacher Silvia Lopez administers the Concepts About Print test in September, after her children have been in school about four weeks. The results provide baseline data about each child's emergent literacy development. The item-by-item analysis is more important and useful than the overall score.

When Silvia reviewed Adam's September data (see Figure 5–1), she saw that he understood book orientation behavior—where the front of the book is located (item 1), that a picture has a bottom (item 8), and that the left page is read before the right one (item 11). This was a good indicator that Adam had noticed what his parents did at home when they read to him and that he understood what Silvia was doing when she modeled this behavior during shared reading. Adam also demonstrated that he understood that the print, not the picture, contains the message (item 2). This is an important benchmark and again indicated Adam's exposure to books and print. Finally, Silvia saw that Adam understood the difference between what a letter is (item 21) and what a word is (item 22). These are essential concepts that Silvia uses in her daily instruction.

By January, Silvia noted that Adam understood print direction (items 3, 4, 5, 9), could match upper- and lowercase letters in context (item 19), was able to locate the first and last letter of a word (item 23), and recognized what the term *capital letter* means (item 24). Thus, both Silvia's modeling of these concepts and Adam's experiences with shared reading and journal writing were beneficial.

By the end of the school year, in May, Adam had acquired more essential concepts for learning to read. He could now match speech to print (item 6) and understood the meaning of the question mark (item 15), the period (item 16), and quotation marks (item 18). Silvia uses these CAP results in parent

CONCEPTS ABOUT PRINT	Name: Adam	Grade: Kindergarten	
ITEM	SEPTEMBER SCORE 6/24	JANUARY 14/24	MAY 18/24
1. Front of book	X	X	X
2. Print contains message	X	X	X
3. Where to start		X	X
4. Which way to go		X	X
5. Return sweep to left		X	X
6. Word-by-word matching			X
7. Concept of *first* and *last*		X	X
8. Bottom of picture	X	X	X
9. Print is upside down		X	X
10. Line order altered			
11. Left page before right	X	X	X
12. One change in word order			
13. One change in letter order			
14. One change in letter order			
15. Meaning of question mark			X
16. Meaning of period			X
17. Meaning of comma			
18. Meaning of quotation marks			X
19. Locate M m H h		X	X
20. Locate *was* and *no*			
21. Show one letter, two letters	X	X	X
22. Show one word, two words	X	X	X
23. Show first and last letter of word		X	X
24. Show capital letter		X	X

FIGURE 5–1   Adam's CAP Results

conferences to give a clear indication of how each child is progressing in understanding how written language works.

Teacher-Created Criterion-Referenced Measures

Teachers also develop their own tasks related to instructional or state standards. Because a criterion-referenced test is a performance measure, instructional objectives should describe the conditions under which the student must perform or demonstrate the learning outcome. Will the student respond orally or in writing? Must the student rely on memory or can she refer to notes? The level of mastery is also specified—the number or percentage of correct items (for example, "Given a written draft with twenty-five misspelled words, the student will circle twenty"). The level of mastery may also include a time limit when appropriate (for example, when measuring oral reading fluency or computation speed). When developing a criterion-referenced test, keep in mind how students have been asked to perform the task in your classroom and design the task or items and conditions accordingly.

In Sue Rosche's fifth-grade class, her students, in collaborative groups, created science vocabulary word splashes during a monthlong unit on populations and ecosystems. They encountered key vocabulary many times and had many opportunities to see how their peers established relationships among the words. While their collaborative work was both thinking evidence and a work sample, Sue later prepared a criterion-referenced test to assess individual progress (see Figure 5–2). For the test, students wrote an essay using the specific vocabulary to demonstrate their understanding of the major concepts. Isabella's essay (see Figure 5–3) highlighted her familiarity with the key vocabulary and her ability to dis-

---

Name _____   Date _____

Unit D
Populations and Ecosystems
Chapter One
WORD SPLASH

Use a sheet of notebook paper to do the following. Be sure to number your paper correctly. Your Word Splash should give *enough information* to show that you understand the vocabulary. **Highlight** each required word once in your Word Splash.

I.   What is an ecosystem? (required)
     Use these vocabulary words to answer this question:
     ecosystem, community, population, biotic, abiotic

II. How are living things in an ecosystems related? (required)
     Use these vocabulary words to answer this question:
     producers, consumers, decomposer, herbivores, carnivores, omnivores

III. How are living things in an ecosystem related?

Choice 1:
     Use these vocabulary words to answer this question:
     parasitism, commensalisms, mutualism

Or, Choice 2:
     Make the necessary Venn Diagrams to compare and contrast these vocabulary words:
     parasitism, commensalisms, mutualism

FIGURE 5–2   Word Splash Criterion Test

cuss the major concepts. In Sue's opinion, Isabella met the benchmark measure for this science unit.

Running Records

Benchmark measures can assess a broader range of behavior than simple content knowledge. Running records, also developed by Marie Clay (2000), assess the strategies readers use when reading a variety of texts over time. From time to time, teachers may take partial running records during guided reading groups. However, a full running record is used as a benchmark to gauge student progress at specified intervals. Clay developed a short-hand teachers can use to record students' word

Isabella — June 2
Science — word Splash

1. An ecosystem is a community of biotic and abiotic things. Biotic is something that is living and abiotic is things that are not real. For example a plant is a living thing so it is biotic and a pencil box is abiotic because it is not living. To know how many there are of something is a population. For example if you look in a geography book it will tell you the population of that country. Population is usually used in terms of people.

2. A herbivor is a organism that only eats plants. A carnivor is just the opposite it only eats meat. Omnivore eats both meat and plants. A producer is like a herbivor because it does not eat meat. A consumer is like a carnivor because they both eat other living things to uptain energy. A Omnivor is like a decomposer because breaks down the plant or meat that it is eating.

FIGURE 5–3 Isabella's Word Splash Test

(continues)

> Chace 3.
> 1
>
> Living or biotic things in a ecosystem
> are related because one of the organisms
> are feeding upon an organism and
> harming an organism or an organism
> can be irritated or nothing might
> not happen to the other organism
> at all. For example parasitism is when
> one organisim is irrated and the
> other organisim feeds upon it. For
> example a dog + a flea. The dog is
> the one who is irritated and the
> flea is the one getting the food
> Commensalism is when one organism
> benifes and the other is harmed.
> mutulism is when both organisms
> benifit. for example the rino +
> the bird that sits on the rinos
> head.

FIGURE 5–3 Continued

recognition strategies and accuracy as well as their fluency and ability to correct miscues (errors). Analyzing the results enables teachers to assess students' reading progress. Running records are particularly sensitive indicators of English language learners' growth in language and literacy (Boyd-Batstone 2003; Escamilla et al. 1996). Teachers in the primary grades or those who work with struggling readers take running records about once a month to monitor student progress (Peregoy and Boyle 1997).

Maria Juez, a second-grade teacher, periodically assesses her students' oral reading accuracy and comprehension by taking running records, followed by retellings. So that the tasks match classroom conditions, each student reads aloud from books at his independent reading level (reading for pleasure during sustained silent reading) and instructional level (reading in guided reading groups). Thus, Maria is able to accommodate the range of reading levels in her class; one book does not have to fit all students. Maria's students also read the actual books—in their original format and font and with all the illustrations—not photocopies or retyped versions. They can therefore employ all the cues—semantic (meaning), syntactical (grammar), letter-sound, and pictorial—they would normally use.

Maria's running records, along with related notations and anecdotal records, let her view student progress in various genres (realistic fiction, fantasy, information) and help her determine whether students are reading materials at an appropriate level—just right, as opposed to too hard or too easy. (The word recognition criterion for independent books is between 95 and 100 percent; for instructional books, it is between 90 and 94 percent.) She also sees what each student can or cannot yet do. Compiling individual results on a chart lets her see at a glance how many students have mastered the instructional objective and helps her plan future instruction.

Figure 5–4 shows results for Carmen, Brandon, Jorge, Leticia, and Derrick. Everyone except Brandon met the criterion Maria had established for both independent and instructional reading. Maria therefore took a closer look at Brandon's oral reading strategies (meaning, syntax, letter-sound matching). Noticing that Brandon consistently used letter-sound cues but ignored semantic and syntactic cues, she planned appropriate

follow-up lessons for him and students with similar problems.

Individual criterion-referenced test results are also useful during student or parent conferences, since the students are being compared with the criterion or standard, not with each other. Maria shares her running records with each student and his or her parents and compares the results over time. Since the running record criteria for independent and instructional levels are constant, Maria can discuss each student's reading performance across genres and highlight consistencies in word recognition strategies as the books become more difficult.

Rubrics

A rubric is a document that describes levels of performance on a particular assignment; it uses a set of criteria and a performance rating

Student and Date	Independent-Level Book (title, author, genre, level) Word Reading Accuracy	Instructional-Level Book (title, author, genre, level) Word Reading Accuracy
Carmen 12/12	*The Doorbell Rang*, Hutchins, realistic fiction, 2nd grade—100%	*Nine True Dolphin Stories*, Davidson, information, 2nd–3rd grade—90%
Brandon 12/12	*And I Mean It, Stanley*, Bonsall, realistic fiction, 2nd grade—90%	*Nine True Dolphin Stories*, Davidson, information, 2nd–3rd grade—80%
Jorge 12/12	*Aunt Eater Loves a Mystery*, Cushman, fantasy, 2nd grade—97%	*Nine True Dolphin Stories*, Davidson, information, 2nd–3rd grade—95%
Leticia 12/12	*Bread and Jam for Frances*, Hoban, fantasy, 2nd grade—95%	*Dolphins*, Holmes, information, 3rd–4th grade—90%
Derrick 12/12	*Hungry, Hungry Sharks*, Cole, information, 3rd grade—100%	*Dolphins*, Holmes, information, 3rd–4th grade—95%

FIGURE 5–4 Ms. Juez's Running Records

scale, from excellent to poor, for each criterion (Goodrich 1996/1997). The rating scale should reflect gradations of quality. Rubrics are usually presented as a matrix, with the criteria listed on the left and the ratings for each criterion described qualitatively on the right. Each criterion is scored separately. In effect, a rubric lets students know what counts in any particular assignment or task.

When we need a new car or home appliance, we probably do some homework to compare the quality and price of various brands. Most of these results are presented as rubrics, with each essential criterion (energy or gasoline costs, repairs, longevity) rated across a scale. Seldom is this rating scale all or nothing; there are gradations of quality for each indicator. Consumers are thus able to be more fully informed as they comparison shop. In schools, rubrics inform educational consumers—students and parents—how a product or performance rates.

A Retelling Rubric

Commercially published rubrics help teachers rate students' performance consistently, especially on periodic assessments. Maria Juez uses Mary Shea's rubric for story retellings (2000) to evaluate her students' comprehension of the books they read while she takes running records. Brandon's retelling results for *And I Mean It, Stanley* are shown in Figure 5–5. Brandon retold the plot without prompting and included all the story grammar elements, so his score for that criterion was 4. Brandon's unprompted retelling included some details, which rated a 3. However, Brandon needed to be prompted for inferences, predictions, and conclusions, as well as for type of fictional selection, so he received scores of 2 in each of these categories. Finally, Brandon did make a few connections to his own life without prompting, which earned him a score of 3 in this category. Overall, Maria considered this text to be at Brandon's instructional level, since his average score was 2.8. Brandon could read *And I Mean It, Stanley* with good comprehension if prompted

by his teacher. Both his word reading accuracy (90 percent) and retelling scores indicated that the book he was attempting to read independently was really a book at his instructional level. Now Maria realized why Brandon had been struggling when reading on his own.

A Holistic Journal Rubric

Once you become comfortable with commercially published rubrics, you may want to develop your own. Even teachers who work with very young children find rubrics useful in keeping track of developing readers and writers. Carmen Fernandez teaches prekindergarten children who are four or five years old. One of their daily activities is recording and illustrating significant events in their journal. When they finish, they read their entry to Carmen, and she records what they say. To capture how the children are progressing and to provide understandable feedback, Carmen devised a holistic rubric, because the task is always the same, even though the content of the entries may change. Her rubric uses two criteria; the child's form of writing and level of communication. The ratings reflect a developmental progression from the earliest attempts to the most sophisticated. Carmen rates the children's entries once a month. (See Figure 5–6.)

Figure 5–6 includes rubrics for four of Dylan's journal entries, made at the beginning, middle, and end of the year. In the "Aliens" entry, Dylan used random letters to record his idea and read this as a label for his picture. By the middle of the year, Dylan was using both invented and conventional spelling and had recorded a one-sentence description. This shows progress not only in learning about English orthography but also in communicating ideas. At the end of the year, Dylan's spelling was primarily conventional and he communicated a sentence with more description. The holistic rubric captured this growth over time.

Formative and Summative Rubrics

A rubric helps evaluate learning and supports communication among the students, the

Name: <u>Brandon</u> Date: <u>12/12</u>

Title: <u>*And I Mean It Stanley*</u>   Reading Level: _____ Ind. __X__ Instr. _____ Frus.

Comprehension Elements	Score of 4	Score of 3	Score of 2	Score of 1
Story Grammar [4]	Without prompting, reader includes all elements of story grammar: ☒ characters, ☒ setting, ☒ problem, ☒ event sequence, ☒ resolution	Without prompting, reader includes most of the elements of story grammar: [] characters, [] setting, [] problem, [] event sequence, [] resolution	With prompting, reader includes most of the elements of story grammar: [] characters, [] setting, [] problem, [] event sequence, [] resolution	Even with prompting, reader is unable to state or confuses elements of story grammar.
Details [3]	Without prompting, reader laces retelling with all significant and accurate details and some minor ones in a subordinate way.	Without prompting, reader laces retelling with some significant and accurate details.	With prompting, reader conveys some accurate details.	Even with prompting, reader does not include details or gives inaccurate details.
Inferences, Predictions, and Conclusions [2]	Without prompting, reader explains critical inferences, predictions, and/or conclusions drawn.	Without prompting, reader explains inferences, predictions, and/or conclusions drawn; however, they are weak or minimal.	With prompting, reader conveys understanding of story inferences, predictions, and/or conclusions.	Even with prompting, reader does not convey understanding of or confuses story inferences, predictions, and/or conclusions.
Connections to Reader's Life and Other Texts [3]	Without prompting, reader explains connections with other texts and/or life experiences that closely relate to this text.	Without prompting, reader explains connections with other texts and/or life experiences that vaguely relate to this text.	With prompting, reader makes connections with other texts and/or life experiences.	Even with prompting, reader is unable to make or confuses connections with other texts and/or life experiences.
Type of Fictional Selection [2]	Without prompting, reader identifies type of fictional selection he read (e.g., fairy tale, fantasy, mystery, historical fiction).	With limited prompting, reader identifies type of fictional selection he read (e.g., fairy tale, fantasy, mystery, historical fiction).	With excessive prompting, reader identifies type of fictional selection (e.g., fairy tale, fantasy, mystery, historical fiction).	Even with prompting, reader is unable to identify type of fictional selection (i.e., fairy tale, fantasy, mystery, historical fiction).

From Shea, M. 2000. *Taking Running Records*. New York: Scholastic. Used by permission.

FIGURE 5–5 Brendon's Retelling Rubric

teacher, and the parents. The same rubric can generate both a formative and a summative assessment (Jackson and Larkin 2002). When the rubric is given to students before they begin the task, it helps them meet the expectations and requirements of the assignment: they can see their progress and recognize whether or not the goal is being met (Valencia 1998). The rubric can also be used to give feedback on first attempts. Based on the rubric, students revise the assignment and submit it for final evaluation. At that point,

Holistic Rubric for Journal Entries

Student   Dylan

Date   9/6

Developmental Level	Proficient	Developing	Early	Emergent
			↔	
Form of Writing: Knowledge of English Orthography/Conventions	Conventional Spelling	Invented Spelling	Letters	Scribble • scribble sentences • word scribble • some letter-like forms
Level of Communication: Level of Message Construction	Several Sentences Focused on Topic	One-Sentence Description • scribbles w/intended meaning	A Phrase • scribbles w/intended meaning	A Label

Date   10/15   "Aliens"

Developmental Level	Proficient	Developing	Early	Emergent
			X	
Form of Writing: Knowledge of English Orthography/Conventions	Conventional Spelling	Invented Spelling	Letters • random letters • letter patterns • uses letters in his name	Scribble
Level of Communication: Level of Message Construction	Several Sentences Focused on Topic	One-Sentence Description	A Phrase • labeled picture w/phrase	A Label X

FIGURE 5–6   Dylan's Journal Entry Rubrics

Date   1/12

Developmental Level	Proficient	Developing **X**	Early	Emergent
Form of Writing: Knowledge of English Orthography/Conventions	Conventional Spelling • some conventional spellings	Invented Spelling • 1st sound only • 1st and last sounds • syllabic—all sounds in word represented	Letters	Scribble
Level of Communication: Level of Message Construction	Several Sentences Focused on Topic	One-Sentence Description X	A Phrase	A Label

Date   5/23

Developmental Level	Proficient	Developing ◄─►	Early	Emergent
Form of Writing: Knowledge of English Orthography/Conventions	Conventional Spelling • words mostly spelled correctly	Invented Spelling	Letters	Scribble
Level of Communication: Level of Message Construction	Several Sentences Focused on Topic	One-Sentence Description • including more description	A Phrase	A Label

FIGURE 5–6   Continued

91

the rubric is used to evaluate the final product and assign the grade. Therefore, both process and product can be evaluated using rubrics.

A rubric gives students specific feedback about their performance and helps teachers tailor instruction. Using a rubric's gradient criteria to evaluate their own performance, students are able to gauge how close they are to being exemplary. They don't have to guess. The features are clearly identifiable, and students are aware of what is needed to improve their performance. Knowing this, they can employ appropriate fix-up strategies and move closer to their goal. Thus, rubrics support the development of students' metacognition.

In Florida, fourth-grade social studies classes focus on state history. Julia Moreno, a teacher in Miami, assigned a culminating project in which each student was to plan a five-day road trip incorporating three stops. They had a budget of twelve hundred dollars to cover the cost of lodging, meals, car rental, gas, and admission to tourist attractions. They kept track of their expenses on a spreadsheet and computed mileage and the cost of gasoline in a separate table. Additional requirements included a journal, an itinerary, a map with the route highlighted, a description of the destination cities, and a rationale for visiting three attractions. Students used the Internet to determine costs of hotel rooms and

restaurant meals and to discover local tourist attractions near the three planned stops.

Figure 5–7 is the rubric for this culminating project. It helped Julia's students plan the project and meet the requirements. After they completed each part of the assignment, they could check it against the rubric. If it didn't match, they knew what they had to fix. The budget sounded like a lot of money to Darin until he started investigating the cost of lodging. He wanted to stay at the Hard Rock Hotel until he saw the room rate: "I can't believe that even a cheap room at this hotel will blow my budget!" he said.

Developing Rubrics

Many teachers develop a rubric along with their students, especially if the purpose is to guide instruction as well as assess student learning. When you develop your own rubric, it is likely to match your teaching style and curriculum very closely. Involving students helps them understand what the task entails and its particular attributes or specifications. For instance, the content and format of, language used in, and audience for a book report are different from those same elements related to a book review. Developing a rubric for each would help students differentiate the two.

Goodrich (1996/1997) identifies the following steps in developing rubrics:

1. Gather some examples of excellent and poor work to share with your students. Discuss what makes each one excellent or poor.
2. List the criteria that evolved from your class discussion. These constitute what counts for quality work on this particular assignment.
3. Articulate gradations of quality by describing the best and worst levels for each criterion. Once you've identified the extremes (excellent and poor), fill in the middle levels using examples from the class discussion as well as your knowledge of students' common difficulties with this characteristic. Try for four levels of quality for each criterion.

Darin's Florida History Project

Project Requirement	Score of 3	Score of 2	Score of 1
Journal	Detailed entries for each day including description of stops, meals, and time. All entries match itinerary.	Entries include brief description of stops, meals, and time. All entries match itinerary.	Entries for each day record some, but not all of the stops, meals, and time. Most entries match itinerary.
Itinerary	Each day's destination, name of hotel with street address, food for each meal and restaurant, and means of transportation are specified. Costs for each item are included.	Each day's destination, name of hotel with street address, food for each meal and restaurant, and means of transportation are specified. Costs for most items are included.	Each day's destination, hotel, meals, and means of transportation are listed. Specific information is provided for most items. Costs for some items are included.
Route Map	Beginning and end of trip indicated, each of five days clearly marked on map. Mileage for each day matches estimated mileage from itinerary.	Beginning and end of trip indicated, each of five days clearly marked on map. Mileage for each day does not match itinerary mileage.	Beginning and end of trip indicated, most of the five days marked on map. Mileage for each day does not match itinerary mileage.
Expense Spreadsheet	Each day's expenses are detailed separately. Individual costs for meals, gas mileage, hotel, car rental, and attractions are listed. Each type of expense is totaled separately and accurately. Final cost of trip is within $1,200 budget.	Each day's expenses are detailed separately. Individual costs for meals, gas mileage, hotel, car rental, and attractions are listed. Final cost of trip is within $1,200 budget.	Each day's expenses are detailed separately. Expenses for meals, gas mileage, hotel, car rental, and attractions are not listed in separate categories. Final cost of trip is within $1,200 budget.
Cities	Description for each city includes detailed information such as the rationale for visiting, relevant historical facts, and unique features. Description is in paragraph form.	Description for each city includes general information such as the rationale for visiting, relevant historical facts, and unique features. Description is in paragraph form.	Description for each city includes most, but not all of the following information: rationale for visiting, relevant historical facts, and unique features. Description is in paragraph form.
Attractions	Detailed description includes the educational purpose for visiting, unique features or shows, basis for selecting, and how attraction operates. Description is in paragraph form.	General description includes the educational purpose for visiting, unique features or shows, basis for selecting, and how attraction operates. Description is in paragraph form.	General description includes most of the following: the educational purpose for visiting, unique features or shows, basis for selecting, and how attraction operates. Description is in paragraph form.

FIGURE 5–7   Rubric for Florida History Project

Use descriptive, specific terms and avoid ambiguous or negative language. There should be measurable, observable differences in the levels of quality.

4. Use the class rubric to rate the models you presented. This will help clarify the assignment's parameters and scoring.

5. Give the students the task or assignment to complete. As they develop their assignment, have them use the rubric to assess their own and their peers' work.

6. Give students time to revise and fine-tune their work based on the feedback they've received.

7. Use the same rubric to assess the student work yourself.

In our era of high-stakes assessment, rubrics provide additional support for meeting performance standards. As students examine exemplary work and compare it with that of lesser quality, they recognize the expectations for performance and the specific qualities needed to receive a higher rating. A rubric removes some of the guesswork about what really counts.

Rubrics on the Web

Some excellent websites provide support and models for developing rubrics. RubiStar (*http://rubistar.4teachers.org*) has rubrics for different purposes, like PowerPoint presentations, that you can customize. The New York State Education Department website's model for a large science project called Seed by Design (*www.emsc.nysed.gov/nysatl/Science /SeedByDesign/html/design6.html*) includes rubrics for graphing and cooperative learning. The Exemplars website (*www.exemplars.com*) presents several rubrics, including ones for very young learners evaluating their own science and math performances. The International Reading Association and the National Council of Teachers of English sponsor the website ReadWriteThink (*www.readwrite think.org*), which includes literacy lesson plans linked to the national English language arts standards. Many of these lesson plans provide scoring rubrics for the activities. For example,

Figure 5–8 is a rubric for center work that includes individual criteria and differentiated levels of performance. Try it out in your classroom and see how it works for you.

Rubrics for Grading

As you can probably already see, rubrics have the potential to streamline your grading of student work, especially complex projects. The time you invest in developing an analytical rubric is time well spent. It helps you assess student work consistently across several dimensions (Whittaker, Salend, and Duhaney 2001) and, when distributed to students at the beginning of the project, makes it more likely that the work submitted will be of high quality (Andrade 2000). The teacher's expectations are clarified: students see what they have to accomplish and more readily plan their work (Jackson and Larkin 2002).

Some teachers develop one grading rubric for an entire project; others may have separate rubrics for each part (Jackson and Larkin 2002). In the latter case, the teacher totals the scores from each of the rubrics to arrive at the final grade. When students are informed about grading through rubrics, they understand how their final grades will be determined. Why someone received an A is no longer a mystery. Grading rubrics can also be used during parent and student conferences to improve communication about student performance and help set future goals.

Special education students in inclusive classrooms, as well as English language learners, benefit from grading rubrics as well because they can focus their efforts on what is important. As they become more familiar with how rubrics work, special-needs students can identify individual strengths and weaknesses (Hall and Salmon 2003).

Todd Miklas and Brian Shea, sixth-grade earth science teachers, give students the option of completing a project in lieu of a final examination. There are four options: completing a model, creating an invention, conducting an experiment, or writing a research report. (See Figure 5–9.) The project,

Criteria	Exemplary 4	Accomplished 3	Developing 2	Beginning 1	Score
Purpose	Creatively and completely addresses the clearly evident purpose (required information).	Appropriately completes the task. The purpose can be concluded.	Attempts to complete the task. Somewhat attends to the intended purpose.	Demonstrates limited awareness of expectations for the task. Limited evidence of intended purpose.	
Understanding	Several interesting, specific facts and ideas are included.	Many facts and ideas are included.	Some facts and ideas are included.	Few facts and ideas are included.	
Artwork/ Presentation	Highly appealing in style and presentation.	Acceptable in style and presentation quality.	Somewhat acceptable in style and presentation.	Lacks appeal in presentation quality.	
Conventions	All grammar and spelling are correct.	Only one or two grammar and spelling errors.	A few more than one or two grammar and spelling errors.	Many grammar and spelling errors.	

ReadWriteThink Copyright 2003 IRA/NCTE. Used by permission.

FIGURE 5–8   Scoring Rubric for Center Assignments

like the final exam, makes up 20 percent of the final grade. Each project option has specific requirements. For example, each inventor needs to state the purpose of the invention, summarize the information used to design the invention, and describe in detail how it was built and how it works. All projects require a proposal, daily log, calendar, oral presentation, bibliography, and exhibit. Students who conduct interviews receive extra credit. Most students begin their projects in March and complete them in May.

A grading rubric is used to evaluate each aspect of the project (see Figure 5–10). Students are given specific guidelines, along with the rubric, at the beginning of the project and can see what they need to accomplish to receive an A, how each element will be rated, and how much time they will need to meet the criteria for each element.

Presentations

The IRA/NCTE Standards for English Language Arts include two for using language. Standard 4 states, "Students adjust their use of spoken, written, and visual language (e.g., conventions, style, vocabulary) to communicate effectively with a wide variety of audiences for a variety of purposes." Likewise,

1. Design a **model, invention, experiment,** or **research report.**
2. Follow the guidelines for a **model, invention, experiment,** or **research report.**
3. Use the provided **daily log** and **calendars** to keep track of your work.
4. Prepare materials for an **oral presentation** of your project.
5. Project boards may be purchased from the school store. (**$3.50**)
6. Prepare your project board including **graphs, tables,** and any other **written information** collected.
7. Refer to the **Science Project Evaluation Sheet** (rubric) as a guide in preparing your presentation.
8. **OPTIONAL:** Conduct an interview with a professional related to the topic of your project for extra credit. **Any extra points earned over the possible 50 for the project will be averaged into the fourth marking period grade.**

FIGURE 5–9   Science Project Guidelines

Standard 12 states, "Students use spoken, written, and visual language to accomplish their own purposes (e.g., for learning, enjoyment, persuasion, and the exchange of information)." Student presentations are a venue in which students can develop competence in both standards. Presentations are important benchmarks.

In the sixth-grade science project mentioned earlier, the grading rubric weights both the exhibit and the presentation equally. Students are given clear guidelines for their oral presentations (see Figure 5–11); they need to demonstrate familiarity with their topic, use scientific vocabulary instead of general terms, and deliver this information as an expert. In addition, they must plan a stand-alone, self-explanatory exhibit that is attractive, logical, and creative. The exhibit and presentation are evidence that Standards 4 and 8 have both been met.

Student presentations can also be videotaped. This option allows students to refine their presentation skills and rerecord as necessary, creating a final presentation that represents their best effort. Third grader Darin presented his February book report as a video commercial for *Everest: The Summit.* First he wrote the script, shown in Figure 5–12. Next he gathered props: a sheet (to cover the rock-climbing wall in his backyard and create the mountain); a parka, goggles, and a pick (winter survival gear); and of course, a microphone and headset. In the video, Darin sounds like a reporter and appears to be climbing the snow-covered mountain, planting his pick to keep from slipping backward. He pauses, pretending to listen to the Weather Service bulletin, before continuing his report. Each element is evidence of careful attention to detail and planning and underscores a benchmark performance—using the language of a commercial, building suspense, and creating audience interest in the book.

The video presentation affords special-needs students and English language learners more control over its quality. Always being able to do it again means the final cut has a much better chance of representing an optimum performance. In addition, the video is an excellent means of self-evaluation and a basis for feedback. In reviewing the product, the student and teacher can highlight what went well and pinpoint what needs to be improved. For English language learners, having evidence of growing competence in a second language supports and sustains learning.

A rubric can rate students' language and rapport with audiences in a variety of presentations. In the ReadWriteThink lesson plan "Heroes Around Us," students learn to differentiate between heroes and idols. In this project, students collaborate on determining the criteria for heroism and then research, write, and present reports on heroes. Figure 5–13 is a teacher's scoring rubric for the hero report presentation. The continuum of ratings reflects growing confidence and competence in communication as well as audience engagement. This student's ratings indicate that while the main idea was effectively explained with supporting information, there was diffi-

Project Title: _____   Name: _____

Possible Points	Points Received/Comments	EXPERIMENTAL DESIGN
20–11		All required elements of the valid experimental design were followed.
10–1		Some required elements were missing from your valid experimental design.

Possible Points	Points Received/Comments	INVENTION
20–11		All required elements of the invention design were followed.
10–1		Some required elements were missing from your invention design.

Possible Points	Points Received/Comments	MODEL
20–11		All required elements of the model design were followed.
10–1		Some required elements were missing from your model design.

Possible Points	Points Received/Comments	RESEARCH REPORT
20–11		All required elements of the research report were followed.
10–1		Some required elements were missing from your research report.

FIGURE 5–10   Science Project Grading Rubric

(continues)

Project Title: _____   Name: _____

Possible Points	Points Received/Comments	PRESENTATION
15–13		Exemplary, confident presentation; proper and effective use of scientific vocabulary and terminology; complete understanding of topic.
12–10		Well-organized, clear presentation; appropriate use of scientific vocabulary and terminology; knowledge of topic.
9–7		Presentation acceptable; adequate use of scientific terms; acceptable understanding of topic.
6–4		Presentation lacks clarity and organization; little use of scientific terms and vocabulary; poor understanding of topic.
3–1		Poor presentation; cannot explain topic; scientific terminology lacking or confused; lacks understanding of topic.

Possible Points	Points Received/Comments	EXHIBIT
15–13		Highly appealing exhibit layout that is self-explanatory and successfully incorporates a good sensory approach; creative and effective use of material.
12–10		Layout logical, concise, and easy to follow; materials used in exhibit appropriate and effective.
9–7		Acceptable layout of exhibit; materials used appropriately.
6–4		Organization of layout could be improved; better materials could have been chosen.
3–1		Layout lacks organization and is difficult to understand; poor and ineffective use of materials.

15–10	Points Received/Comments	EXTRA CREDIT INTERVIEW

Total pts. _____

Point Breakdown: A = 46–50   B = 41–45   C = 36–40   D = 31–35

Overall Comments:

FIGURE 5–10 Continued

Oral Presentation Guidelines

1. Speak loudly and clearly. Make eye contact with your audience.
2. State what you worked on.
3. Explain how you decided to investigate your project.
4. Show examples of your equipment and/or work.
5. Show the tables and graphs of your results on large charts.
6. Explain the meaning of your results.
7. Point out your successes and show how the results led to your conclusion.
8. Note any difficulties or failures you had and explain what caused them if you can.
9. Did your conclusion answer the problem statement? If not, can you explain why it does not?

FIGURE 5–11   Oral Presentation Guidelines

Script for Commercial

I'm here at 27,000 feet above sea level climbing Mount Everest with the temperature at 100 degrees below zero.

I'm a reporter with the Dolphins Daily.

I'm approaching the infamous Dominic Alexis who is 5,000 feet from being Everest's youngest Summiteer.

I left Advanced Base Camp (ABC) after getting permission from the Nepalese government to join Dominic Alexis.

I'm looking forward to asking him what it's like being a summiteer of Everest.

ALERT!!!

I'm getting a transmission from the national weather service. They're reporting that there is a massive storm 2,000 feet above us.

I hope Dominic got the transmission.

It would be dangerous to climb in a storm as massive as this one.

If Dominic is climbing he could die!

If you want to find out what happens to Dominic, read the book, *Everest: The Summit*.

FIGURE 5–12   Darin's Script for Video Commercial Presentation

Connor's Project on Solar Power

Criteria	Exemplary 4	Accomplished 3	Developing 2	Beginning 1	Score
Expresses ideas clearly	Clearly and effectively communicates the main idea or theme and provides support that contains rich, vivid, and powerful detail.	Clearly communicates the main idea or theme and provides suitable support and detail.	Communicates important information, but not a clear theme or overall structure.	Communicates information as isolated pieces in a random fashion.	3
Maintains audience attention	High level of audience engagement	Acceptable maintenance of audience engagement	Some maintenance of audience engagement	Limited maintenance of audience engagement	2

ReadWriteThink Copyright 2003 IRA/NCTE. Used by permission.

FIGURE 5–13   Rubric for Hero Report Presentation

culty keeping the audience focused and tuned in to the presentation.

A follow-up conference with this student can give him feedback on how to improve his delivery for his next presentation. Perhaps he did not practice the material enough in order to be able to maintain eye contact with the audience, or maybe he didn't speak loudly enough. The rubric can also help special-needs and English language learners plan specific goals or techniques to support improved performance.

Summing Up

In-the-classroom benchmarks are ways of recognizing student growth and competence. These tools support appropriate instruction for learners who are making progress as well as those who may be struggling. Since the data are obtained on a regular basis, teachers can address students' confusions or problems as they arise. Along with thinking evidence and work samples, in-the-classroom benchmarks fairly capture what students can do under normal classroom conditions. Together, these three forms of assessment data balance the results of norm-referenced tests to present a composite picture of student learning.

By using multiple assessments, teachers can be more confident about the important decisions they make about students. The decision of whether to promote or retain a student cannot and should not be made on the basis of a single piece of evidence. How we assess and evaluate student learning should be developmentally appropriate, multidimensional, and longitudinal.

Norm-Referenced and Other Statewide Standardized Achievement Tests

This chapter is neither a minicourse on measurements and statistics nor an evaluation of current testing policies. Rather, it describes types of standardized achievement tests typically used in schools, how information gathered from them is used, and their place in an assessment-*for*-learning system.

The three categories of portfolio data we've talked about so far—thinking evidence, work samples, and in-the-classroom benchmarks—are collected in the classroom by teachers and students or sometimes provided by parents and/or caregivers through informal conversations, notes, or conferences. The fourth category—norm-referenced standardized achievement tests and other statewide or locally used standardized achievement tests—comprises information that comes from assessment instruments created outside the classroom.

Lyman (1998) describes a *standardized* test as one that "has set content, the directions are prescribed, and the scoring procedure is completely specified. And there are norms against which we can compare the scores of our exam-

inees" (27). *Achievement* tests are designed to evaluate a test taker's current level of knowledge, skill, and/or competence in a given area. The three types of commonly used *standardized achievement tests* (SATs) vary in format and content (*SAT* here refers to general tests with these characteristics and should not be confused with the Stanford Achievement Test or the Scholastic Aptitude Test). They are

1. off-the-shelf, norm-referenced standardized achievement tests (NR/SATs)
2. customized criterion-referenced standardized achievement tests (CCR/SATs)
3. hybrid-augmented standardized achievement tests (HA/SATs) (Quality Counts 2004)

Each type of test has distinct features.

It's important to understand the tests used in one's state in order to prepare students for taking them and to determine the extent to which results should inform day-by-day instruction. It's also important to realize that just because tests are approved or mandated by the state, they are not necessarily of high quality. Popham (2004a) states, "Sadly, in some of our fifty states—probably in *most* of our fifty states—the wrong kind of achievement tests will be selected to implement NCLB [federal testing requirements related to the No Child Left Behind legislation]" (7–8). Appendix 6–1 summarizes critical state-by-state information related to testing. It identifies subject domains tested by grade level, whether states have adopted strong standards and aligned tests to them, whether the state sanctions or rewards schools based on test performance, and, last, whether there's a test requirement for high school graduation. Despite differences, these statewide assessments meet the definition of standardized achievement tests.

Why Do We Need Standardized Achievement Tests?

The No Child Left Behind legistation calls for *standardized statewide tests*, tests that are "administered and scored in a standard, pre-determined manner" (Popham 2001b, 39). A statewide test can be supplanted by local tests (tests designed at the district level) *if* the tests are technically equivalent. The local tests "must represent an equally difficult challenge. . . . As a practical matter, that sort of technical equivalence is almost impossible to attain for a collection of locally developed assessments" (17). Therefore, NCLB's assessment requirements are most easily satisfied with statewide tests based on state-created learning standards.

The U.S. Congress Office of Technology further defines a *standardized* test as one that follows uniform procedures for administration and scoring in order to ensure that results across test takers are comparable. Any testing format, including essays, multiple-choice questions, and oral examinations, can be standardized. "Standardized means that the test is always developed, administered, and scored the same way. Consistent questions are asked and the same directions are given for each test. Specific time limits are set and each

student's performance may be compared with all the other students taking the same test under the same conditions" (McGrawHill 2004a, 2). Standardized tests are also *secured*; questions are kept secret until the time of testing to ensure fairness (ThinkQuest 2000).

Many states' achievement tests are rigidly secured even after they've been administered. Other states release parts of previously administered CCR/SATs or HA/SATs to be used for practice. The specific content of many state tests changes yearly, while the format remains relatively consistent. Teachers typically have students practice on parts of released old tests to increase their familiarity with the format and types of tasks. This test practice also helps teachers identify potentially *at-risk-for-failure* students, who then receive remedial instruction and/or are taught with alternative instructional methods. Such steps are critical when the stakes attached to success and failure are high (e.g., sanctions and rewards for schools).

Most states require standardized tests for statewide testing of student achievement at designated grades. Kohn (2000) claims that "standardized testing has swelled and mutated" (1). Teachers need to be fully aware of the types of tests used in their state for accountability as well as in their district for screening purposes *and* understand the scores.

What Type of Test Is Your State Using?

Understanding the language surrounding specific testing policies, the types of tests used, and the way scores are analyzed in a climate of accountability is a daunting but doable task. The annual special edition of *Business First*, with its detailed ranking of local schools, boldly brings home the fact that districts and schools are running a horse race! The outcome affects the real estate market and other aspects of the local economy, so the whole community is paying attention. It's critical that teachers know, in detail, what's expected of them and their students.

Education Week conducted a survey to determine the types of tests states were using (see Appendix 6–2; the descriptors *standardized* and *achievement* have been added to each test moniker to characterize them more accurately as well as reflect what they have in common). Forty-two states use customized criterion-referenced standardized achievement tests designed to match each state's standards in specific grades and/or subject areas. Twenty states and the District of Columbia use off-the-shelf, norm-referenced standardized achievement tests in at least some grades. Twelve states use hybrid-augmented standardized achievement tests that include norm-referenced and criterion-referenced portions. The criterion-referenced portion relates to the standards of the particular state for which the hybrid is designed; the normed portion is constructed by modifying an NR/SAT so that it contains items related to a specific state's curriculum framework (Skinner and Staresina 2004). "A test publisher can use a state's academic standards to augment an existing norm-referenced test so that the test taker's results can be used for both comparisons to a reference group and assigning performance levels" (Zucker 2003, 7). Clearly, all achievement tests are not created equal.

NR/SATs

Norm-referenced standardized achievement tests, sometimes called *normed tests,* are commercially developed for general use. NR/SAT results are used to rank students, groups, and/ or schools. The scores of students who take the test after its publication are compared with the scores (*norms*) of a *norming group* (large *representative* national sample of students given the test prior to its availability to the public) (Lyman 1998; McMillan 2004; Zucker 2003). It's important that the test's norming group appropriately represents (geographically, demographically, and socioeconomically) the students with whom scores will be compared (McMillan 2004).

General-use NR/SATs cover a broad range of what test takers are expected to know and be able to do within a subject area (Zucker 2003). Although NR/SATs are expected to measure knowledge and skills commonly taught in schools as well as students' ability to apply them, they are not designed to match precisely any given curriculum or single instructional program (McGrawHill 2004b). There is, however, considerable controversy about just how much they measure school knowledge and how much they measure out-of-school knowledge. "If you were to review the actual items in a typical standardized achievement test, you'd find many items whose correct answer depends heavily on the socioeconomic status of a child's family" (Popham 2001a, 2). The California Achievement Test (CTB/McGraw Hill), the Iowa Test of Basic Skills (Riverside), and the Metropolitan Achievement Test (Psychological Corporation) are commonly used NR/SATs (Bond 1996). NR/SATs are also designed to highlight achievement differences across and between students and produce a dependable ranking of high achievers to low achievers (Bond 1996). Students' raw scores (number of items correct) are converted to derived scores, standard scores, and/or scaled scores for the purpose of comparison.

Classroom teachers receive externally scored NR/SAT results that have to be filed in students' permanent folders. These typically report percentiles, normal curve equivalent scores, stanines, and grade equivalent scores (for definitions, see Figure 6–1). Scoring manuals for NR/SATs corrected on-site (e.g., NR/ SATs used in the Title I program) typically contain tables that convert raw scores to percentiles, stanines, normal curve equivalents (NCEs), and grade equivalent scores (GEs). A segment of a conversion table is shown in Figure 6–2.

CCR/SATs

The same companies that market national achievement tests design most of the state customized achievement tests (Popham 2001b). Unlike NR/SATs, which cover subject areas

Percentile rank: A percentile is the percent of scores in a set of data that are at or below a certain score. Percentiles indicate how a pupil compares with other children in the same grade or age level. For example, a percentile score of 74 means that the student did as well or better than 74 percent of the group with whom the comparison is being made.

Normal curve equivalent (NCE) scores: NCE scores are based on percentile ranks that have been converted to a *normalized* scale representing equal units. A difference of 10 NCE units represents the same difference in achievement between any two points along the scale. *Normalized* refers to standard scores that have been transformed to a normal distribution or bell curve. NCE scores resemble standard or normalized scores. They range from 1 to 99, have a mean of 50, and describe a student's performance in relation to a group at the same grade level.

Stanine: Stanines are normalized standard score scales divided into nine sections, ranging from a low of 1 to a high of 9. Stanines 4–6 represent average performance. Each stanine represents a range of scaled scores.

Grade equivalent (GE) score: A GE score indicates the grade level at which the raw score was the median score obtained by the norming population. Grade equivalent scores are given in years and tenths because there are ten months in the academic year (September = 0.0 and June = 0.9). For example, assume that the median raw score for a norming group who took the test in the *beginning* of its third-grade year was 10. That median score of 10 would then be assigned a grade equivalent score of 3.0 for beginning third grade. A grade equivalent score of 3.6 would indicate that the test taker's raw score is the same as the *estimate* (estimated from existing scores of norming group) median score for students that have been in grade 3 for six months. Grade equivalent scores have several limitations.

Sources

Cooper, J. D., and N. Kiger. 2001. *Literacy Assessment.* New York: Houghton Mifflin.
Harris, A., and E. Sipay. 1990. *How to Increase Reading Ability.* New York: Longman.
Heiman, G. 2001. *Understanding Research Methods and Statistics.* 2d ed. New York: Houghton Mifflin.
MacGinitie, W., R. MacGinitie, K. Maria, and L. Dreyer. 2000. *Gates–MacGinitie Reading Test, Level 3, Forms S and T: Manual for Scoring and Interpretation.* Itasca, IL: Riverside.
McMillan, J. 2004. *Classroom Assessment.* New York: Pearson Education.

FIGURE 6–1 Score Definitions

very broadly, CCR/SATs are *customized* to focus on a state's established learning standards (Quality Counts 2004). But they are much different from the classroom criterion-based tests discussed in the previous chapter, which are used to determine how well students are doing on specifically stated classroom instructional objectives.

Grades on classroom criterion-referenced tests (CRTs) may be expressed as pass/fail, a percentage, or a letter grade. Scores may be based on an evaluator's overall impression of the work, determined by how well the student's work matches the criteria on a rubric, or reported as a number of correct items. Regardless of how scores on such *nonstandardized* CRTs are reported, they express individual success with the content tested.

CRTs measure *precise* behavior taught in the classroom (Cohen 1988), while CCR/SATs often cause teachers and students to "play a guessing game regarding which content standards will be assessed on a given year's standards-based tests" (Popham 2004a, 79). CCR/SATs are explicitly designed to measure students' performance in relation-

Raw Score (RS)	Percentile Rank (PR)	Stanine (S)	Grade Equivalent (GE)	NCE Score
63	51	5	3.8	50
64	53	5	3.8	52
65	54	5	3.9	53
66	56	5	4.0	53
67	58	5	4.1	54
68	60	6	4.2	55
69	61	6	4.3	56
70	63	6	4.4	58

Adapted from: MacGinitie, W., R. MacGinitie, K. Maria, and L. Dreyer. 2000. Gates–MacGinitie Reading Test, Level 3, Forms S and T: Manual for Scoring and Interpretation. Itasca, IL: Riverside.

FIGURE 6–2   Sample Conversion Table for NR/SAT Scores

ship to statewide learning standards but *also* to rank individuals, groups, and schools based on the scores (FairTest 2004).

How CCR/SATs Compare Students' Performance

Comparisons are possible when raw CCR/SAT scores are converted to scaled scores linked to performance levels. In other words, the scaled scores report test results at various levels on a single common scale. They can be compared across forms and levels of a test and are useful in measuring change in achievement over time. They are not, however, directly comparable from one subject to another (Harris and Sipay 1990).

For example, an English language arts (ELA) CCR/SAT designed by CTB/McGraw Hill, as used in New York State, has scaled scores linked with four performance levels (see Figure 6–3). Total raw scores are calculated by adding up all the correct multiple-choice and open-ended items on the test. Each multiple-choice item is worth one point. Open-ended items are scored with a four-point rubric and are worth the number of points they receive. Raw scores are then matched to scaled scores and performance levels for comparisons across students and

schools (see Figure 6–4). Scaled scores permit year-to-year comparisons, since the scales represent the same level of achievement regarding state standards even when there are slight changes in the difficulty of test questions (NYSED 2004a). The established performance levels define the competencies and skills students must demonstrate to reach beginning, basic, proficient, or advanced levels (NYSED 2004b). Similarly, the table in Figure 6–5 shows raw score conversions for the October 2003 Grade 3 Ohio Reading Test. Ohio, however, has five performance levels: limited, basic, proficient, accelerated, and advanced (OHSED 2004).

State education department websites for other states with CCR/SATs typically have links to similar conversion tables, along with explanations of the process used to construct them. States are making these statistical conversions to prepare for federal reporting of student achievement by level. The state conversion tables facilitate the reporting of students' and schools' standards-related progress, but the discussion and public reporting begins to simulate the ranking aspect of NR/SATs.

The NCLB Act established that all students should reach "proficient" levels on state tests by the 2013–14 academic year (Rebora

New York Grade 4 English Language Arts (Reading, Writing, and Listening Items) Performance Levels (NYSED 2004b)

Performance Level	Descriptions
4 SS Range: 692–800	Students consistently demonstrate understanding of written and oral text beyond the literal level. They can analyze and interpret a variety of texts, identify significant story elements, compare and synthesize information from related texts, and form insightful opinions, using extensive supporting details. Students' writing is well organized, thoroughly developed, and uses sophisticated and effective language, with few or no errors in spelling, grammar, or punctuation.
3 SS Range: 645–691	Students demonstrate understanding of written and oral text with some attention to meaning beyond the literal level. They can gather information, make inferences, identify theme or main idea, understand character actions, and make connections between two related texts, providing some supporting information. Students' writing is generally focused and organized, with minor errors in spelling, grammar, or punctuation that do not interfere with readability.
2 SS Range: 603–644	Students demonstrate partial understanding of written and oral text at a literal level. They can recognize basic story elements, make some inferences, and identify some similarities and differences in two related texts, providing limited supporting information. Students' writing shows some focus and basic organization, and uses simple sentence structure and vocabulary. Students follow some rules for correct spelling, grammar, and punctuation, but errors sometimes interfere with readability.
1 SS Range: 455–602	Students demonstrate minimal understanding of written and oral text. They can locate and recall some stated information, and attempt to construct short and extended responses. Students' writing consists of brief, general, or repetitive statements, and reveals difficulty in organizing thoughts. Errors in spelling, grammar, and punctuation interfere with readability and comprehension.

The performance level indicates that the student can perform the majority of what is described for that level as well as what is described for the levels below. The student may also be capable of performing some of the things described in the next higher level, but not enough to have reached that level of performance.

The skills and knowledge described in the next higher level are the competencies a student needs to demonstrate to show academic growth.

FIGURE 6–3   Conversion of Scaled Scores to Performance Levels

2004). The National Assessment of Educational Progress (NAEP) policy definition of *proficient* is a level that "represents solid academic performance for each grade assessed. Students reaching this level have demonstrated competency over challenging subject matter, including subject-matter knowledge, application of such knowledge to real-world situations, and analytical skills, appropriate to the subject matter" (AASA 2004, 1). How-

	Raw Score Range 2004	Scale Score Range	Performance Level
ELA Grade 4	0–14	455–602	1
	15–26	603–644	2
	27–36	645–691	3
	37–42	692–800	4

FIGURE 6–4   Comparison of February 2004 New York Grade 4 English Language Arts (ELA) Test Scores (NYSED 2004)

ever, individual states are allowed to construct their own definition, since Congress didn't define the term (AASA 2004). Nor did Congress give the U.S. Department of Education regulatory powers over states that might appear to be watering down their definitions of *proficiency* (Hoff 2002).

All this raw-score gymnastics causes people to wonder how CRT-like commercial CCR/SATs tests really are. Rather than directly state that their tests *are* CRTs, some publishers merely claim that their tests have some of the features of CRTs (Cohen 1988).

The CCR/SAT Business

Commercial CCR/SATs have been available for a while. Measured Progress, a company that claims to be a pioneer in designing CCR/SATs, has done assessment work in more than half of our nation's states (Measured Progress

Ohio October 2003 Grade 3 Reading Achievement Test

Retrieved from *www.ode.state.oh.us/proficiency*
(Search for 2003 Grade 3 Reading Achievement Test)

Cutoff points for limited, basic, proficient, accelerated, and advanced levels

Standard	Raw Score	Scaled Score
Limited	Below 25	Below 385
Basic	25	385
Proficient	33	400
Accelerated	38	415
Advanced	43	432

Number and Percentage of Students by Performance Levels from October 2003 Test Administration

Standard	Number of Students	Percent
Limited	34,730	26.4
Basic	26,199	19.9
Proficient	23,183	17.6
Accelerated	26,984	20.5
Advanced	20,605	15.6

FIGURE 6–5   Raw Score Conversions for Ohio Reading Test

2004). Olson (2004) reports that three New England states (New Hampshire, Vermont, and Rhode Island) have cooperatively contracted with Measured Progress to devise joint reading and mathematics tests for grades 3–8 that meet federal NCLB requirements. These tests, including a writing test for grades 5 and 8, will be field-tested in the fall of 2004 and will be fully implemented beginning in the 2005–2006 academic year for a cost of a little more than six million dollars per year. This market seems bearish!

Instructional Objectives Exchange (IOX) Assessment Associates also develops CCR/SATs for states and school districts. Dr. James Popham, professor emeritus and expert on assessment, formed IOX in 1968 (IOX 2004). However, if accountability through testing maintains its hold, many more testing companies are likely to seek a corner of the market.

HA/SATs

Hybrid-augmented standardized achievement tests, also called *standards-referenced tests*, are both normed to a reference group and aligned to a set of state content and performance standards, thus incorporating elements of both NR/SATs and CCR/SATs (Zucker 2003). HA/SATs are explicitly designed to measure students' performance in relation to particular statewide learning standards. The NR/SAT elements used are constructed from commercial NR/SATs that have been modified to better reflect the state's standards. "This framework enables states to report standards-based information (content standard scores), performance levels (cut scores), and percentile rank information for every student" (Zucker 2003, 6–7). By using HA/SATs, schools can accomplish two things with one test:

▶ Students' attainment of state learning standards can be determined through scores on the criterion-referenced portion. Statewide comparisons (of students and schools) can be completed with the established cutoff—the passing total score or

state reference point (FairTest 2004; Williams 1989).

▶ Testing time can be reduced (Williams 1989). However, unless modified NR/SATs produce norm-valid scores, they "cannot provide test results that reflect true changes in achievement" (4).

The State of Your State

State assessments typically include a number of ways in which to respond. That is, learners might demonstrate their knowledge and skill by

▶ conducting experiments

▶ making calculations

▶ answering multiple-choice questions

▶ providing short answers (filling in the blank, completing a sentence, or writing a *short* response to a question or a prompt)

▶ providing extended responses (writing an essay based on a question or a prompt)

Forty-nine states and the District of Columbia include multiple-choice items on state tests. Multiple-choice items, sometimes called *selected responses*, provide a group of three or four possibilities from which students try to select the correct answer (Zucker 2003). These items are clearly limited in the kind of achievement they can measure. For example, multiple-choice items cannot determine students' ability to apply critical-thinking skills or successfully complete complex tasks.

Performance tasks, however, *can* measure students' application of knowledge and skills (Zucker 2003). Performance tasks measure how well students are able to carry out tasks that require the application of state-established content standards (e.g., writing an essay, conducting an experiment) (NEA 2004). About half of our nation's states use standardized achievement tests that include tasks in which the correct answers are not embedded in a group of possible choices

(Doherty 2004). At this time, just two states (Vermont and Kentucky) currently include portfolio compilations of student work as a statewide measure of students' achievement (Doherty 2004).

Of course, it's *real* change toward *real* achievement that *really* matters. Do your state tests reveal that? Understanding a test's type, content, and format, as well as the meaning of the resulting score, is a prerequisite for using it in a meaningful way. The chart in Figure 6–6, comparing NR/SATs and CRTs, is a place to start. With these characteristics in mind, you can examine your state's tests to determine which breeds or mutations thereof are in use. Do the characteristics in one column best describe the tests used in your school, or are your tests hybrids that fall somewhere in between?

Value-Added Assessment

Along with understanding the kind of test used in your state, you must be aware of data analysis techniques used to determine teacher effectiveness and whether students achieve *adequate yearly progress* (AYP). Statistical procedures for comparing year-to-year growth in achievement are gaining recognition.

Twelve states and numerous school districts in many others have begun to apply *value-added assessment* in their analysis of teacher effectiveness and student progress (SAEE 2000). Tennessee has taken the lead in this regard, working closely with William Sanders and researchers from the University of Tennessee, who developed a statistical procedure that uses scaled scores to construct individual profiles of academic achievement (Pipho 1998). Hill (2000) suggests that Sanders has designed a procedure for isolating and measuring the yearly value added to a child's learning, something conscientious teachers and administrators have always done informally.

Definitions of value-added assessment vary, as well as opinions on its usefulness.

Joanne Yatvin (2004), a member of the National Reading Panel (NRP) and retired Oregonian principal, described how she computed students' year-to-year growth on standardized testing measures to help the school's teachers, the community, and herself identify "that there was significant growth" in students' learning. She was interested in how well students were learning and "not at all interested in evaluating teachers through the process—especially because [the] teachers worked in teams that shared students and supported each other." She found that in her school, in which 70 percent of the pupils came from low-income households, most students showed considerable growth between grade 3 and grade 5 and many had achieved the state standards set for grade 8 (see Figures 6–7 and 6–8).

Not everyone agrees, however, that such profiles should concentrate on year-to-year statistical calculations, since these are insufficient measures of *all* the value added to a child's development. The Vermont Superintendents Association (VSA) asserts in its April 2004 position paper that "learning should be measured by looking at how much students grow in their knowledge, civic values, and skills from the time they enter school until the time they leave the school" (1). Furthermore, the VSA suggests that a comprehensive process must be used to evaluate student achievement, as well as teacher and school effectiveness, accurately—a process that respects the unique qualities of individuals and institutions rather than one that moves in a rigid, lockstep march.

Meyer (2000) defines *value-added assessment* as a process that measures school and program effectiveness "using a statistical regression model that includes, to the extent possible, all of the nonschool factors that contribute to growth in student achievement, in particular, prior student achievement and student, family, and neighborhood characteristics" (2). The qualifier "to the extent possible" in this definition is the problem. Without

Dimension	Criterion-Referenced Tests (CRTs)	Norm-Referenced Standardized Achievement Tests (NR/SATs)
Purpose	• To determine if individual students have acquired specific learning outcomes for a unit or course of study • To assess students' strengths and weaknesses with specific concepts and/or skills in order to plan for further instruction	• To compare individual students' scores against scores of standardization group • To rank students with respect to achievement in broad areas of knowledge • To determine those at extremes—high and low performing
Content	• Selected on the basis of its significance in relationship to the curriculum that was taught • These skills are identified locally by teachers and/or through textbooks used	• Selected by how well it discriminates among students • Broad skill and concept areas, identified by outside experts from a sampling of textbooks and other curricular resources, are measured • Typically measures much general world knowledge
Item Characteristics	• Each skill is tested by a minimum of four items to have an adequate sampling and to minimize the effects of guessing • The items that test a particular skill or concept are equivalent in difficulty	• Each skill is tested by fewer than four items • Items vary in difficulty levels • Items are selected for their ability to create a range of scores that sort out the high and low achievers
Score Interpretation	• Individuals' performances are matched to the preset educational outcomes for the unit or course of study • Scores expressed as raw scores, percents, or rubric scores	• Individuals' scores are compared with scores of the test's original norming group • Scores expressed as standard scores—percentiles, stanines, and/or grade equivalents

Adapted from Popham, J. 1975. Educational Evaluation. Englewood Cliffs, NJ: Prentice-Hall.

FIGURE 6–6 CRTs Versus NR/SATs

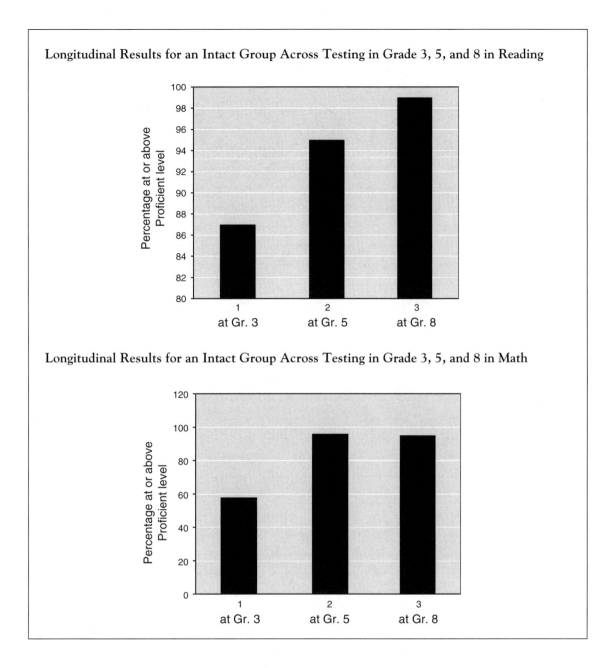

FIGURE 6–7 Logitudinal Results

controlling for socioeconomic status, demographics, family factors, and other such *extraneous variables* mainly related to students, incorrect conclusions about their achievement can be easily drawn. Extraneous variables are variables "that can influence the results. . . . Such variables come from four components of a study—the researcher, participants, environment, and measurement task" (Heiman 2001, 59). Along with student factors, extraneous variables in the

environment—those related to teachers and schools—must also be controlled. The danger is that these critically important controls might be inadequately applied or not applied at all in AYP or value-added assessment calculations. "Failure to account for differences across schools in these characteristics could result in highly contaminated indicators of performance" (Meyer 2000, 2).

Sanders and his colleagues also reached a conclusion in their research that few would

Spring Statewide Reading Assessment Comparison of Scores (Class Average):
Local School Tracking Scores with Scores of Other County Schools in Same SES Band and State Average

Local School Tracking Scores = L
Other Schools in the County in Same SES Band = O
State Average = A

Score	Grade 3	Grade 5	Grade 8
236			
235			L
234			
233			O
232			O
231			
230			O O O O
229			O O A
228			O
227			
226			
225			
224			
223			
222			
221		O	
220		O O	
219		O O O O	
218		O O O O O O	
217		L O O O O	
216		O O O O A	
215		O	
214			
213		O	
212			
211			
210	O	O	
209	O		
208	O O		
207	O O		
206	O O O O O O O O O A		
205	O O O O O		
204	O		
203			
202	O		
201	L O		
200			
199	O		
198			
197			

FIGURE 6–8 Comparison of Scores

challenge: it's the teacher that makes the difference—she or he is the most influential variable in any statistical equation (Pipho 1998). However, the downside of giving accolades for success to individual classroom teachers is that their work is often supported by other professional and/or paraprofessional colleagues—and, one hopes, by parents and the community. Students' successes in the best situations are the result of collaborative, harmonious effort. Attributing achievement gains to individual effectiveness excludes the contributions of others in the process (J. K. Mora 2004). Teachers in schools with limited resources are struggling to play multiple roles in meeting students' needs. Typically, these are needs that must be met before achievement is even possible. Is it fair to conclude that these teachers are not as effective as those with a merry band of assistants because their students' AYP indicators are lower?

Value-added assessments have the potential to be informative when the data they yield are integrated with other factors that contribute to or inhibit students' learning. Classroom teachers usually have responsibilities in the school's testing regime that produces this data and are also most aware of mitigating circumstances that should be factored into the equation.

Dealing with Tests

Administering, Scoring, Analyzing, and Filing

Classroom teachers are usually responsible for administering achievement tests according to prescribed protocols. Teachers typically don't select the test used; that decision is more often made at administrative levels in the district or state. Nor do teachers typically correct them, especially NR/SATs.

However, performance tasks on tests are designed to elicit such competencies as critical thinking, problem solving, and/or the use of communication skills. Students' performance as they construct short or long essays and show the processes they used to solve

math problems, perform scientific work, or organize portfolios of a year's work demonstrates their ability to apply specific state content standards, and each completed task must be evaluated. Classroom teachers are often asked to do so, and the required time and training creates another cost, which may influence a state's decision about test type. "Concerns with the costs of performance-based tests, the reliability of scorers' judgments, and the difficulties of covering the breadth of standards all may be reasons why performance-based assessments have been in short supply among state testing programs" (Doherty 2004, 2).

Whether corrected within or outside the school, test results need to be gathered for filing and reporting. Students' permanent folders typically include individual achievement test results that provide a profile of individual achievement relative to norms and/or state standards. Students' scores on standardized tests may also be used to verify the appropriateness of local curriculum, the efficacy of current teaching methods, teaching effectiveness, and/or the need for interventions. We suggest that students' portfolios should also contain the normed and/or other standardized test results that accumulate during their school career. A review of test information in students' folders allows teachers to identify at-risk students, plan interventions, and/or test practice activities accordingly, and identify appropriate support services.

Computers now allow aggregated and disaggregated scores to be easily stored at every level—school, district, and state. Educators can analyze as well as report scores by individuals, by groups within the school or district, by school, or by district.

New or Known Information?

Test data often confirm what teachers have already concluded from ongoing assessment of the teaching and learning in their classrooms. After a few weeks of school, good teachers have gotten to know all about their students—as learners, yes, but also as people.

Each day, they witness and document the mini- and maxi-evolutions that learning stimulates. Working anthropologically, teachers have the privilege of prolonged engagement with and persistent observation of their community of learners. Teachers question whether they really need an outside measure that gives possibly misleading or redundant information, especially assessments that are insensitive to the uniqueness of learning communities. We must always consider the usefulness of test scores in the context of our particular situation.

Accountability

Testing has been around for decades. We probably all have memories of the spring ritual of taking and, later, administering standardized achievement tests. However, it's a memory that is no doubt overshadowed by the many other exciting things we did as a class during the year. Testing week was just an interruption in our lively schedule. We prepared, if you could call it that, by uncovering curriculum all year long. But times have changed!

That change seemed to arrive during the late eighties. Scores on statewide tests became a major concern. Considerable time was spent focusing on test formats and taking practice tests, and there was lots of associated stress. Now the federal testing mandate associated with the NCLB legislation has been added to the mix (NEA 2004). Some may argue that, technically, the NCLB legislation doesn't *mandate*, since a state can say no, thank you, to the federal funding tied to this legislation. Nevertheless, most states currently have established schedules for statewide testing of students' progress related to identified learning standards and benchmarks for achievement.

The most important sections of NCLB are those that refer to *accountability* and *testing*. Accountability sections in the legislation are intended to "hold public school educators directly responsible for the effectiveness of their instructional efforts. *Assessment* . . . is simply a ritzy word for testing" (Popham 2004a, 15). State-designated consequences related to *failure* are another important aspect of this legislation that educators should be aware of as NCLB is implemented in their schools. Some states reward schools with acceptable scores, some sanction schools with unacceptable scores, and other states do both (see Appendix 6–1).

It is not in the purview of this text to argue for or against the use of standardized achievement tests (NR/SATs, CCR/SATs, or HA/SATs), although that debate is still ongoing nationwide. We do, however, encourage educators to pay attention to the kinds of tests used in their state and to consider whether these purported assessments *of* learning in any meaningful way act as assessments *for* learning. Teachers need to know

▶ what the measures show or do not show
▶ how the tests impact day-to-day instruction and curriculum
▶ how results affect job security, their position, and/or their status
▶ how they should file data
▶ how and to whom they should report data

For them, there is much at stake and therefore much to learn

Talking the Talk: The ABCs of Statewide Standardized Achievement Testing

In order to be players in testing and accountability conversations, teachers need to understand the acronyms used and the implications of school report cards. State education department (SED) websites provide numerous links with general information, guidelines, and regulations related to statewide achievement testing. They also commonly have links to aggregated and disaggregated scores. The acronymic alphabet soup includes some common terms and others that are state specific. Teachers could use a *vade mecum*, a book or manual that provides background and simplified explanations for technical terms, processes, and calculations. For example, teachers may hear or read about AYP (annual yearly progress), AMOs (annual measurable objectives), RCI (regional cost index), SPI (state performance index), and SRP (state reference point)—and that's the tip of the iceberg. Comprehending the relevance and impact of a student's or group's converted score(s) on a state test usually requires a modicum of technical expertise regardless of the kind of test. With stakes this high, teachers need to surf their SED site and become well versed in the measures and measuring processes used locally.

Are the Tests Useful?

Test experts, or psychomatricians, advertise (sometimes even tout) the level of a test's *validity* and *reliability*. (For definitions of these terms and examples of what they mean, see Appendix 6–3.) However, another attribute also needs to be considered when evaluating a test: its *usability* or instructional utility. In other words, is it practical in terms of cost, time required, and ease of scoring? Most important, does it contribute to instruction in a meaningful way? It should yield *instructionally beneficial* data—data that effectively informs day-to-day teaching (Lyman 1998; Popham 2003).

There's a *shelf life* to tests as well. As instructional methods evolve to match current research, new ways of assessment measure new competency benchmarks. For example, a notable change in the new edition of the venerable SATs (now referred to only by the acronym, since the term *scholastic aptitude* has become suspect) is the addition of a student-written essay designed to measure writing competency. The class of 2006 will be the first to take the new version, in the spring of 2005 (College Board 2004).

Popham (2004a) emphasizes the need for *instructionally supportive* accountability tests that are *instructionally sensitive*. Such measures provide accurate information with which to evaluate a state's schools and improve instruc-

tional methods in ways that meet the unique needs of students. However, he also warns that "education officials in most states have chosen NCLB tests, either national exams or state-customized ones, that are essentially insensitive to the detection of instructional improvement. Instructionally insensitive tests simply can't identify instructional improvements—even if such improvements are actually present" (2004b, 40).

Instructional utility, usefulness, and sensitivity all relate to the degree that a test yields specific information that can meaningfully inform practice in the classroom—information a teacher can use in planning purposeful subsequent lessons for learners. Such lessons evolve from identified strengths and needs, allowing teachers to reinforce and extend students' learning in efficient ways. Each test much be examined individually and thoroughly to determine its degree of instructional utility and sensitivity.

So What's the Answer?

Balance
Balance, a relatively simple concept, is critical for harmony in the universe, world, home, and school. *Balance* is essential in the processes that fuel any assessment system. Information gleaned should clearly identify learners' strengths and instructional paths. Useful information is *triangulated* in the sense that it results from different tasks in different settings in order to provide a comparative, holistic perspective. These tasks allow for more than one acceptable solution, reflect what is valued in the learning community, have curricular relevance without being restricted to the curriculum taught, allow multiple performances, and consider the *processes* students use as well as their *products* (Eisner 1998). "Multiple measures are needed for monitoring and accountability systems" (Linn 2000, 9).

The assessment system described in this text is built on the integration of multiple forms of categorical data (to include standardized achievement test results) but does not place test information at center stage. *All* relevant pieces of data are melded to create up-to-the-minute individual profiles of learning.

Not a Single Score or Score Type

Alone, standardized achievement tests provide uncorroborated data and therefore should never be the sole determiners of achievement (AERA 2000). The American Education Research Association spells this out emphatically:

> Decisions that affect individual students' life chances or educational opportunities should not be made on the basis of test scores alone. Other relevant information should be taken into account to enhance the overall validity of such decisions. As a minimum assurance of fairness, when tests are used as part of making high-stakes decisions for individual students such as promotion to the next grade or high school graduation, students must be afforded multiple opportunities to pass the test. More importantly, when there is credible evidence that a test score may not adequately reflect a student's true proficiency, alternative acceptable means should be provided by which to demonstrate attainment of the tested standards. (AERA 2000)

We are glad the AERA does not stand alone in this. Even a testing company like CTB/McGrawHill advocates multiple measures of data for determining students' achievement: "A comprehensive assessment program may include several different measures. . . . No single test can ascertain whether all educational goals are being met. . . . No one kind of test can tell us all we need to know about a student's learning" (McGrawHill 2004b, 2). The Standards for Educational and Psychological Testing cite the misuse of a test as its highest crime: "Testing is a largely self-policed industry, constrained ultimately only by the victims of bad testing" (Sacks 1999, 100).

Stiggins (2004) proposes that the "belief in the power of standardized testing has blinded public officials and school leaders to a completely different application of assessment—day-to-day classroom assessment—that has been shown to trigger remarkable gains in student achievement" (23). In the assessment system proposed throughout this text, standardized achievement test results are but one of four data categories, and their legitimate function is integrated and their dangers are, we hope, controlled.

Self-Study

It's not likely that standardized achievement tests in schools will be eliminated in the near future. In fact, there is more and more testing, and there are ever more tests, along with frequent instances of grade retention, school dropouts, and schools rated as failing that are directly related to students' performance on these tests. Therefore, we need to think about what can be done to minimize these tests' negative impact:

1. Speak up. Speak out. You might be dubbed your school's resident radical, but consider it a compliment even if it isn't meant that way! Question every test that is used. Research test reviews. Ask to see the test if you aren't familiar with its format. We don't need to kill the messenger, but we do need to question him. Too often, administrators and/or specialists on study teams address the group in *authority speak* (the tone and language of *I know best*) even when they don't mean to. People feel intimidated. Don't be. Doing your homework is *critical* if you are to advocate successfully on behalf of students, and the Internet has made it much easier to do that homework.

2. Be ready with a well-documented *counterpoint.* Just as we need to match what's taught in the classroom with the skills assessed on tests, we need to establish policies that require multiple quality indications of locally determined standards of performance. Classroom data deserve a respectful place at the table. Portfolios allow teachers and other

student advocates to present their alternative data in an organized and professional way.

3. Get smart! Classroom teachers *must* be prepared to recognize, examine, and report any tests that appear questionable. We need to be test savvy. As the ad says, "An educated consumer is our best customer." We've got to become this educated test consumer who can't be fooled by achievement tests that are snake oil in slick packages.

4. Know what standardized achievement tests *can* and *cannot* show. Depending on the type, they can help parents identify how their child "compares with a nationally representative sample of children with respect to what is measured by such tests [and] . . . in a very rough way, identify a child's relative strengths and weaknesses" (Popham 2000, 66). A recent statement by Grover Whitehurst, assistant secretary for research and improvement at the U.S. Department of Education, should send chills up our spines: "We know for example, that many states are now looking at the fourth-grade reading performance scores in terms of predicting how much prison space they are going to need ten or twelve years later" (Whitehurst 2004, 1).

Assessment, Accountability, and Testing

National testing policies direct that students must be tested every year as an effective and efficient way to ensure they are learning and schools are doing their job. Stiggins (2004) states that the national regime of standardized testing protocols we're expected to adhere to represents a "fundamentally flawed set of beliefs about how to use assessment for educational improvement" (23). Policy makers and supporters of the NCLB legislation seem to assume that this testing *is* assessment. It's not! It's merely a thin slice of the assessment pie. Testing produces scores that require interpretations about students' current level of knowledge and skills as measured *on particular instruments* (Popham 2004a); assessment is a much broader, comprehensive *process* that informs day-to-day instruction.

To be sure they are learning, we should assess students constantly, not just yearly. Clearly, *assessed* is different from *tested*. Assessment involves an ongoing gathering of data as students go about their daily learning. These data are analyzed and compiled before evaluative conclusions are formed. Such a gradual and thorough kind of investigation tells teachers whether or not students are learning and, possibly, where support is needed. "The assessment process involves much more than just testing. It uses all teaching and learning experiences, as well as tests, in determining where students are and what they need to support their growth" (Cooper and Kiger 2001, 4).

Effective teaching and learning is a partnership, a dance rooted in sound pedagogy and creatively choreographed to meet the identified needs of individual learners. Good teachers have always taught dynamically, constantly monitoring learners' performance and adjusting instruction as needed. Useful assessment creates an *assess-teach-perform-assess* cycle that continuously informs instruction.

Teachers, typically focused on teaching and learning with the students in their classrooms, must now focus on how *others* are assessing their students. We aren't testing experts, but as professionals, we *must* acquire a basic knowledge of specific tests, the testing process, and the testing culture currently suffocating schools. The national mandate is not a *system* of assessment—either of or for learning. It is a testing policy. Clearly, balanced assessment systems are needed in the classroom, schools, and the nation.

State of the States

Adapted from Public Broadcasting System. 2004. *Frontline*: "Testing Our Schools: In Your State." Retrieved from *www.pbs.org/wgbh/pages/frontline/shows/schools/state.* Information at source was based on *Education Week*, "Quality Counts 2002"; American Federation of Teachers, "Making Standards Matter 2001."

State	Subjects tested by grades?	Has the state adopted standards in core academic subjects?	Are the state's standards considered strong based on AFT* criteria?	According to the AFT, are all of the state's tests "aligned" with the standards?	What types of items are used on the tests?	Does this state sanction and/or reward schools?	Do students have to pass a test in order to graduate from high school?
AL	*English:* K–11 *Math:* 3–11 *Science:* 9–11 *Social Studies:* 9–11	Yes	Yes	No	Multiple choice, extended response	Yes, both	Yes
AK	*English:* 3, 4, 6, 7, 8, 10 *Math:* 3, 4, 6, 7, 8, 10 *Science:* No testing *Social Studies:* No testing	Yes	No	Yes	Multiple choice, short answer, extended response	No, neither sanctions nor rewards schools	Yes
AZ	*English:* 1–10 *Math:* 2–10 *Science:* No testing *Social Studies:* No testing	Yes	Yes	Yes	Multiple choice, short answer, extended response	No, neither sanctions nor rewards schools	Yes
AR	*English:* 4–8, 10, 11 *Math:* 4–10 *Science:* 5, 7, 10 *Social Studies:* 5, 7, 10	Yes	No	No	Multiple choice, short answer, extended response	Yes, both	No
CA	*English:* 2–11 *Math:* 2–11 *Science:* 9–11 *Social Studies:* 9–11	Yes	Yes	Yes	Multiple choice, extended response	Yes, both	Yes

State	Subjects/Grades			Test Format	Sanctions/Rewards	
CO	*English:* 3–10 *Math:* 5–10 *Science:* 8 *Social Studies: No* testing	Yes	Yes	Multiple choice, short answer, extended response	Yes, both	No
CT	*English:* 1–4, 6, 8, 10 *Math:* 4, 6, 8, 10 *Science:* 10 *Social Studies: No* testing	Yes	Yes	Multiple choice, short answer, extended response	No, neither sanctions nor rewards schools	No
DE	*English:* 2–10 *Math:* 3–10 *Science:* 4, 6, 8, 11 *Social Studies:* 4, 6, 8, 11	Yes	No	Multiple choice, short answer, extended response	Only rewards schools	Yes
FL	*English:* 3–10 *Math:* 3–10 *Science: No* testing *Social Studies: No* testing	Yes	Yes	Multiple choice, short answer, extended response	Yes, both	Yes
GA	*English:* K–8, 11 *Math:* K–8, 11 *Science:* 3–8, 11 *Social Studies:* 3–8, 11	Yes	Yes	Multiple choice, extended response	Only rewards schools	Yes
HI	*English:* 3, 5, 8, 10 *Math:* 3, 5, 8, 10 *Science: No* testing *Social Studies: No* testing	Yes	No	Multiple choice, short answer, extended response	No, neither sanctions nor rewards schools	No

APPENDIX 6–1   State of the States

State	Subjects tested by grades?	Has the state adopted standards in core academic subjects?	Are the state's standards considered strong based on AFT* criteria?	According to the AFT, are all of the state's tests "aligned" with the standards?	What types of items are used on the tests?	Does this state sanction and/or reward schools?	Do students have to pass a test in order to graduate from high school?
ID	*English:* K–11 *Math:* 3–11 *Science:* 3, 5, 8, 9 *Social Studies:* 3, 5, 8, 9	Yes	Yes	No	Short answer, extended response	No, neither sanctions nor rewards schools	No
IL	*English:* 3, 5, 8, 11 *Math:* 3, 5, 8, 11 *Science:* 4, 7, 11 *Social Studies:* 4, 7, 11	Yes	Yes	Yes	Multiple choice, extended response	Only sanctions schools	No
IN	*English:* 3, 6, 8, 10 *Math:* 3, 6, 8, 10 *Science:* No testing *Social Studies:* No testing	Yes	Yes	Yes	Multiple choice, short answer, extended response	Yes, both	Yes
IA	*English:* 4, 8, 11 *Math:* 4, 8, 11 *Science:* 8, 11 *Social Studies:* No testing	No	No	No	Multiple choice	No, neither sanctions nor rewards schools	No
KS	*English:* 2, 5, 8, 11 *Math:* 4, 7, 10 *Science:* 4, 7, 10 *Social Studies:* 6, 8, 11	Yes	Yes	No	Multiple choice	No, neither sanctions nor rewards schools	No

State	Grades Tested			Item Types	Accountability	
KY	English: 3, 4, 6, 7, 9, 10, 12 Math: 3, 5, 6, 8, 9, 11 Science: 4, 7, 11 Social Studies: 5, 8, 11	Yes	Yes	Multiple choice, short answer, extended response, portfolio	Yes, both	No
LA	English: K–10 Math: 3–10 Science: 3–9, 11 Social Studies: 3–9, 11	Yes	No	Multiple choice, short answer, extended response	Yes, both	Yes
ME	English: 4, 8, 11 Math: 4, 8, 11 Science: 4, 8, 11 Social Studies: 4, 8, 11	Yes	No	Multiple choice, short answer, extended response	No, neither sanctions nor rewards schools	No
MD	English: 2–6, 8–10 Math: 2–6, 8–10 Science: 3, 5, 8, 10 Social Studies: 3, 5, 8, 10	Yes	Yes	Multiple choice, short answer, extended response	Yes, both	Yes
MA	English: 3, 4, 7, 8, 10 Math: 4, 6, 8, 10 Science: 5, 8, 10 Social Studies: 5, 8, 10	Yes	Yes	Multiple choice, short answer, extended response	Only sanctions schools	Yes

APPENDIX 6–1 Continued

State	Subjects tested by grades?	Has the state adopted standards in core academic subjects?	Are the state's standards considered strong based on AFT* criteria?	According to the AFT, are all of the state's tests "aligned" with the standards?	What types of items are used on the tests?	Does this state sanction and/or reward schools?	Do students have to pass a test in order to graduate from high school?
MI	*English:* 4, 5, 7, 8, 11 *Math:* 4, 7, 11 *Science:* 5, 8, 11 *Social Studies:* 5, 8, 11	Yes	No	No	Multiple choice, short answer, extended response	Only rewards schools	No
MN	*English:* 3, 5, 8, 10 *Math:* 3, 5, 8 *Science:* No testing *Social Studies:* No testing	Yes	No	No	Multiple choice, short answer, extended response	No, neither sanctions nor rewards schools	Yes
MS	*English:* K–8, 10, 11 *Math:* K–5, 7–9, 11 *Science:* 10 *Social Studies:* 11	Yes	No	Yes	Multiple choice, short answer, extended response	Only sanctions schools	Yes
MO	*English:* 3, 7, 11 *Math:* 4, 8, 10 *Science:* 3, 7, 10 *Social Studies:* 4, 8, 11	Yes	No	Yes	Multiple choice, short answer, extended response	Only sanctions schools	No
MT	*English:* 4, 8, 11 *Math:* 4, 8, 11 *Science:* 4, 8, 11 *Social Studies:* 4, 8, 11	Yes	No	No	Multiple choice	No, neither sanctions nor rewards schools	No

State	Grade levels tested				Test format	Accountability	
NE	English: 4, 8, 11 Math: 4, 8, 11 Science: 4, 8, 11 Social Studies: 4, 8, 11	Yes	No	No	Extended responses	No, neither sanctions nor rewards schools	No
NV	English: 3–5, 8, 10–12 Math: 3–5, 8, 10, 11 Science: 4, 8, 10, 11 Social Studies: No testing	Yes	Yes	No	Multiple choice, short answer, extended response	Only sanctions schools	Yes
NH	English: 3, 6, 10 Math: 3, 6, 10 Science: 6, 10 Social Studies: 6, 10	Yes	Yes	No	Multiple choice, short answer, extended response	No, neither sanctions nor rewards schools	No
NJ	English: 4, 8, 11 Math: 4, 8, 11 Science: 4, 8, 11 Social Studies: 5, 8, 11	Yes	No	No	Multiple choice, short answer, extended response	Only rewards schools	Yes
NM	English: 3–10 Math: 3–10 Science: 3–10 Social Studies: 3–10	Yes	Yes	No	Multiple choice, short answer, extended response	Only rewards schools	Yes
NY	English: 4, 8, 11 Math: 4, 8, 10 Science: 4, 8, 9 Social Studies: 5, 8, 10, 11	Yes	Yes	No	Multiple choice, short answer, extended response	Only sanctions schools	Yes

APPENDIX 6–1 Continued

State	Subjects tested by grades?	Has the state adopted standards in core academic subjects?	Are the state's standards considered strong based on AFT* criteria?	According to the AFT, are all of the state's tests "aligned" with the standards?	What types of items are used on the tests?	Does this state sanction and/or reward schools?	Do students have to pass a test in order to graduate from high school?
NC	*English:* 3–8, 10 *Math:* 3–8, 10 *Science:* 10 *Social Studies:* 10	Yes	Yes	No	Multiple choice, extended response	Yes, both	Yes
ND	*English:* 4, 6, 8, 10, 12 *Math:* 4, 6, 8, 10, 12 *Science:* 4, 6, 8, 10 *Social Studies:* 4, 6, 8, 10	Yes	No	No	Multiple choice, short answer	No, neither sanctions nor rewards schools	No
OH	*English:* 4, 6, 9, 10 *Math:* 4, 6, 9, 10 *Science:* 4, 6, 9, 10 *Social Studies:* 4, 6, 9, 10	Yes	No	System under development	Multiple choice, short answer, extended response	No, neither sanctions nor rewards schools	In development
OK	*English:* 1–3, 5, 8, 10 *Math:* 3, 5, 8, 10 *Science:* 5, 8, 10 *Social Studies:* 5, 8, 10	Yes	Yes	Yes	Multiple choice, extended response	Yes, both	No
OR	*English:* 3, 5, 8, 10 *Math:* 3, 5, 8, 10 *Science:* 5, 8, 10 *Social Studies:* 5, 8, 10	Yes	Yes	Yes	Multiple choice, extended response	No, neither sanctions nor rewards schools	No

PA	*English:* 5, 6, 8, 9, 11 *Math:* 5, 8, 11 *Science:* No testing *Social Studies:* No testing	Yes	Yes	Multiple choice, extended response	Only rewards schools	Yes
RI	*English:* 3, 4, 7, 8, 10, 11 *Math:* 4, 8, 10 *Science:* No testing *Social Studies:* No testing	Yes, but only in 3 of 4 core subject areas	No	Multiple choice, short answer, extended response	Only sanctions schools	No
SC	*English:* 3–10 *Math:* 3–10 *Science:* 3–10 *Social Studies:* 3–10	Yes	No	Multiple choice, short answer, extended response	Yes, both	Yes
SD	*English:* 2, 4, 5, 8, 9, 11 *Math:* 2, 4, 8, 11 *Science:* 2, 4, 8, 11 *Social Studies:* 2, 4, 8, 11	Yes	No	Multiple choice, extended response	No, neither sanctions nor rewards schools	No
TN	*English:* 3–9, 11 *Math:* 3–10 *Science:* 3–8, 10 *Social Studies:* 3–8, 10	Yes	No	Multiple choice, extended response	Yes, both	Yes
TX	*English:* 3, 8, 10 *Math:* 3, 8, 10 *Science:* 8, 10 *Social Studies:* 8, 10	Yes	Yes	Multiple choice, short answer, extended response	Yes, both	Yes

APPENDIX 6–1 Continued

State	Subjects tested by grades?	Has the state adopted standards in core academic subjects?	Are the state's standards considered strong based on AFT* criteria?	According to the AFT, are all of the state's tests "aligned" with the standards?	What types of items are used on the tests?	Does this state sanction and/or reward schools?	Do students have to pass a test in order to graduate from high school?
UT	English: 1–11 Math: 1–11 Science: 3–11 Social Studies: 3, 5, 8, 11	Yes	Yes	No	Multiple choice, short answer, extended response	No, neither sanctions nor rewards schools	Yes
VT	English: 2, 4, 5, 8, 10 Math: 4, 8, 10 Science: 5, 9, 11 Social Studies: No testing	Yes	No	No	Multiple choice, short answer, extended response, portfolio	Only sanctions schools	No
VA	English: 3–6, 8–11 Math: 3–6, 8–10 Science: 3, 5, 8, 10 Social Studies: 3, 5, 8, 10	Yes	Yes	Yes	Multiple choice, extended response	No, neither sanctions nor rewards	Yes
WA	English: 2–4, 6, 7, 9, 10 Math: 3, 4, 6, 7, 9, 10 Science: 5, 8, 10 Social Studies: No testing	Yes	No	No	Multiple choice, short answer, extended response	No, neither sanctions nor rewards	Yes
WV	English: K–11 Math: K–11 Science: 3–11 Social Studies: 3–11	Yes	Yes	No	Multiple choice, extended response	Only sanctions schools	No

WI	English: 3, 4, 8, 10, 11 Math: 4, 8, 10, 11 Science: 4, 8, 10, 11 Social Studies: 4, 8, 10, 11	Yes	No	No	Multiple choice, short answer, extended response	No, neither sanctions nor rewards	Yes
WY	English: 4, 8, 11 Math: 4, 8, 11 Science: No testing Social Studies: No testing	Yes	No	No	Multiple choice, short answer, extended response	No, neither sanctions nor rewards	No

*American Federation of Teachers

APPENDIX 6–1 Continued

Types of Standardized Achievement Tests: State by State and District of Columbia

State	Tests Aligned to State Standards		Off-the-Shelf Commercial Tests Not Aligned to a Specific State's Standards
	CCR/SATs	HA/SATs	NR/SATs
Alabama (AL)	X		X
Alaska (AK)	X		X
Arizona (AZ)	X		X
Arkansas (AR)	X		X
California (CA)	X		X
Colorado (CO)	X		
Connecticut (CT)	X		
Delaware (DE)		X	
District of Columbia (DC)			X
Florida (FL)	X		X
Georgia (GA)	X		X
Hawaii (HI)		X	
Idaho (ID)	X		
Illinois (IL)	X	X	
Indiana (IN)	X		
Iowa (IA)			X
Kansas (KS)	X		
Kentucky (KY)	X		X
Louisiana (LA)	X		X
Maine (ME)	X		
Maryland (MD)	X	X	
Massachusetts (MA)	X		
Michigan (MI)	X		
Minnesota (MN)	X		
Mississippi (MS)	X		X
Missouri (MO)	X	X	
Montana (MT)		X	X
Nebraska (NE)	X		
Nevada (NV)	X		X
New Hampshire (NH)	X		
New Jersey (NJ)	X		
New Mexico (NM)	X		X
New York (NY)	X		
North Carolina (NC)	X		
North Dakota (ND)		X	
Ohio (OH)	X		
Oklahoma (OK)	X		X
Oregon (OR)	X		
Pennsylvania (PA)	X		
Rhode Island (RI)	X	X	
South Carolina (SC)	X		
South Dakota (SD)	X	X	X
Tennessee (TN)	X	X	
Texas (TX)	X		
Utah (UT)	X		X
Vermont (VT)	X		
Virginia (VA)	X		
Washington (WA)	X		X
West Virginia (WV)	X		X
Wisconsin (WI)	X	X	X
Wyoming (WY)		X	
Column Totals	42	12	21
	21 of 51 (states + DC), or 41 percent, use CCR/SATs only		30 of 51 (states + DC), or 59 percent, use NR/SATs in off-the-shelf or modified form (HA/SATs)

Adapted from Quality Counts. 2004. "Standards and Accountability: Types of Tests." Education Week. Retrieved from www.edweek.org/sreports/qc04/reports/standacct-tlb.cfm.

APPENDIX 6–2 Types of Standardized Achievement Tests: State by State and District of Columbia

Legend
Types of standardized achievement tests used for statewide testing:
CCR/SATs (customized criterion-referenced standardized achievement tests) are tests explicitly designed to measure identified statewide learning standards. They may be locally or commercially produced.
NR/SATs (norm-referenced standardized achievement tests) refer to commercially developed or off-the-shelf tests that have not been modified to reflect a specific state's standards.
HA/SATs (hybrid-augmented standardized achievement tests) are tests that incorporate elements of NR/SATs and CCR/SATs. They are also explicitly designed to measure identified statewide learning standards. The NR/SATs used are constructed from commercial NR/SATs that have been modified to better reflect a specific state's standards.

Validity and Reliability Definitions and Examples

Validity

Category	What It Means	Type	Definition
Criterion-related validity	The degree to which the test relates to a particular criterion or standard performance separate from the test	Predictive	Tests such as the SAT and ACT claim that the correlation of students' test scores with earned GPAs provides evidence of the test's predictive validity or ability to predict future performance.
		Concurrent	If high scorers on a writing test are indeed good writers when judged by current criteria for standard performance, that writing test would have concurrent validity.
Construct-related validity	How well the test reflects the hypothetical construct it claims to measure		For example, when the construct is *reading*, a test reporting scores of *general reading ability* would require significant reading of continuous text with demonstrated comprehension rather than a compilation of subtests of separate reading-related skills.
Content-related validity	How well the content of the test matches the content that it is supposed to cover or, more specifically, knowledge and skills deemed important to a particular area of study		Human judgment in test item analyses is the basis for concluding whether a test has content validity. Items are match to the curricular content to determine the degree of match.

Reliability

Category	What It Means	Example
Equivalent-form reliability	A test taker's score would be statistically similar if given the alternate form of a test at the same level.	If a test has an A form and a B form at a particular level, a student's score would be statistically the same regardless of which form is used.
Similar-test reliability	The test is consistent with other tests that measure the same skill or construct.	A student's scores on this test and another test of reading comprehension are statistically similar.
Split-halves reliability	The test has internal consistency—all items are aimed at measuring the same skill or construct.	If every other item in a test were extracted to form a second test, a student's scores on both, when taken close in time and without intervening instruction, would be statistically similar.
Test-retest reliability	Given the same test at two different administrations, close in time, a test taker's score would be statistically similar.	A student is retested using the same test without feedback on the first administration of it or intervening instruction, and the student's second score is statistically similar to the first.

Sources: Heiman 2001; Lyman 1998; Popham 2000.

APPENDIX 6–3   Validity and Reliability Definitions and Examples

Analyzing and Evaluating Data

You're attending a local health fair. At the various stations, you have your bone density checked, have blood drawn and analyzed for glucose and cholesterol levels, have your hearing and vision tested, have your body fat measured, and have your blood pressure taken. With each piece of data, you learn how your particular reading relates to a "normal" one, but no single test deems you healthy or unhealthy. Normal blood pressure is not necessarily more important than your glucose or cholesterol level. Nor does a bone density T-score outweigh the importance of your body fat index. All the results have to be considered collectively to assess overall health. Then, regarding the less positive results, you need to consider what action to take. Should you change your diet, meditate more often, or lift more weights? After all, why gather all the data if you have no intention of improving your health? It's a waste of your time and the health care professionals' expertise.

Likewise, when you assess children, one piece of data or one test cannot adequately indicate whether or not learning has taken place (Linn 2000). You rely on several sources of data to make your evaluation. If you teach special-needs or English language learners, the need for multiple data sources is even greater (Rueda and Garcia 1997). Gathering the data also implies that you will be responsible for acting on the results. You don't assess children in order to fill up a grade book or a portfolio. Your assessment informs your decisions about instruction and the goals you set with the student. Sometimes it also prompts you to take a closer look at your assessment system (Bauer and Garcia 2002; Harlin and Lipa 1996).

The A in CARP

Remember that skillful assessment takes time and organization. The CARP system—in which you collect data (to include thinking evidence, work samples, in-the-classroom benchmarks, and norm-referenced and other standardized achievement tests), analyze data, report data, and plan instruction—is a critical component of good teaching. It is process oriented and flexible, designed to show the change in students from dependence to independence, production to reflection, and teacher-directed learning to self-directed learning, as well as prompt the move from isolated to collaborative assessment. After you've collected the data, you need to analyze and evaluate them—the A phase in the CARP system.

Data analysis is much easier if you collect the necessary information day by day; otherwise, you'll be overwhelmed at the end of the month or a grading period. (This involves mainly the *T*, *W*, and *I* in TWIN evidence, since the *N* is collected only as these tests are administered.) A schedule for *what* and *how* you'll collect data ensures you'll have balanced information to analyze.

When she taught third grade, Sue Rosche developed a system for data collection and analysis that enabled her to use her time efficiently (see Figure 7–1). Notice how her planning helped her make the best use of her time during the school day as well as after school and ensured that she collected information on *all* her students. Sue also analyzed each piece of data shortly after collecting it. This meant she could accurately record the student's responses and use the results in planning follow-up instruction. Sue's systematic approach to collection and analysis made the data broader and richer and therefore increased their value in portraying student learning. Her system also streamlined end-of-the-quarter reporting, making it easier to match data sources to learning outcomes.

Triangulating Evidence of Skill and Competency

The assessment data you collect are integrated, interdependent elements that are relevant to identified learning goals. By having a variety of assessment formats available, you increase students' chances of *showing* or *demonstrating* their knowledge and skills (Harlin and Lipa 1995). When data sources are aligned with state learning standards, student products, performances, and proficiency become the body of evidence for meeting the learning goals. Furthermore, the thinking evidence, work samples, and in-the-classroom benchmarks help you assess students' progress toward the same learning standards that are evaluated on your state's norm-referenced or other standardized achievement tests.

How can you best interpret all these data?

First, make an inventory of all of your data sources. You may be surprised by how much evidence you really possess and how varied it

is. What thinking evidence is produced in your classroom? Anecdotal records, conference notes, reading logs? How about work samples? Are there journal entries, summaries, learning logs? What about benchmarks? Have you collected running records, rubrics, projects, and presentations? Once you've listed them, gather your data sources together in one place and sort them by student. Decide how many students you will evaluate per day. By distributing your work over several days, you will be able to focus on one student at a time and evaluate many dimensions of progress toward each learning standard.

A minimum of three data sources collected over time and from different types of tasks can be triangulated to assess student growth in a particular skill or area of knowledge. Your first step is to identify one of your learning outcomes and locate the relevant data sources. Labeling your evidence as you collect it streamlines the sorting process. Some teachers use colored sticky flags on which they jot down the standard to which the piece of data relates. It is entirely possible that something like a retelling rubric will be labeled and coded for several standards or more than one kind of learning behavior, such as knowing the elements of story grammar; explaining inferences, predictions, and conclusions; and making connections between the text and the reader's life.

Cross-Checking Data

If you're like Sue Rosche, you've spent your time wisely, collecting the significant artifacts that represent your skillful teaching and your students' learning. Now is the time to create a composite picture. What can your students do now? What strategies do they use independently? How do they solve problems? Which concepts have they internalized? Can they apply what you think you've taught? Some of these questions may be answered by your data sources. Your goal is to locate demonstrations of your students' learning (Bauer and Garcia

Data Source	Time Frame for Collection and Analysis
Journals (Work Sample)	Dialogue with one student a day for a total of five per week during silent reading. Do random sampling at end of day depending on prompt (in the classroom after school). Make note of some journals to see more often.
Independent Reading Log (Work Sample)	Review one a day for a total of five per week during silent reading.
Running Record (Benchmark Measure)	Do one a day during silent reading. Collect one each quarter (nine weeks) for early readers. Evaluate that evening.
READ and RETELL (Benchmark Measure)	Collect one each quarter minimum. Begin with fiction piece with whole class to introduce procedures and purpose. Continue throughout the year in connection with content area instruction or assigned in small groups of fluent readers. District requires one representative sample a year for fluent readers. Evaluate within two or three days for whole class; that evening for small group.
Reading Conference Record (Thinking Evidence)	One a day during silent reading in connection with taking a running record or in a small book talk group (focus notes on one child). Evaluate that evening.
Anecdotal Records (Thinking Evidence)	As needed in all language arts and content areas. Use flip cards. Looking at grade-level expectations, may have specific children in mind for particular lesson. Take notes on journals and log review/evaluation and writing conferences. Highlight "follow-up required." Weekly review to consider future instruction, and so on.
Survey (Interests, Reading, and Writing) (Thinking Evidence)	Done at the beginning of the year for my information. Reviewed by children in last quarter to notice growth.
Self-Evaluation of Independent Reading Log (Benchmark Measure)	Students do this quarterly to note: number of books read during daily silent reading number of fiction/nonfiction number of picture books and title of favorite one number of chapter books and title of favorite one number of easy/just right/too hard books (child estimates own level of difficulty) current just right/challenging book which read-aloud books are reread goal to make log (paper/record) better* goal to become a better reader* Self-evaluation referred to during reading conference (book talks) at the beginning or middle of quarter as a reminder of goals and to discuss grade.
Writing Conferences (Work Sample and Thinking Evidence)	Methodically plan to see everyone once a week. Individual conferences for content, process, evaluation. Conferences direct instruction by identifying needs (for a small group or the whole class) and also who (child/teacher) can teach the minilesson!

As a class, we brainstorm possible responses. Children need this guidance from one another and me.

FIGURE 7–1   Schedule for Data Collection and Analysis

2002; Shepard 2000). You need an approach for systematically weighing the evidence you've collected.

One way to begin to synthesize your data is to develop an organizational framework, perhaps based on the state learning standards for your grade level. Elena Rodriguez, a second-grade teacher, made a chart of Florida's standards for language arts and matched them with the corresponding pieces of evidence she had collected (see Figure 7–2). Then she compiled these pieces of evidence student by student.

Let's look at how Elena Rodriguez analyzed Jackie's progress, beginning with her anecdotal records taken during small-group reading instruction (thinking evidence). As Elena read through them, she noted several entries containing information that she matched to different standards. Spotting a stack of student reading response journals (work samples), she quickly read through Jackie's entries. Another work sample, Jackie's reading logs for independent reading, provided not only a list of the books Jackie had read but also information on how she had selected each book and a rating for that book ("4 stars = a great book and I would read other books by this author; 3 stars = I would recommend it and probably read other books by this author; 2 stars = it was okay, but I like other authors better than this one; 1 star = I probably would not read another book by this author"). Then Elena skimmed Jackie's running records (benchmarks). Finally, she looked at her reading conference notes to see what they revealed about Jackie's performance on the learning standards. Elena had multiple data sources to evaluate Jackie's progress on each of the three standards shown in Figure 7–2. This increased the likelihood that they would fairly represent what Jackie could do and decreased the weight of any one performance.

State Language Art Learning Standard	Data Source
Uses prior knowledge, illustrations, and text to make and confirm predictions	• Teacher's anecdotal records during directed reading-thinking activities 10/20; 10/27; 11/4 • Student's reading response journal entries 9/17; 9/23; 10/1; 10/15 • Student reading conferences 9/10; 9/21; 10/8
Cross-checks visual, structural, and meaning cues to figure out unknown words.	• Running records 9/8; 10/8 • Teacher's anecdotal records during guided reading 9/1; 10/3 • Student reading conferences 9/10; 9/21; 10/8
Selects material to read for pleasure, as a group or independently.	• Teacher's anecdotal records during daily sustained silent reading time 9/5; 9/26; 10/15 • Student's reading log for independent reading • Student reading conferences 9/10; 9/21; 10/8

FIGURE 7–2 Matching Learning Standards to Data Sources

Elena Rodriguez's next step was to cross-check the data from each source, which represented different contexts. Comparing each data source to the learning standard, she focused on what Jackie *could do* as a reader. Figure 7–3 shows Elena's analysis of three data sources as they relate to one of the language arts learning standards. She found that Jackie consistently used illustrations, prior knowledge, and text information to make and confirm predictions; demonstrated her proficiency with folktales, realistic fiction, and informational genres; and, more important, employed effective prediction strategies

---

Florida State Standard: Uses prior knowledge, illustrations, and text to make and confirm predictions.

Data Source	Analysis
Teacher's anecdotal record, 10/20, on directed reading-thinking activity *Miss Nelson Is Missing!* Jackie made predictions based on the cover illustration and justified her response. She was quite confident making predictions at each place in the story. When asked to prove whether or not they came true, she could support her response with events from the story.	• Can make predictions • Bases predictions on illustration and text information • Can prove predictions using illustrations and text information
Reading conference with Jackie, 9/10 Question: When you pick up a book for the first time, how can you guess what might happen in that book? Answer: Sometimes I look at the picture on the cover and think, "What is that person going to do?" Question: Do you ever do anything else? Answer: Well, if it's an author that I know because last year's teacher read those books or my mom read them to me, I can make a pretty good guess. Question: How do you make your guesses while you're reading a book? Answer: I think about what I would do if I had that problem.	• Uses illustrations to make predictions during independent reading • Uses prior knowledge of author and books to make predictions • Uses prior knowledge (own experiences) to make predictions
Jackie's reading response journal, 10/15 *Skinny Bones* I'm at the part where Alex goes to get his haircut but Mr. Peoples is in a relly bad mode. Mr. Peoples pracktley made Alex bold! Alex was not to happy about that. I predict that Alex will get relly mad at Mr. Peoples and he will run home and show his mother.	• Makes prediction during independent reading based on knowledge of plot and characters.

FIGURE 7–3 Analysis of Jackie's Documents

when she was reading different kinds of books on her own. Thus, Jackie was moving from dependence on her teacher toward independent use of the strategy and was well on her way toward meeting this particular language arts standard.

When you cross-check information, you're looking for evidence of a strategy or learning standard in different forms: *If the student can do this in one time and place, can she do it in others?* You cannot base your conclusions solely on one document or one instance. What you are seeking is consistent performance, which can be supported only by triangulating your data—collecting several pieces of evidence. Do not allow one piece of data to distort the picture. Sometimes this may mean that you will read and reread the documents you collected. You will become aware of what each document *shows* about the student: *How does she think? What does she do? When can she do this independently?* As you become more familiar with the documents and the process, your analysis will become more reliable and less tedious.

Data-Based Decision Making

As you evaluate a student's learning on the basis of multiple sources, the link between assessment and instruction becomes obvious. For each learning standard the student meets, you can assume that your instruction has been appropriate and that there were sufficient experiences for the student to become proficient. Now you need to build on this successful performance. For each grade level, the demands for meeting the standard increase, and students are expected to read more genres and more difficult texts.

Use New Texts

For Elena Rodriguez, a logical decision might be to expand Jackie's experiences into other contexts and provide additional opportunities to apply what she has learned. Perhaps Elena might introduce Jackie to more genres— biographies and mysteries, for example. Can Jackie adjust her prediction strategies to these

new genres? Are there changes in how and when she makes predictions? Or Elena could decide to have Jackie read chapter books instead of picture books, increasing the difficulty of making predictions. Elena is aware that the standardized achievement test used in her state includes several genres. Thus, she wants to be sure that Jackie and her other students are familiar with each one.

Continue to Teach Instructional Strategies

In either case—changing genres or choosing more difficult texts—Elena Rodriguez first must provide modeling and instruction during guided reading to demonstrate how one makes and confirms predictions in these varied contexts. For example, when you read a mystery, you need to focus on the details. They provide the salient information with which to solve the mystery. As Elena works with Jackie's guided reading group, she must be sure to model this focus consistently. This means Elena must make some strategic decisions about *how* she will show this as well as *which texts* she will use to introduce students to the genre. Finding the appropriate mysteries means reading several titles to find the ones that best exemplify the genre and are developmentally appropriate for Jackie's group, then assembling an ample supply for independent and guided reading. Based on what she learned from Jackie's evaluation, Elena should also gauge how frequently to model predictions with this new genre.

Create New Tasks or Formats

The new genre, mysteries, may also mean designing and introducing a new format for the reading response journals. Elena Rodriguez might decide to have her students use double entries, with clues listed on the left side and predictions based on the clues recorded on the right. Then their reading response journals would support these second graders in becoming more conscious of the importance of details in solving mysteries. The new format would also be useful when Elena reviewed her students' journals for evidence of the learning standard with this new genre.

Once her students have read and discussed several mysteries, Elena Rodriguez may use their familiarity with the genre as a basis for guided or independent writing. Jackie and the others will now be aware of which authors and titles they like best, and their enthusiasm will be a lead-in to discussing what a good mystery should contain and modeling how to create a story map to plan a group-authored mystery. Through guided writing, Jackie and the others can apply what they've learned about style, details, and plot. Learning opportunities connecting reading and writing could further prepare Jackie and her peers to write more effectively on state-mandated tests. The models provided by published authors and analyzed under the guidance of Elena would support Jackie's development as a writer.

Dealing with Unmet Standards

Of course, the learning standards are not always met. Sometimes when you analyze your data sources, you may not find enough evidence to show that your students are meeting a given standard. What should you do?

Examine Time Management

First, take a deep breath and gather all your data sources together—thinking evidence, work samples, and in-the-classroom benchmarks. Select one of your students to review, and separate the appropriate sources for one of your learning standards. Make sure you have evidence from each data category. You are looking for consistency across different classroom contexts and tasks in which the amount of support available to the student varies. This consistency is especially critical in relation to your low-achieving students and special-needs and English language learners. Check to see that you matched the source with the standard when you initially analyzed it.

This second analysis may reveal evidence you overlooked the first time or suggest additional sources of data. In other words, perhaps you have the evidence you need, but your analysis needs to be more methodical when you sort through your documents initially. The solution is to take more time synthesizing your data and, following Sue Rosche's example, analyze the data as you collect them.

Determine Whether Learning Opportunities Are Appropriate

If time management is not the problem, you need to look for another explanation for your students' failure to meet a learning standard. One of your next questions should be, Are there sufficient opportunities in my classroom for students to meet this standard? Review your anecdotal records and your lesson plans to identify how often you introduced and modeled a strategy and allowed your students to practice it. If you were Elena Rodriguez, for example, how many times did you plan a directed reading-thinking activity (DRTA) related to prediction? Did you use this strategy with *all* your students or only some groups? Which groups had guided practice with this strategy? How often?

Perhaps you had planned to use a DRTA five times but instead modeled it twice during the last nine weeks. For your second graders two lessons were probably not enough; they need several demonstrations to become familiar with making and proving predictions. You also need more than two opportunities to observe your students during a DRTA to record anecdotal records that will help you monitor how each student responds to the strategy. You could address the problem by planning more frequent DRTA lessons for each of your groups during the next nine weeks, thus increasing the number of demonstrations and providing equal learning opportunities for all your students. Equal opportunities are of even greater concern for your English language learners and your low-achieving and special-needs students. No students should be held accountable for something that wasn't taught, should they?

How often did your students have a chance to *apply* what you taught them? For most students, independent practice, perhaps during drop everything and read (DEAR), is their chance to apply the strategies you've taught, such as making and proving predictions. When you look at your anecdotal records and student reading conference notes and at the students' reading response journals, what do you see? How many students had time each day to read the books they chose? Did your English language learners and special-needs students have DEAR time? There may have been several days in a row when no one but the best readers had this experience. They may have been the only students to meet the learning standard because they were the only ones who had enough practice. If you find that this is true in your classroom, change your schedule. Maybe if you begin each day with DEAR, you can ensure that each student has an opportunity for independent practice every day. Both instruction and practice must be consistent in your classroom.

Although this may sound obvious, when your students have not met a learning standard, you should also check whether the task or the texts you used were appropriate. For example, when you model or have students practice a strategy like prediction in a DRTA, the text they read should be *unfamiliar*. How can you practice predicting an event when you already know what happens in the story? Even if the text is unfamiliar, the plot may be obvious; for example, if there is only one way the character's problem could be solved. When you select texts for your students to use to learn a new strategy, be sure they match up with the strategy you're teaching.

For special-needs and English language learners, matching texts and strategies appropriately is even more important. If the texts are too difficult or are inappropriate, these students will be unable to apply the strategies they've learned. The goal of your assessment system is to portray an accurate and fair picture of all students' abilities. Special learners are unable to show what they can do if they are frustrated by the texts they read (Rueda and Garcia 1997).

Look for Ambiguous Data

Maybe your problem is not the number of opportunities to meet the standard but the way you record your data. If you reviewed your anecdotal records for the DRTA, what would you find? Are there records for each student in the group or just a few? What information did you record for each student? Perhaps the appropriate information was not entered or lacks detail. Anecdotal records for a DRTA should resemble what Elena Rodriguez recorded for Jackie in Figure 7–3. She noted how Jackie made and supported her predictions, along with the title of the text Jackie read. This information helped her determine whether or not Jackie used more than one source of information as the basis for predicting. Noting the title also helped her determine in which genres Jackie could make logical predictions.

To solve this problem, you need to plan the information you will record during instruction. This may mean developing a record-keeping system that reminds you to note the important details. Figure 7–4 is an example of a helpful format for DRTA anecdotal records. First, listing each student in the guided reading group reminds you to enter information for *each child* as the group members share their predictions, not to focus on only one or two. Second, designating space for recording what the child said when stating a prediction and what evidence the child provided to support each prediction ensures that you will have essential details when you assess each child's progress. Don't be tempted to just record a check mark when a student makes or proves a prediction. That kind of recording is too ambiguous to be worthwhile. Third, noting the date, title, and genre of the book allows you to compare your data across DRTA sessions.

In addition, audiotaping the guided lesson will let you verify the accuracy of what you wrote on the anecdotal record form.

Once you refine the way you record and collect your data, their value will increase. Always be sure to add the details that

Directed Reading Thinking Activity Anecdotal Record

Title of Text: *Cam Jansen and the Ghostly Mystery* (Adler) **Genre:** *Mystery* **Date:** *11/1*

Student	Prediction 1	Proof 1	Prediction 2	Proof 2
Brittany	The ghost takes Cam's money.	Cam has money in her hand in the picture on the cover of the book.	The police will catch the ghost in the train station.	The ghost ran into the train station.
Jorge	A ghost is scaring people at a play.	It says box office in the picture on the cover.	The old man helped the robber get away.	Cam said the ghost had a plan and she will look for the old man.
Pamela	Cam wants to find out who the ghost is.	The title says ghostly mystery.	The man's fingerprints on glasses will help police catch him.	That's what they do on TV. Police match fingerprints.
Kyle	A ghost keeps trying to scare Cam.	Cam looks scared in the picture.	The police will find the robber by looking at his shoes.	The ticket lady told the cops the robber had on sneakers.
Courtney	Cam wants to find out why the ghost is scaring people.	Cam solved mysteries in the other books we read.	Cam follows the old man to the robber's house.	At the end of chapter 4, Cam said she would look for the old man.

FIGURE 7–4   Anecdotal Record System for DRTA

complete the picture. For example, go beyond scoring your running records and analyze the student's miscues, noting your observations of the reader's confidence, expression, and fluency and adding comments to the retelling rubric. Now this classroom benchmark supplies the rich data you will need for future evaluation. This is also a good time to code the running record to the appropriate learning standard.

Seek Alternative Data Sources
You cannot adequately evaluate students' progress toward any learning standard when there are fewer than three sources of evidence. In this situation, you have two choices. One is to delay your evaluation until a later date when you expect to have more data. (For example, your students may be about to complete a unit project and present their findings.) If you know that additional information will be available within two weeks, it makes sense to wait. If not, then you should seek alternative data sources.

Fourth-grade teacher Rosario Blanco was faced with this problem. She had collected a few pieces of thinking evidence and some work samples but had no in-the-classroom benchmarks. Although uncomfortable with rubrics, Rosario tried a retelling rubric designed by a colleague who taught second grade. When she scored her students' retellings on the borrowed rubric, she discovered it didn't capture the appropriate elements. For example, there wasn't a category for story grammar or for differentiating unprompted and prompted responses. Frustrated, Rosario abandoned the rubric.

About a month later, Rosario attended an inservice workshop on assessing comprehension. She learned not only how to structure the retellings but also how to use rubrics for oral and written samples. The workshop leader provided rubrics for narrative and informational texts for both primary and intermediate students. Rosario's problem was solved. She now had appropriate rubrics for her fourth graders. In addition, she had an alternative strategy for written retellings, which enabled her to collect the data from several students at once. Rosario became more comfortable with the rubrics and more consistent in using them. She increased her performance data and added a needed dimension to her assessment strategies.

When your students are English language learners or have special needs, it's more than likely you'll need to explore alternative assessment strategies. Your English language learners' fluency in their second language will determine whether or not they should be assessed in their native language. For example, a first-grade teacher may need to use the Spanish version of the Concepts About Print test. Assessing first graders' knowledge of written language concepts such as book orientation and print direction in their native language precludes making false assumptions about the extent of their understanding. And you may want to consult with the resource teachers about alternatives and accommodations that will make your planned assessment developmentally appropriate for your special-needs students.

What if you have no evidence at all for some of your learning standards? One very good place to start is to meet with your fellow teachers to discuss alternatives. Your peers may be able to suggest some alternatives you've overlooked. Myra Jackson, a new fifth-grade teacher, found that neither she nor her peers had ways to assess New York State's science standards. She decided to check the department of education's website for information. For each standard, she discovered several indicators, among them student work samples accompanied by an analysis that evaluated the performance and explained how each aspect of the standard was met. Myra shared these with her fifth-grade team. Together they designed their evaluation plan and identified the evidence they all would collect. Now Myra not only understood the standards more completely but also felt more confident in how she would provide opportunities for her students to meet those standards.

Reporting Acquisition and Mastery

Once you have collected, analyzed, and cross-checked your assessment data, how do you synthesize and report your results? Your goal is not only to use the data for instructional planning but also to keep track of your students' progress at regular intervals. While your assessment is ongoing, your evaluation of the data occurs at specified times, usually at nine-week intervals. State-mandated tests are usually administered during the last nine weeks of the year. Therefore, you need to know how close your students are to meeting the learning standards those tests measure.

A realistic way to report your data regarding student acquisition and mastery of standards is by way of a developmental continuum. Elena Rodriguez and her colleagues use a reporting system that indicates the amount of assistance needed or independence in relation to particular standards. Jackie's level of mastery of three standards is reported in Figure 7–5. Based on her earlier analysis of the assessment data related to the first standard (Figure 7–3), Elena rated Jackie's performance at the independent level. Jackie made predictions during guided reading as well as on her own during independent reading. However, Jackie couldn't do this yet with all of the grade-level texts or genres. Similarly, Elena's analysis of running records, anecdotal records during guided reading, and student reading conferences revealed that Jackie's word recognition strategies, particularly those related to structural cues, needed to be prompted. Therefore, Jackie's rating was "can perform with assistance." For the third standard, Elena's analysis of the anecdotal records for sustained silent reading, Jackie's reading log, and student conference notes confirmed that Jackie frequently and independently chose the books she read for pleasure. Her rating for this standard was "can perform independently."

During the next nine weeks, Elena Rodriguez continued to collect evidence related to these three standards as well as the others. The instructional and learning experiences she planned for Jackie and her other students provided further opportunities to develop competence with each standard. The CARP cycle does work for busy teachers! The following chapter discusses reporting on students' progress in more detail.

Florida State Standards
Language Arts—Second Grade

Child's Name: *Jackie*   Teacher: *Ms Rodriguez*   Date: *November 3*

Learning Standard	Not Assessed	Can Perform with Assistance	Can Perform Independently	Can Perform with Grade-Level Texts
Uses prior knowledge, illustrations, and text to make and confirm predictions			X	
Cross-checks visual, structural, and meaning cues to figure out unknown words		X		
Selects material to read for pleasure, as a group or independently			X	

FIGURE 7–5   Reporting for Student Mastery

Reporting Achievement and Planning the Next Instructional Step

I (Mary Shea) receive regular reports on my modest investment portfolio. I try to read each one and make informed decisions, but the foreign and confusing accountant language sabotages my effort every time. Although my financial adviser patiently answers questions (when I can formulate them), my brain frequently shuts down while processing her explanations. I've also tried watching Suze Orman, a TV financial analyst who puts things in practical terms. Suze talks too fast for my brain to absorb it all, so I decided to read her book, in order to be able to control the rate of information. However, I still struggled through her discussions of annuities and equities.

Specialty language and presentation can keep people from understanding any message in spite of their intelligence and reading competency. We need to avoid this communication roadblock when reporting assessment data, both in the classroom and in the community of which our schools are a part.

My conversion to pragmatic reporting began right after I finished a degree in literacy education. I'd just accepted a position as a reading specialist in an elementary school and had worked diligently on reports for students' files. In fact, I was quite proud of their professional quality. However, Joe Mitchell, a Title I auditor, commented during his debriefing to the district that student reports tended to be *reader unfriendly*. They were too long, excessively detailed, and filled with technical language—much like a financial adviser's explanations. Of course I felt reprimanded, but I knew Joe had made an important point. However unintentionally, I hadn't considered my audience when writing those reports. The first responder to them was no longer a professor and not necessarily another reading specialist. I had to speak to my audience—classroom teachers and parents. Joe Mitchell's constructive feedback reminded me that participants in any form of communication have to first *understand* each other's message. I was making my readers feel like I do when I read Fidelity's quarterly report.

But What Does That Mean?

Reporting involves telling or communicating ideas. Good reporting is based on having something worth sharing and doing so in a way that's clear, accurate, and concise. The title of Chris Tovani's book *I Read It, but I Don't Get It* (2000) pops into my mind when I think about some educational reporting I've encountered (and even created!). Reports on children's progress, no matter how comprehensive and accurate, are not successful unless they are *used*. Sadly, too many are unread and filed away because the reader gets hopelessly bogged down in the first paragraph or two. Oral reports can numb an audience just as easily. Ironically, it's more difficult to write or present the kind of report that confuses rather than enlightens. I had to try very hard to achieve the academic tone I used in those early evaluations.

Now I remind myself to just say it in plain English, in a conversational tone. It's important to limit technical language; use it only when necessary and then explain all terms fully but succinctly. Naturally, there will always be situations when a particular word encapsulates a broad concept critical to the discussion. Teachers and administrators can build a common educational vocabulary with parents by introducing these terms gradually and repeating them, respectfully, in context.

As essential as the right words are to coherence, they are not enough. Successful communicators also consider the visual aspects of effective communication. Warm, sensitive gestures motivate audience response and participation: people speak volumes through their body movements. In addition, visual aids—headings, captions, charts, graphics, tables—reinforce or expand central ideas. They synthesize information and represent it in a logical array of key components and interconnections. Well-designed, wisely used visual aids focus the message and help readers and listeners understand.

Learning Standards: The Common Threads in Educational Reporting

Even when one is mindful of the need to present information clearly and interestingly, it's difficult to decide how to support ideas without overstating them; there is so little time and so much to share. There is no universal pattern, no silver bullet. However, while every report should be customized to the unique information being conveyed, there are some common denominators in *what* is shared.

In previous chapters, we've discussed the TWIN model for collecting evidence. We've suggested methods for organizing and categorizing the collected data. And we've discussed the importance of triangulated evidence in forming a clear and accurate picture of what students know and can do related to designated *learning standards*. These standards—local and/or state specific—are the warp and woof of each tapestry depicting student achievement.

We've also stressed the importance of assessment *for* learning: using collected information to plan for the most efficient next step in instruction, the one that propels students' learning. On their journey toward reaching outcomes or standards, learners receive feedback that is *in the moment*, within the lesson, and that reports incremental progress, recognizes efforts, and draws the student forward. This kind of response shapes learning as it's unfolding; it's *formative* feedback, specific in content and sensitive in tone (Hanna and Dettmer 2004; Wiggins 1998). Although students are the primary recipients, snippets can be shared with caregivers as well. Sending home a *happy gram* to celebrate daily accomplishments or a request for information takes little time, and it can have big payoffs in building home-school rapport.

However, to be truly formative—capable of enhancing development—feedback must be something students and teachers can and will *use*. Black et al. (2004) state that "assessment becomes 'formative' assessment when the evidence is actually used to adapt the teaching work to meet learning needs" (10). They also report that researchers have concluded that such formative assessment unequivocally raises standards and emphasize that the tone and specificity, rather than quantity, is critical. Comments can be useful only if they encourage learners with genuine affection and respect, direct them to where practice needs to be applied, and guide their approximations as they work toward mastery and independence.

Teachers are not the only ones who deliver feedback. Reflective discussion is, *continuously*, a two-way street. Students' feedback reflects their understanding of learning goals and their metacognitive evaluation of their progress toward them. It also informs the teacher what students think they need and what would therefore be a more appropriate next instructional step (Black et al. 2004).

Effective formative feedback, whether from the teacher, a peer, or a teacher-student discussion about performance, "should make more explicit to students what is involved in a high-quality piece of work and what steps they need to take to improve" (Black et al. 2004, 19).

In-the-classroom benchmarks summarize what students have learned in large blocks of curriculum like units of study. Norm-referenced and other standardized achievement tests assess students' year-to-year learning or learning across several academic years. When reporting such assessments *of* learning, we provide *summative* feedback—feedback that describes students' leaps of progress toward learning standards (Hanna and Dettmer 2004; Wiggins 1998). Summative feedback comes in all the forms discussed in Chapters 5 and 6 (e.g., benchmark measures and standardized achievement tests). It is also delivered as written and verbal reports describing students' learning leaps (or lack of them) that are distributed to students, parents, school committees or teams, the board of education, and the community. There's a lot of telling to be done!

But in-the-classroom benchmarks and norm-referenced and other standardized achievement tests also contribute to plans *for* learning. Black et al. (2004) suggest that summative measures can be used for formative purposes when students are allowed to reflect on their performance in a way that enables meaningful, focused, and detailed planning for improvement.

From the Inside Out: Flow of Reporting on Assessment

Letting Learners Lead

Which stakeholders do we address first? Like a river, reporting should begin at the source. Since most data originate in the classroom, the classroom is the place to begin. Learners deserve to be the first ones informed about their performance, even when it's not worthy of accolades. Students can handle the truth when it's sensitively delivered.

I love this story my friend Terry tells about one of her first graders. Maria was the youngest in the class and therefore less mature in all areas of development; that was only natural. However, at midyear, Maria was becoming frustrated with the academic difficulty she continued to experience. Terry sat down with her to discuss the situation. She started by asking Maria to describe the things she'd learned since their last talk. Maria lamented that she was not a good reader or writer anymore; others were reading hard books, and she didn't know the words in those books. Maria had even intuited her parents' concern. Though they hadn't said anything, she knew they were worried, because her brother could read those hard books when he was in first grade. Her perceptions were right on target. We can't fool those who know us well—children read us loud and clear!

We can all learn coaching tips from Terry's response.

Terry agreed that, yes, those books, as well as some other skills they'd recently been working on in class, were hard right now. But after briefly reiterating core principles she'd shared with her students early in the year, Terry reminded Maria about the goals they'd set during their last conversation.

First, Terry explained that she didn't expect first graders to run a learning race; races were for the playground or physical education class. Learning is finding out about our world, others, and ourselves. Doing it well doesn't mean getting to the head of a line; it's about keeping at the task with our best effort. Then, Terry displayed the evidence she'd collected about Maria's growth in reading, writing, math, and other areas, including social and emotional descriptors that were part of the school's report card. Maria's body language ever so slowly began to change from slumped to upright, to the point of interjecting, "Did you get it down that I know how to write a sentence now?"

Soon after, when her parents came for their conference with Terry and Maria, Maria began with an air of authority. She immediately addressed her parents' unspoken concern. "I can't read hard books yet, like Sally, but I *will* be able to because I'm practicing and getting better. I did do a lot of things that *were* hard and they're in my portfolio." Maria *owned* what she was saying and was therefore able to communicate it effectively. Right from the start, students' voices can and should be involved in reporting their achievement.

Preparation and Organization

Assessing Literacy with the Learning Record (Barr et al. 1999) is an excellent source for reporting forms. Other schools in your area may be willing to share the forms they use; setting up professional sharing networks benefits everyone involved. Or do an Internet search. You'll find numerous sites that provide suggestions for conferring with parents as well as printable forms that are in the public domain. These should of course be adapted to meet the context of your particular classroom. It's a good idea, however, to use forms that are somewhat consistent throughout the school and throughout the year. Students and parents become increasingly adept at reading and completing a predictable form. Nevertheless, it does make sense to have separate primary and intermediate forms that highlight developmental expectations at these levels.

Having notepaper, sticky notes, and writing tools readily available ensures that you will be able to record agreed-on points and/or negotiated new goals before they're forgotten. Review items on the checklists and, when

evidence warrants, mark and date them. (See Figures 3–12 through 3–16.)

An inviting ambience is also needed. Such an environment respects participants and supports honest, open talk. Prepare a quiet place in the classroom where reporting conferences can be held and try to make it nonintimidating. Instruct other students not to interrupt such conversations unless there's an emergency, and come to a consensus on what constitutes an emergency. Sitting at a small table or at the student's desk, where participants can interact eye-to-eye, rather than at your desk reinforces the equal status of contributions and ideas.

The Ebb and Flow

I let the student begin the conversation, since it's a report of his learning. However, I like to remember that it's also an indirect report on my teaching. If this student hasn't learned, what do I need to do or find out to make it happen? The teacher's most important task at this point is to listen, listen, listen to the student's comments, claims, or queries before responding in a way that demonstrates the quality of that listening: "I heard you say thus and so."

In like manner, the student's most important task at this point is to listen, listen, listen to the teacher before responding and moving the conversation forward. And on and on it goes. This two-way reporting reveals, uncovers, discovers, points out; it's a critique—a detailed evaluation—without criticism.

Once the teacher and student each understand how the other views the reported achievement, they can evaluate the status of previous goals, set new goals, and establish a plan of action. Then they're prepared to report in tandem to parents and/or caregivers.

Give-and-Take Leads to Win-Win

The reporting stream (see Figure 8–1) begins with a *dialogue* between two people who interchange the teacher and learner roles. Each informs and instructs the other. Such reciprocity continues as the stream widens. The key word is *dialogue*. Monologues by the

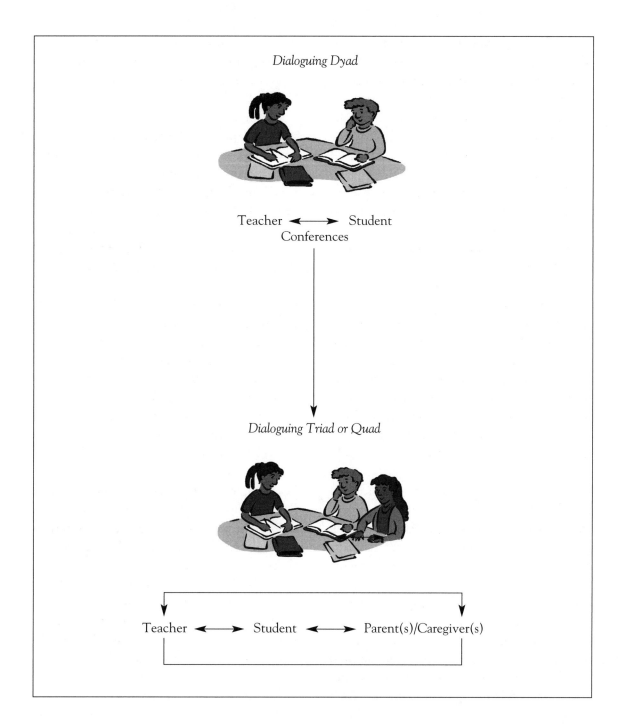

Dialoguing Dyad

Teacher ◄——► Student
Conferences

Dialoguing Triad or Quad

Teacher ◄——► Student ◄——► Parent(s)/Caregiver(s)

FIGURE 8–1   Flow of Reporting

teacher, committee chair, administrator, or board of education president—anyone who usurps control of the exchange—threaten the democratic intent of these discussions, as well as the progress of the child. Each participant reports progress to the other from a personal perspective; each learns about his or her per-

formance and identifies ways to help the other perform better.

Teacher–Student Conferences: It Takes Two to Tango

Even very young children can contribute to the reporting process when the discussion is geared to their level of understanding. Such interactions initiate and reinforce metacognitive behavior and encourage responsibility for one's learning. They also contribute to two essential elements for learning; self-efficacy and optimism (Sagor 2002). But good conversationalists aren't born; it's a learned behavior.

Lots and lots of modeling of good conversation *must* be provided. Children also need ample time to practice democratic dialogues before genuine reporting exchanges can take place. Outlining instruction that will develop critical conversational skills is beyond the scope of this text, but readers will find *Knee to Knee, Eye to Eye: Circling in on Comprehension* (Cole 2003) an essential resource for advice on how to nurture young discussants and reporters. When developing these skills becomes a schoolwide initiative, everyone wins. Children improve their comprehension and learning in all areas of the curriculum while acquiring skills for living in the world effectively.

Chapter 3 includes the form (Figure 3–7) Sue Rosche has students complete before their assessment discussion. After engaging in the reflection this form prompts, students are organized, focused, and ready to report progress from their point of view. Students also come to the conference with writing folders, showcase portfolios, or other sources of evidence that support their claims. Likewise, Sue comes prepared with work samples, benchmark measures, anecdotal notes, and checklists of learning outcomes for each student. (See Figures 3–1, 3–2, and 3–3.) She also integrates information collected by other teachers with her own classroom data.

Team Teachers and Student

The teacher side of the reporting group can include more than one person. The classroom teacher is the central trunk of a tree with many branches. In my job as a reading specialist and then a language arts coordinator, I frequently met with teachers (as well as students) to share data related to students'

reading progress. I once explained to Marcia Cleary, a first-grade teacher in my district, a numeric confusion I had uncovered and clarified.

John and Kyle were buddies in her class who sometimes socialized when they should have been working. One day, when I arrived to help in their writing workshop, John and Kyle were huddled in the corner. John had just passed Kyle a small piece of paper and seemed to be discussing its contents. When I asked what they were doing, Kyle told me that John had just given him Abraham Lincoln's phone number and they were going to call him that night. I said, "Really! Where did you get that, John?"

He quickly responded, "In a book," with a tad of indignation, seemingly offended that I'd challenge the authenticity of his information.

Puzzled about how he came to this conclusion, I said, "Gee, I never saw *that* in a book. Would you show me?"

John immediately got one of the reference books Marcia had brought into the classroom for the February research projects. He opened it up to the page with a biographical sketch on Abraham Lincoln and said, "There. It's right there!" pointing to 1809–1865.

"Oh," I said. "That does look like a phone number starting with one eight zero nine and then having that dash line, but let me tell you what it really means. I'm afraid Mr. Lincoln won't answer if you try to dial that number."

After Marcia and I shared a chuckle, Marcia planned a lesson on numerical patterns and configurations we see every day (e.g., life spans, dates of birth, phone numbers, ZIP codes).

In many of today's schools, teachers regularly team-plan, team-teach, team-assess, and team-report. When my son Brian taught second grade, he and a special education teacher worked together full-time to meet students' needs in their inclusion class. There were also several other teachers and resource personnel who visited the classroom daily, fulfilling individualized education plan (IEP) objectives. Their successes were the direct result of continuous open communication with one another, the children, and their parents. These teachers found, as I had, that using standard forms made essential reporting exchanges comfortably predictable as well as efficient.

Conferences Between the Teacher, the Student, and Parents

Sue Rosche and Nancy Gantz have their students' parents or guardians complete a form in preparation for conferences (see Figure 3–6). Caregivers' thoughtful responses become fuel for meaningful give-and-take exchanges like those described previously. In these three- or four-way dialogues, the learner also initiates the conversation. Once discussions begin, participants' ideas have an equal status; each is addressed respectfully. This doesn't mean parents don't have ways to share information at other times as well. Parents should be regularly invited to contribute insights and queries to the collection of data on learners and their learning. The telephone, notes, letters, and e-mail are all viable avenues parents and teachers can use to communicate.

Reports on students' development should not typically be *classified*, privy only to adult stakeholders. Learners have a right to know the conclusions drawn about their performance. However, *always* and *never* are tricky words; there are few absolutes. There may be situations in which some information must remain privileged, but I suspect these are rare.

Reporting Student Progress Within the School

When assessment reporting is addressed schoolwide, and faculties work together to determine the tone, protocols, and forms they want to use, the process becomes organic and pervasive. It's applied in all assessment discussions, wherever and whenever they occur. We would hope each school's adopted process is a democratic one.

Accepted reporting processes begin to guide interactions within and among several types of committees and faculty teams that function to fulfill specific needs of the school as a whole. These include child-study teams, grade-level teams, the faculty as a whole, and special education committees. As in every other assessment dialogue, it's important to give the learner a voice in the conversation, to every extent possible. The voices of parents and the classroom teacher, who have had prolonged and persistent engagement with the learner, should also be front and center at these meetings.

Respecting Voices

As the student's academic advocate, the classroom teacher has a critical role in sharing varied forms of assessment data that represent performances in day-to-day classroom activities. Activities like those described in previous chapters provoke demonstrations of *knowing* not usually influenced by stress (e.g., new surroundings, new people, a formal test). Parents attending such meetings need to advocate strongly for their child, sharing insights gleaned from watching the child behave in the family and community. Too often, this information has been given a lower status of importance. Denny Taylor's *Learning Denied* (1991) is a testimony to what can happen when the voices of those who work most closely with the child refuse to be muted. Teachers and parents, addressing education committees as vocal advocates for students, allow committee members to make fully informed decisions that are based on multiple viewpoints rather than on a singular point of view.

Exponential Power of Group Problem Solving

In one middle school, members of a pupil service team came up with a creative solution to frequent behavior problems. They set up a before-school program, supervised by the physical education teacher, in which, with parental permission, ten students could swim, play basketball, and use the gymnasium equipment every morning from seven o'clock until the beginning of home room. A significant behavioral infraction during program hours or the school day resulted in a hearing at which a student's membership in the program could be revoked. The students' behavior dramatically improved, as did their attention in class, the amount of homework they completed, and their overall achievement. The teachers' willingness to assess the problem, think outside the box, and cooperatively experiment with a proposed solution was key to this success story.

Wide-Angle View

Schoolwide committees have a special view of student achievement, because their information comes from sources with varied perspectives. It also comes in many forms. Committee members may be analyzing aggregated or disaggregated data. Or they may be examining collective conclusions about the match of methodology, materials, and objectives for individual learners. After reporting *what is* (the learner's current level of achievement), these teams are in a position to suggest what *can be* (achievement possible with well-matched instruction).

After reviewing group data, committee reports generally include recommendations relative to schoolwide, grade-level, and occasionally individual instruction. As important as these recommendations are, they should not mark the end of a committee's work. At future meetings, members must review progress made as a result of their recommendations and modify them when appropriate.

Reporting Student Progress to Administrators or Special Personnel

As a classroom teacher and reading specialist, I was occasionally asked to meet with the principal, school psychologist, or school social worker to discuss a child's achievement. Sometimes the child's parents were included; at other times these meetings were held to prepare for a conference with the child's parents. I was expected to be prepared—to share my

insights *succinctly*. A well-organized portfolio became my road map. It helped me present information in a way that was focused, evidence based, and professional. Administrators and teachers appreciate that immensely!

Reporting Student Progress to the Board of Education

Although it often makes their knees rattle, teachers are in the best position to share students' achievements with the district board of education (BOE). They're closest to the action.

A superintendent in a small school district had each grade level and special area (art, PE, music, resource, reading, etc.) sign up for a thirty-minute presentation to the BOE that outlined the highlights of their program. Of course, students' achievements were the highlight. As part of every BOE meeting during the school year, board members had an opportunity to meet teachers and pose questions.

A few years ago my son Andrew gave a PowerPoint presentation to his BOE outlining students' performance on the new eleventh-grade state test in English. The only eleventh-grade English teacher in a small rural district, Andrew works with all the grade 11 ELA test takers. Using graphics, Andrew respectfully told board members about the characteristics of the test, the district's curriculum, students' aggregate achievement, and the school's plans for dealing with areas of concern. Interactions between teachers and the BOE like this support everyone with a stake in student achievement: armed with this information, BOE members are better prepared to answer questions posed to them by the community.

Teacher Jay Basham shared the miniresearch and Web quests his seventh graders completed with BOE members in his district. He demonstrated how the students' reports and presentations integrated skills in English and social studies. He was also able to point out how inclusion students were effectively involved in the learning partnerships associated with these projects. This kind of information is helpful for BOE members who want and need to know how well teachers are meeting the diverse needs of students and meaningfully uncovering curriculum.

Some BOE meetings in my area are televised on a local-access cable channel. These broadcasts and newspaper reports of BOE meetings disseminate presentations like those I have described to a wider audience. Educators need to encourage more voices at BOE meetings and comprehensive reporting to ensure that more perspectives are considered.

Reporting Student Progress to the Community

Reporting to the community through board of education meetings is an excellent way to affirm or refute school and student progress as measured by outside formulas, such as *Business First*'s annual ranking of schools by performance (which real estate agents use as a sales tool). An open house is a great opportunity for students to strut proudly, impressing parents with their accomplishments and current projects. Invite the paparazzi. Let the cameras flash and the stories be printed!

Newspapers are another way to bring students well-earned broader recognition for their performances. My son Brian calls the *Journal Register* (in Medina, New York) to cover the story when sixth graders in Wise Middle School present their end-of-year science projects (see Figure 8–2). Students are impressed when interviewed by a *real* reporter, and seeing their names (and faces) in print all over town is a great bonus!

Many school districts regularly publish newsletters that report on a wide range of topics that are of interest to the school community. Student work is sometimes included, and data demonstrating student achievement are often given considerable space. Such publications help connect schools and the community in which they reside.

Reporting Student Progress to the State

Formats for reporting student achievement to the state are typically governed by specific requests for information and formats for presentation. Some of this information is mandated. Achievement report parameters are defined for general and special populations. Generally, state reports for the general population focus on some type of aggregated test results—by grade level, gender, race, or some other type of special classification. Little, if any, consideration is given to the other categories of data discussed in this book except in the few states that include portfolios. (See Appendix 6–1.)

States use the data in ways that may or may not significantly impact students. States are now required to report cumulative data to federal authorities. The state's disaggregated data are the source of the evaluative evidence requested on applications for government grants, vouchers, and other funding sources. States also use the data to plan statewide educational initiatives focused on the collective needs of their constituents.

Completing the Loop: Informing the Next Instructional Step

The purpose of assessment reporting is twofold. First, it informs recipients about the progress learners have made. However, its second purpose is fundamental to the *future* success of learners. Assessment reporting should enlighten; it should make clear a logical next step for instruction. This means that a teacher's plans should flow from assessment data that have been collected, analyzed, and reported rather than follow generic scripts. This reporting of learning serves as a baseline for the next learning step. That is, the next step in a lesson is determined by your assessment of students' performance on the current step. We must drop back and punt if it's not going well or go for the pass if students are ready to run with the ball. Tomorrow's teaching is grounded in what we've learned about students today.

Minilessons That Follow In-the-Moment Assessment

My book *Taking Running Records* (Shea 2000) includes a list of "If . . . thens," as I call them,

NO MORE PENCILS

Wise sixth-graders turn in projects instead of taking final exam

BY AKIKO MATSUDA
matsudaa@gnnewspaper.com

William Zink, a sixth-grader at Wise Middle School, explains the Earth's structure confidently using his hand-made three-dimensional model.

"This shows magma comes up," Zink said, pointing at a piece of red-colored cotton in his model.

Getting the idea from his mother, Zink created his model Earth with a fishbowl and aquarium rocks.

"Once magma comes out, (it creates a plate and) goes into the trenches, and it's basically recycled," Zink said. "That's why the Earth is not getting any bigger."

Zink studied the sea-floor spreading theory as his science final project, doing research on the Internet and in books for a couple of months. The project takes the place of a final exam in science.

The changeover from a traditional exam to a hands-on demonstration of learning took place last year. Completing the projects requires a lot of time and effort, but the idea of not having written exams is popular with students.

"Our motivation behind it is that by the time kids get to sixth grade, they're burned out," said Todd Miklas, science teacher. "Subjects start getting heavier. We start losing a bit of fun. But we want to encourage students (to know) that science and school can be fun through 12th grade."

With his colleague, Brian

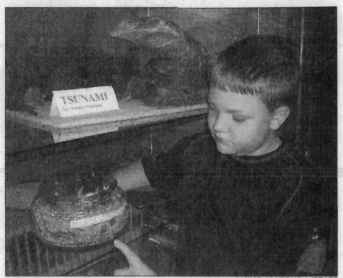

AKIKO MATSUDA/STAFF

NO EXAM: Wise Middle School sixth-grader William Zink explains the concept of sea-floor spreading using his hand-made model. He did the project instead of taking the exam.

Shea, Miklas teaches earth science to sixth-graders. Fun is valued, but expectations are high, the teachers say. After researching their chosen science topic, students had to make poster boards and models to present their results.

Miklas said he and Shea expect students to "speak as authorities" in making their presentations. "They have to be able to answer questions and speak very intelligibly."

Zink gave a Power Point presentation.

"His presentation brought everything together," Miklas said. "(Power Point) made his presentation flow, and he spoke like he was giving a workshop. It's impressive for a sixth-grade student."

So impressive, Zink earned a grade of 100.

Sixth-grader Michael Wengrzycki also received a 100 on his final project, which concerned the San Andreas Fault in California.

"I was interested how much

damage earthquakes and tidal waves can do," Wengrzycki said. "Part of California will break off and will create tidal waves."

Or, he theorized, the plate will keep moving up until it hits Alaska.

"You cannot be sure what's going to happen," he said.

Wengrzycki said he preferred the labor-intensive final project over a written exam.

"(The project) is a whole lot better," he said. "Then you don't have to study forever for exams."

Shea said eight students of his class chose to tackle questions raised by Towne School kindergarten students. They will present their results to the kindergartners Tuesday.

"Students are very excited about going back and sharing their findings," Shea said. "They really did a lot of research on it."

Contact Akiko Matsuda
at (585) 798-1400, Ext. 2226.

FIGURE 8–2 *Medina Journal Register* Article by Akiko Matsuda (June 14, 2004)

premised on possible learning scenarios: "*If* the child demonstrates/doesn't demonstrate [a learning outcome or behavior], *then* we should [proposed activities for further instruction]." (See Figure 8–3 for a few examples.) As always with teaching advice, this idea must be used mindfully. By no means are these scenarios absolutes. Rather, they are meant to suggest a way of thinking: analyses of children's performances should trigger several sound instructional responses as logical next steps.

This doesn't mean that all scripts and teaching suggestions should be ignored and abandoned. Remember that *always* and *never* are tricky words. It does, however, imply that nothing is appropriate *as is*. Authors of these materials are writing for a general audience. They cannot possibly know the needs of individual learners. When teaching ideas are pedagogically sound, teachers can adapt or combine them to meet their students' specifically identified needs. Scripts can't know where individual students are in their learning—what the *teachable moment* calls for. A teacher does.

Two Heads Are Better than One

At one point a few inclusion students in my son Brian's second grade were having difficulty grasping the regrouping sequence of adding and subtracting two- and three-digit numbers. The children were getting very frustrated. Brian and his coteacher, Jan, analyzed the children's work, researched how other teachers had dealt with this problem, and adapted the suggestions they found to a customized plan for these particular students. They brought in manipulatives (counters) and color-coded the place value positions: ones, green; tens, yellow; and hundreds, red. When children worked at the board, the appropriate-color chalk was used for the numerals in each position. The clouds of confusion didn't disappear overnight, but gradually and surely, with caring, creative instruction, the sun broke through. When Carl's parents came in for a conference with the Committee on Special

Education, Carl proudly subtracted a five-digit number on the board, *in all white chalk*. He had insisted on doing a problem that was harder than those they'd been practicing so he could impress his parents. Carl accomplished that and met and surpassed an IEP objective as well!

Planning with Parents

First-grade teacher Nancy Roberts noticed during the first few days of school that Alan was struggling as a reader and a writer. In fact, his written messages were incomprehensible. And she immediately recognized that Alan's demeanor was unlike that of his outgoing, gregarious older brother. Alan shied away from his classmates and tried to participate as little as possible. When he did speak, his articulation was muffled and contained impediments. Nancy made careful notes.

One day, as Nancy was circling the room while children wrote in their journals, she stopped at Alan's desk. He was starting to write a story title "My Favorite Place on the Planet." Stymied by the seemingly random strings of letters, Nancy asked Alan to read aloud what he had started to write. He read a beautifully descriptive sentence—the kind that repeats over and over in your mind: "The water at Sunset Bay tickles my toes when the sun sets." Nancy exclaimed, "Oh, Alan! That's beautiful. Your words painted that picture in my head! Why don't you write that right here?"

Accustomed to being misunderstood in school, Alan responded with an edge of irritation, "But, Mrs. Roberts, I *did* write it! Right there."

Nancy quickly and graciously repaired her faux pas. She was also prompted to take a closer look at writing that wasn't a string of random letters as she had assumed! Alan's writing was phonetically matched to his pronunciations. Decoding his cryptographic-like writing required careful attention to his speech patterns, since he was representing what he heard after sounding words out.

Targeting Individual Needs

When . . .	If . . .	Then . . .
Before Taking the Running Record	the child appears anxious	go over the purpose of RRs (also a good topic for a whole-class meeting). Explain that each child is different and is at a different reading level. Practicing the hard things we find in this reading will help him improve just like practice in sports improves an athlete's performance.
		remind the child of his strengths (e.g., "You're great at catching your own errors and correcting them."). Let him know you'll notice strengths as well as needs when he reads and that any mistakes he makes will help you both decide what kind of help will work best right now.
During the Oral Performance	the child fails to self-correct	the child may not understand what she is reading or may be unaware that it's the reader's job to use fix-up strategies when meaning is lost. Failure to self-correct is a significant indicator of reading difficulty.
		explicitly teach fix-up strategies. Provide lots of modeling and then abundant scaffolding when she first uses a strategy. If the child stops in her tracks while reading, prompt her to use specific strategies taught, helping as needed. Gradually fade support when she appears ready to self-initiate strategies and use them effectively.
During Retelling	the child needs a few prompts	give appropriate prompts and note what type they were, where they were needed, and how successful they were in guiding the child's retelling.
		praise the reader's successful use of your prompts. Tell him that you hope to see self-prompting (using the posted checklist) during the next RR.
		review the checklist for retelling procedures and components. Go over how to start the retelling, what to tell, and how to conclude.

(Adapted from Shea 2000, 117; 199, 124. Used with Permission.)

FIGURE 8–3   If . . . Then Scenarios for Instructional Planning

Nancy needed to know how informed Alan's parents were about his difficulties and strengths. They told Nancy that Alan's kindergarten teacher had recommended Alan for speech services but that they felt she was overreacting. They understood him. In fact, with four other little ones at home, Alan's parents were used to deciphering immature speech. They believed that his articulation errors were developmental and he would correct them himself in time. Nancy asked them to rethink their position.

The speech teacher, who also attended the meeting, described the assessments she could use and the kind of information each would yield. Nancy shared Alan's writing and pointed out the beautiful messages he had constructed filled with personal voice and wonderful language. Alan's parents talked about interests and strengths he displayed outside school. The picture of the learner that emerged was collectively examined and used to set up an immediate three-way plan for intervention. The regime included focused instruction from the speech teacher, Nancy's nurturing of Alan's beautiful use of language, and at-home reinforcement from his parents to accelerate his development in all areas. Alan was on a path to catch on and catch up!

Planning with a Team

Identifying the problem and devising solutions are critical steps for success. However, finding time for this is difficult and often requires broader negotiations. After implementing schoolwide curricular changes to improve students' writing and math skills, eighth-grade teachers at one middle school determined that some students needed reinforcement in smaller groups if they were to be successful with the state tests *and* in the classroom. But there wasn't enough time in the daily schedule.

The idea of an after-school program surfaced, but most wondered how they'd motivate students to participate. Then someone remembered the old adage You catch more flies with honey than vinegar. They had to make the program attractive.

The teachers decided to have high school students taking an SAT prep class, a college student (the daughter of one of the eighth-grade teachers) preparing for a certification exam, and a lawyer who had recently passed the bar exam speak to an assembly of eighth graders. The presenters described how they prepared for comprehensive exams and how their preparations helped them succeed. They noted that even the best students usually took advantage of test preparation programs or guides. (The eighth graders were also told that getting a test score below the state cutoff point meant they'd have to attend a daily remediation class in that subject the following year, which might cramp their high school schedule. There was a small stick along with the carrot.) The group was primed!

Then these eighth-grade teachers described an *opportunity* they'd created just for their students. The students could prepare for tests just like these speakers had and, most likely, improve their daily work in the process. The teachers detailed a four-day-per-week after-school *enrichment* program; two days would focus on math and two on reading and writing. Since late buses would be scheduled, transportation wouldn't be a problem. *Anyone* who wanted to be included could sign up. Teachers realized, however, students would need parental permission and, just maybe, some parental nudging before enrolling.

The teachers sent letters to parents explaining the program and its rationale. The turnout was amazing. It was a truly heterogeneous student group that worked well cooperatively. Enriching content, interesting materials (movies, CDs, text sets), and stimulating resources (computers, tutors, guest speakers) built skills and sparked motivation. Overall, test scores improved. More important, these after-school sessions complemented daily instruction, extending and reinforcing the curriculum. And there was no stigma attached to getting additional practice in *enrichment* classes.

Summing Up

Genuine dialogue is at the core of successful assessment reporting and planning for further instruction. Respectful listening and sharing characterizes these *functional* exchanges. That is, they aren't simply window dressing to give the appearance that all stakeholders have a voice. Rather, everyone's ideas and opinions are truly considered and then *used*. Collaborative assessment reporting and instructional planning isn't easy, but the pay-offs are huge!

Students take ownership of their learning. They live metacognitively in school and in their world. They grow in their understanding of others. They learn the steps and body movements in the delicate dances of human relationships. Parents' critical role as partners in their children's learning is recognized and celebrated. Parents are invited to report as well as to reinforce follow-up instruction.

Triangulated assessment data from multiple sources reach their full value in meaningful, thoughtful, and respectful collaborative assessment reporting and instructional planning.

Afterword

Assess what you value and value what you assess. —Grant Wiggins

The term *assess* is derived from a word meaning *seated beside*, emphasizing its collaborative and supportive intention. The assessor and the learner should be working together diagnostically and dynamically throughout the cycle— teach, practice, observe, record, analyze, conclude, plan, and return to teach or reteach. Assessment is the road map for instruction.

The system proposed in this book attempts to mirror this fundamental meaning of assessment. In any teacher–learner relationship, the oath Do no harm applies, just as it does in doctor–patient ones. Instructional interactions with all learners must maintain a vigilant focus on providing sensitive and knowledgeable guidance as learners take the appropriate next step on their journey toward competency.

Useful assessment is part of the instructional process rather than separate from it. It's used in ways that inform teachers, learners, parents, and the community with considerable specificity. Such educative assessment "is a major, essential, and integral part of teaching and learning" (Wiggins 1998, 8).

Moving toward educative assessment is a personal journey. Like their students, some teachers move in small increments while others move quickly and steadily toward the goal. Not surprisingly, the learning curve is just as ragged. Teachers' initial feelings of limited competence for and/or resistance to the journey may be directly related to their perception of its difficulty. But, as Piaget (1969) points out, "The heartbreaking difficulty in pedagogy . . . is, in fact, that the best methods are the most difficult ones" (69). A first—and probably most difficult—step must be taken if the journey is to begin.

Teachers can begin with methods that are comfortable. They should find a point of readiness, start there, and keep raising the ceiling. Most important, however, teachers must believe that the process will help them identify learners' strengths and needs (Tomlinson 2001).

Making the Case for Competence

Students continuously provide evidence of their learning. Grasping this evidence before it slips away unnoticed is the shared responsibility of all stakeholders. It's important, however, for everyone to clearly understand that learning evidence doesn't come only from tests or reside solely in grades and scores. Overemphasis on tests as sources of learning evidence narrows instruction. It also gives educational control to authorities outside the classroom. Yetta Goodman (2004) points out that the control of education through current testing regimes and number manipulations "is also anti-intellectual, as those who control education build a mythology that ignores teachers' expertise—both their knowledge and experience." In schools, as in the world, evidence of successful performance is found in multiple venues.

To exemplify how we make our own case for competence in the world, I ask college students to write down three nouns that describe roles they currently fulfill. This could be sister, brother, parent, friend, teacher, part-time employee. Next, I ask them to circle one in which they feel particularly competent. Then, I tell them: "I'm from Missouri, the show-me state. Prove to me that you're really effective in that role." I give them time to write down the preponderance of evidence they'd present to demonstrate their competence beyond a reasonable doubt. Most of the evidence they come up with is qualitative. For example, to prove she's a good mother, a student might list things like "Teachers have said my children are well adjusted. Neighbors and family members have said my children are well behaved and kind. I spend a lot of time with my children. I help them with homework. My children come to me with problems. I read to them regularly." (This is, after all, a reading class!) On and on, like this, it goes. Obviously, some of these measures could be quantified, but that's not the point. Students hardly ever mention a standardized achievement test for motherhood, fatherhood, sisterhood, friendship, or any other role. They have a clear picture of the varied kinds of evidence the world accepts and expects as proof of competency.

Visualizing Assessment and Learning

Learning is like breathing. When we're healthy, it happens so silently we're hardly aware of it. But if we listen closely and tune in to our body, we hear the lungs filling and exhaling and feel the chest expand

and contract. An understanding of quietness is required for the close listening necessary in assessment for learning. "Quietness is less about not talking than about learning to listen and being attuned to nonverbal clues" (Fredston 2001, 103).

If learning looks like breathing, what then does assessment look like?

Assessment for learning is a process overflowing with verbs—we're watching, waiting, recording, prompting, asking, collecting, sharing, reflecting, analyzing, cross-checking, "what-iffing," connecting, evaluating. As a verb, *assess* implies action. Reeves (2004) suggests that when this action is appropriately carried out, it is qualified by *creatively*, *constructively*, and *meaningfully* rather than equated with *rate*, *rank*, *sort*, and *humiliate!* There's too much riding on winning the case for meaningful educative assessment. We have to get it right—*right now*.

Tour de France or Tour de Lance?

Lance Armstrong has overcome seemingly impossible obstacles, to the point that the race he's won over and over (too frequently, say the French) has been dubbed the Tour de Lance. Teachers must train and work with equal vigor and determination to improve assessment and learning for all students. It can be done. And doing so is accepting real accountability, or accountability that really means something! As professionals, we can't reject accountability for our work. We'd look silly if we tried. But we must stand firm in proclaiming that real accountability is based on so much more than testing.

If all we did were transform low-performing schools' test scores without changing practices, it would be like losing weight through anorexic behavior rather than over time through healthy diet and exercise. Anorexic behavior achieves a goal of weight loss, but the goal won't be maintained. Worse, the behavior destroys one's health. The same principle applies to improving schools' overall performance and individual children's attainment of expected competencies. We can get scores up, but the behavior that accomplishes that goal may be very unhealthy (Reeves 2004). Teachers know that all the right things they're doing to improve students' achievement would stay in place even if NCLB accountability were gone tomorrow. Politicians don't legislate teachers' deep-rooted, personal sense of real accountability. Unfortunately, testing advocates aren't typically patient; they see testing as the quick fix for school improvement.

There will be obstacles to the method of assessment we propose here, and they will seem formidable. However, there's also hope. Although only two states, Vermont and Kentucky, currently have statewide portfolio systems, Nebraska has recently persuaded federal education officials to approve its portfolio process for measuring student progress (Dell'Angela 2004). Nebraska's education commissioner, Douglas Christensen, is quoted as saying, "Nebraska's system is unusual because it rests on a revolutionary concept: that teachers know better than tests whether students are learning, and that they can be trusted to make that happen" (2). It's a small step forward, but perhaps it's a sign that the tide is turning.

Only persistent work toward the goal of positive, purposeful assessment will ensure lasting success. I like the way Jill Fredston puts it in her book *Rowing to Latitude* (2001). In reflecting on her self-propelled journeys along the coasts of Greenland, Norway, and Alaska in all kinds of conditions, she concludes, "Any obstacle, no matter how formidable, becomes insignificant once it has been surpassed" (214). Self-efficacy as professionals comes from stretching ourselves to reach goals we once believed were beyond our reach. The goal now is excellence in assessment *for* and *of* learning. We can assess effectively in order to teach effectively. We can and must share, equally with the rest of education's stakeholders, meaningful accountability as well as kudos for learners' success.

Bibliography

American Association of School Administrators (AASA). 2004. "Resources and Best Practices for Implementing No Child Left Behind." Retrieved 24 June 2004 from *www.aasa.org /NCLB/AYP_def.htm.*

American Educational Research Association (AERA). 2000. "AERA Position Statement Concerning High-Stakes Testing in PreK–12 Education." Retrieved 24 June 2004 from *www.aera.net/about /policy/stakes.htm.*

Andrade, H. G. 2000. "Using Rubrics to Promote Thinking and Learning." *Educational Assessment* 57: 13–18.

Anthony, R., T. Johnson, N. Mickelson, and A. Preece. 1991. *Evaluating Literacy: A Perspective for Change.* Portsmouth, NH: Heinemann.

Assessment Reform Group. 1999. *Assessment for Learning: Beyond the Black Box.* Cambridge, England: University of Cambridge.

Atkins, J. M., P. Black, and J. Coffey. 2001. *Classroom Assessment and the National Science Education Standards.* Washington, DC: National Academy Press.

Ayers, W. 2001. *To Teach: The Journey of a Teacher.* New York: Teachers College Press.

Barr, M., D. Craig, D. Fisette, and M. Syverson. 1999. *Assessing Literacy with the Learning Record.* Portsmouth, NH: Heinemann.

Bauer, E., and G. Garcia. 2002. "Lessons Form a Classroom Teacher's Use of Alternative Literacy Assessment." *Research in the Teaching of English* 36: 462–94.

Black, P., C. Harrison, C. Lee, B. Marshall, and D. Wiliam. 2004. "Working Inside the Black Box: Assessment for Learning in the Classroom." *Phi Delta Kappan* 86: 9–21.

Black, P., and D. Wiliam. 1998. "Inside the Black Box: Raising Standards Through Classroom Assessment." *Phi Delta Kappan* 80: 139–48.

Bond, L. 1996. "Norm- and Criterion-Referenced Testing." *Practical Assessment Research and Evaluation* 5 (2). Retrieved 11 August 2003 from *http://pareonline.net/getvn.asp?v=5tn=2*.

Boyd-Batstone, P. 2003. "Reading with a Hero: A Mediated and Literate Experience." In *English Learners: Reaching the Highest Level of English Literacy*, ed. G. G. Garcia, 333–56. Newark, DE: International Reading Association.

Bromley, K. 1998. *Language Arts: Exploring Connections*. Boston: Allyn and Bacon.

Burns, P., B. Roe, and E. Ross. 1999. *Teaching Reading in Today's Elementary School*. New York: Houghton Mifflin.

Calkins, L. 2001. *The Art of Teaching Reading*. New York: Longman.

Chappuis, S., and R. Stiggins. 2002. "Classroom Assessment for Learning." *Educational Leadership* 60: 40–43.

Clay, M. 1987. *The Early Detection of Reading Difficulties*, 3d ed. Portsmouth, NH: Heinemann.

———. 1989. "Concepts About Print in English and Other Languages." *The Reading Teacher* 42 (4): 268–76.

———. 1995. *An Observational Survey of Early Literacy Achievement*. Portsmouth, NH: Heinemann.

———. 2000. *Running Records for Classroom Teachers*. Portsmouth, NH: Heinemann.

Clemmons, J., L. Laase, D. Cooper, N. Areglado, and M. Dill. 1993. *Portfolios in the Classroom*. New York: Scholastic.

Cohen, S. A. 1988. *Tests: Marked for Life?* New York: Scholastic.

Coladarci, T. 2002. "Is It a House . . . or a Pile of Bricks?" *Phi Delta Kappan* 83: 772–74.

Cole, A. 2003. *Knee to Knee, Eye to Eye: Circling in on Comprehension*. Portsmouth, NH: Heinemann.

College Board, The. 2004. "The New SAT[(r)] 2005." Retrieved 24 June 2004 from *www.collegeboard.com/newsat/index.html*.

Cooper, J. D. 1997. *Literacy: Helping Children Construct Meaning*, 3d ed. New York: Houghton Mifflin.

Cooper, J. D., and N. Kiger. 2001. *Literacy Assessment*. New York: Houghton Mifflin Company.

Crooks, T. J. 1988. "The Impact of Classroom Evaluation on Students." *Review of Educational Research* 58: 438–81.

DeFina, A. 1992. *Portfolio Assessment*. New York: Scholastic.

Dell'Angela, T. 2004. "Nebraska Schools Skip Mandatory Tests." *Chicago Tribune*, 12 April. Retrieved 17 April 2004 from *www.webmail.aol.com/mgsview.adp?folder=SU5CT1g=&seq=2*.

Doherty, K. 2004. "Assessment." *Education Week* (17 June). Retrieved 20 June 2004 from *www.edweek.org/context/topics/issuespage.cfm?id=41*.

Dynneson, T. L., and R. E. Gross, 1999. *Designing Effective Instruction for Secondary Social Studies*. Upper Saddle River, NJ: Merrill/Prentice Hall.

Edwards, S. 2002. "Achieving Standards Without Sacrificing My Own." *Voices from the Middle* 10: 31–34.

Eisner, E. 1998. *The Kind of Schools We Need*. Portsmouth, NH: Heinemann.

Epstein, A. 2003. "Portfolio Assessment: Design and Implementation." Retrieved 31 March 2003 from *www.teachervision.com/lesson-plans/lesson-4535.html*.

Escamilla, K., A. Andrade, A. Basurto, O. Ruiz, and M. Clay. 1996. *Instrumentos de Observacion: De Los Logors de la Lecto-escritura Inicial*. Portsmouth, NH: Heinemann.

FairTest. 2004. "Criterion- and Standards-Referenced Tests." The National Center for Fair and Open Testing. Retrieved 28 May 2004 from *www.fairtest.org/facts/csrtests.html.*

Farr, R., and B. Tone. 1998. *Portfolio and Performance Assessment.* New York: Harcourt Brace College.

Fredston, J. 2001. *Rowing to Latitude.* New York: North Point Press.

Fu, D., and L. Lamme. 2002. "Assessment Through Conversation." *Language Arts* 79: 241–50.

Gardner, H. 1981. *The Unschooled Mind: How Children Think and How Schools Should Teach.* New York: Basic Books.

Gillet, J., and C. Temple. 2000. *Understanding Reading Problems: Assessment and Instruction.* 5th ed. New York: Longman.

Goodman, K., Y. Goodman, and D. Hood. 1989. *The Whole Language Evaluation Book.* Portsmouth, NH: Heinemann.

Goodman, Y. 1986. "Children Coming to Know Literacy." In *Emergent Literacy: Reading and Writing,* ed. W. H. Teale and E. Sulzby, 1–14. Norwood, NJ: Ablex.

———. 2004. Personal communication on listserv "Literacy for All," 29 August.

Goodrich, H. 1996/1997. "Understanding Rubrics." *Educational Leadership* 54: 14–17.

Hall, E., and S. Salmon. 2003. "Chocolate Chip Cookies and Rubrics: Helping Students Understand Rubrics in Inclusive Settings." *Teaching Exceptional Children* 35: 8–11.

Hancock, J., J. Turbill, and B. Cambourne. 1994. "Assessment and Evaluation of Literacy Learning." In *Authentic Reading Assessment: Practices and Possibilities,* ed. S. W. Valencia, E. H. Heibert, and P. Afflerbach, 46–70. Newark, DE: International Reading Association.

Hanna, G., and P. Dettmer. 2004. *Assessment for Effective Teaching.* New York: Pearson/Allyn and Bacon.

Harlin, R., and S. Lipa. 1995. "How Teachers' Literacy Coursework and Experiences Affect Their Perceptions and Utilization of Portfolio Documents." *Reading Research and Instruction* 35: 1–18.

———. 1996. "A Model for Preparing Preservice and Inservice Teachers to Interpret and Utilize Portfolio Assessment." In *Literacy Assessment for Tomorrow's Schools,* ed. B. Moss and M. Collins, 110–22. Harrisonburg, VA: College Reading Association.

Harris, A., and E. Sipay. 1990. *How to Increase Reading Ability.* New York: Longman.

Heiman, G. 2001. *Understanding Research Methods and Statistics.* 2d ed. New York: Houghton Mifflin.

Hein, G. E., and S. Price. 1994. *Active Assessment for Active Science.* Portsmouth, NH: Heinemann.

Henson, J., and C. Gilles. 2003. "Al's Story: Overcoming Beliefs That Inhibit Learning." *Language Arts* 80: 259–67.

Hill, D. 2000. "He's Got Your Number." Retrieved 27 August 2004 from *www.teachermagazine.org/tmstory.cfm?slug=08sanders.h11.*

Hilliard, A. 1989. *Testing and Tracking.* Video. Available from National Association for the Education of Young Children, 1509 Sixteenth Street, NW, Washington, DC 20036.

Hoberman, M. A. 1982. *A House Is a House for Me.* New York: Puffin.

Hoff, D. 2002. "States Revise the Meaning of 'Proficient'." *Education Week* (9 October). Retrieved 26 June 2004 from *www.edweek.org/ew/ewprintstory.cfm?slus=06tests.h22.*

Instructional Objectives Exchange (IOX). 2004. "About IOX: Who We Are." Retrieved 1 June 2004 from *www.ioxassessment.com/cgi-bin*

/iox.cgi?ACTION=ENTER&thispage=about_us.html&ORDER ID=!ORDERID!

Jackson, C., and M. Larkin. 2002. "RUBRIC: Teaching Students to Use Grading Rubrics." *Teaching Exceptional Children* 35: 40–45.

Jane Goodall Institute. 2003. Home page for Jane Goodall Institute. Retrieved 25 April 2003 from *www.janegoodall.org/*.

Jimerson, S., and A. Kaufman. 2003. "Reading, Writing, and Retention: A Primer on Grade Retention." *The Reading Teacher* 56: 622–33.

Johnston, P. 1992a. *Constructive Evaluation of Literate Activity*. New York: Longman.

———. 1992b. "Nontechnical Assessment." *The Reading Teacher* 46: 60–62.

Kane, M., T. Crooks, and A. Cohen. 1999. "Validating Measures of Performance." *Educational Measurement: Issues and Practices* 18: 5–7.

Kohl, H. 1994. *I Won't Learn from You*. New York: New Press.

Kohn, A. 1999. *The Schools Our Children Deserve*. New York: Houghton Mifflin.

———. 2000. *The Case Against Standardized Testing*. Portsmouth, NH: Heinemann.

Langer, G., A. Colton, and L. Goff. 2003. *Collaborative Analysis of Student Work*. Alexandria, VA: Association for Supervision and Curriculum Development.

Linn, R. 2000. "Assessments and Accountability." *Educational Researcher* 29: 4–16.

Lyman, H. 1998. *Test Scores and What They Mean*. 6th ed. Boston: Allyn and Bacon.

MacGinitie, W., R. MacGinitie, K. Maria, and L. Dreyer. 2000. *Gates–MacGinitie Reading Test, Level 3, Forms S and T: Manual for Scoring and Interpretation*. Itasca, IL: Riverside.

McGrawHill. 2004a. "Designing Assessment Systems: A Primer on the Test Development Process." McGrawHill. Retrieved 1 June 2004 from http://nclb.mheducation.com:2000/pdf/primer_quality.pdf.

———. 2004b. "A Guide for Effective Assessment." Retrieved 27 June 2004 from *www.ctb.com/articles/article_information.jsp?JSESSION ID=AfMtYQwC0wtozHZxqUy5kUzIK7qLjIcYEMLhwEEYtDOG AjSm64CV!-411954294!-970123149!5008!6008&CONTENT% 3C%3Ecnt_id=43387&FOLDER%3C%3Efolder_id=39863&bmUID= 1088359597841.*

McMillan, J. 2004. *Classroom Assessment*. New York: Pearson.

Measured Progress. 2004. "About Us." Retrieved 1 June 2003 from *www.measuredprogress.org/AboutUs/Overview.html*.

Meyer, R. 2000. "Value-Added Indicators: A Powerful Tool for Evaluating Science and Mathematics Programs and Policies." *NISE Brief* 3: 1–8. National Institute for Science Education (NISE), University of Wisconsin–Madison. Retrieved 26 August 2004 from *www.wcer .wisc.edu/nise/publications/Briefs/Vol_3No_3*.

Middle States Commission on Higher Education. 2002. *Assessment of Student Learning: Options and Resources*. Philadelphia: Middle States Commission on Higher Education.

Mora, Jill Kerper. 2004. Personal communication on listserv "Literacy for All," 26 August.

National Academy of Sciences. 1996. *National Science Standards*. Washington, DC: National Academy Press.

National Council for the Social Studies. 1999. *Curriculum Standards for Social Studies*. Retrieved 27 June 2004 from *www.ncss.org/standards /2.1.html*.

National Education Association (NEA). 2004. "Accountability and Testing." *NEA News and Action*. Retrieved 2 December 2004 from
www.nea.org/accountability/index.html.

New York State Education Department (NYSED). 1996. *Learning Standards for Social Studies*. Albany: State of New York University at
Albany NYSED Publication.

————. 2004a. "February 2004 Grade 4 English Language Arts (ELA)
Test." Retrieved 1 June 2004 from *www.emsc.nysed.gov/osa/elaei
/G4ELA04convertable.htm*.

————. 2004b. "Grade 4 English Language Arts (Reading, Writing, and
Listening Items)." Retrieved 1 June 2004 from *www.emsc.nysed.gov
/osa/elaei/elaeiarch/gr4eladescrip.htm*.

Newmann, F. M. 2000. "Authentic Intellectual Work: What and Why?"
Research/Practice 8 (1). University of Minnesota, Center for Applied
Research and Improvement. Retrieved 24 January 2004 from
*http://education.umn.edu/CAREI/Reports/Rpractice/Fall2000/
newmann.htm*.

Nolan, K. 2000. Prologue: "Why Is Looking at Student Work Important?" In *What Story Does the Work Tell?* ed. C. Cantrill, D. Glass,
and A. Sparks. Philadelphia: Philadelphia Educational Fund. Retrieved 27 October 2003 from *www.philaedfund.org
/slcweb/prolog.htm*.

Ohio State Education Department (OHSED). 2004. "October 2003
Grade 3 Reading Achievement Test." Retrieved 24 June 2004 from
*www.ode.state.oh.us/search.asp?q1=October+2003+Grade+3+Reading+
Achievement*.

Olson, L. 2004. "Three States in New England to Produce Common
Tests." *Education Week* 23 (May): 10.

Ormrod, J. 2000. *Educational Psychology: Developing Learners*. Upper Saddle River, NJ: Merrill/Prentice-Hall.

Paris, S., R. Calfee, N. Filby, E. H. Hiebert, P. D. Pearson, S. W. Valencia,
and K. Wolf. 1992. "A Framework for Authentic Literacy Assessment."
The Reading Teacher 46: 88–98.

Peregoy, S., and O. Boyle. 1997. *Reading, Writing, and Learning in ESL*. 2d
ed. New York: Longman.

Perrone, V. 1991. "On Standardized Testing." *Childhood Education* 67:
131–42.

Piaget, J. 1969. *The Mechanisms of Perception*. London: Routledge and
Kegan Paul.

Pikulski, J. 1994. "Commentary on Assessment and Evaluation of Literacy
Learning." In *Authentic Reading Assessment: Practices and Possibilities*,
ed. S. W. Valencia, E. H. Heibert, and P. Afflerbach, 46–70. Newark,
DE: International Reading Association.

Pipho, C. 1998. "The Value-Added Side of Standards." *Phi Delta Kappan*
79: 341–42.

Popham, J. 1975. *Educational Evaluation*. Englewood Cliffs, NJ:
Prentice-Hall.

————. 2000. *Testing! Testing!* Boston: Allyn and Bacon.

————. 2001a. "Standardized Achievement Tests: Misnamed and Misleading." *Education Week* (19 September). Retrieved 20 June 2004 from
www.edweek.org/ew/ewprintstory.cfm?slug=03popham.h21.

————. 2001b. *The Truth About Testing*. Alexandria, VA: Association for
Supervision and Curriculum Development.

————. 2003. *Test Better, Teach Better: The Instructional Role of Assessment*.
Alexandria, VA: Association for Supervision and Curriculum
Development.

———. 2004a. *America's "Failing" Schools*. New York: Routledge Falmer.

———. 2004b. "Shaping Up the 'No Child' Act." *Education Week* 23 (May): 40.

Public Broadcasting Service (PBS). 2004. *Frontline:* "Testing Our Schools: In Your State." Retrieved 20 June 2004 from *www.pbs.org/wgbh/pages /frontline/shows/schools/state*.

Quality Counts. 2004. "Standards and Accountability: Types of Tests." Retrieved 22 June 2004 from *www.edweek.org/sreports/qc04/reports /standacct-tlb.cfm*.

Rebora, A. 2004. "No Child Left Behind." *Education Week* (3 March). Retrieved 6 March 2004 from *www.edweek.org/context/topics /issuespage.cfm?id=59*.

Reeves, D. 2004. "Assessment and Accountability. Holistic Accountability: Placing Test Scores in Context." Faces of Education Series, CD# 504356. Alexandria, VA: Association for Supervision and Curriculum Development.

Rueda, R., and E. Garcia. 1997. "Do Portfolios Make a Difference for Diverse Students? The Influence of Type of Data on Making Instructional Decisions." *Learning Disabilities Research and Practice* 12 (2): 114–22.

Sacks, P. 1999. *Standardized Minds*. Cambridge, MA: Perseus.

Sagor, R. 1993. *At-Risk Students: Reaching and Teaching Them*. Swampscott, MA: Watersun Press.

———. 2002. "Lessons from Skateboarders." *Educational Leadership* 60: 34–38.

Shea, M. 2000. *Taking Running Records*. New York: Scholastic.

———. 2003a. "Heroes Around Us." From *www.readwritethink.org/lesson _images/lesson171/rubrics.pdf*. Newark, DE: International Reading Association/National Council of Teachers of English.

———. 2003b. "Paul Revere, American Patriot." From *www.readwritethink .org/lesson_images/lesson220/center.pdf*. Newark, DE: International Reading Association/National Council of Teachers of English.

———. 2004. "Tenement Life: Mapping Texts and Making Models." From *www.readwritethink.org/lesson_images/lesson302/Rubric.pdf*. Newark, DE: International Reading Association/National Council of Teachers of English.

Shepard, L. A. 2000. "The Role of Assessment in a Learning Culture." *Educational Leadership* 29: 4–14.

Skinner, R., and L. Staresina. 2004. "State of the States." *Education Week* (8 January). Retrieved 1 June 2004 from *www.edweek.org/sreports /qc04/article.cfm?slug=17sos.h23*.

Society for the Advancement of Excellence in Education (SAEE). 2000. "Value-Added Assessment." *Education Analyst* 3: 1–2. Retrieved 27 August 2004 from *www.saee.bc.ca/200032.html*.

Spinelli, C. G. 2002. *Classroom Assessment for Students with Special Needs in Inclusive Settings*. Upper Saddle River, NJ: Merrill/Prentice-Hall.

Sternberg, R. J. 2003. "What Is an 'Expert Student'?" *Educational Researcher* 32: 5–9.

Stiggins, R. 1999a. "Assessment, Student Confidence, and School Success." *Phi Delta Kappan* 81: 91–198.

———. 1999b. "Learning Teams for Assessment Literacy: A Concept Paper." Reprint from *Journal of Staff Development* 20 (3): 17–21. Retrieved 3 July 2004 from *www.hawaiiassessmentmatters.org/pdf_files /literature/literacy.pdf*.

———. 2001. *Student-Involved Classroom Assessment*. 3d ed. Upper Saddle River, NJ: Merrill/Prentice-Hall.

————. 2002. "Assessment Crisis: The Absence of Assessment *for* Learning." *Phi Delta Kappan* 83: 758–69.

————. 2004. "New Assessment Beliefs for a New School Mission." *Phi Delta Kappan* 86: 22–27.

Stiggins, R., and N. Conklin. 1992. In *Teachers' Hands: Investigating the Practice of Classroom Assessment*. Albany: State University of New York Press.

Taylor, D. 1991. *Learning Denied*. Portsmouth, NH: Heinemann.

ThinkQuest. 2000. "Academic Achievement Tests." Retrieved 28 May 2004 from *http://library.thinkquest.org/C005704/content_la_testing _academic.php3*.

Tomlinson, C. 2001. *How to Differentiate Instruction in Mixed-Ability Classrooms*. Alexandria, VA: Association for Supervision and Curriculum Development.

Tompkins, G., and L. McGee. 1986. "Visually Impaired and Sighted Children's Emerging Concepts About Written Language." In *Metalinguistic Awareness and Beginning Literacy: Conceptualizing What It Means to Read and Write*, ed. D. Yaden and S. Templeton, 259–75. Portsmouth, NH: Heinemann.

Tovani, C. 2000. *I Read It, but I Don't Get It*. Portland, ME: Stenhouse.

United School District of De Pere, Wisconsin. 2004. "Benchmarks for Learning." Retrieved 9 July 2004 from *www.depere.k12.wi.us /district/teachers/benchmarks.php*.

U.S. Congress, Office of Technology Assessment. 1992. *Testing in America's Schools: Asking the Right Questions*. OTA-SET-519 Washington, DC: U.S. Government Printing Office.

Valencia, S. 1998. *Literacy Portfolios in Action*. Fort Worth, TX: Harcourt Brace College.

Valencia, S., E. Hiebert, and P. Afflerbach. 1994. *Authentic Reading Assessment*. Newark, DE: International Reading Association.

Vermont Superintendents Association. 2004. Position Paper: "No Child Left Behind." Retrieved 27 August 04 from *www.aasa.org/NCLB /VT_supe_assoc.pdf*.

Webster's New Universal Unabridged Dictionary. 1996. New York: Barnes and Noble.

Whitehurst, G. 2004. "Writing and Spelling: An Interview with Russ Whitehurst." Retrieved 2 June 2004 from *www.pbs.org/launchingreaders /writingandspelling/meettheexperts_2.html*.

Whittaker, C., S. Salend, and D. Duhaney. 2001. "Creating Instructional Rubrics for Inclusive Classrooms." *Teaching Exceptional Children* 34: 8–13.

Wiggins, G. 1991. "Standards, Not Standardization: Evoking Quality Student Work." *Educational Leadership* 48: 18–25.

————. 1993. *Assessing Student Performance*. San Francisco: Jossey-Bass.

————. 1998. *Educative Assessment: Designing Assessments to Inform and Improve Student Performance*. San Francisco: Jossey-Bass.

Williams, P. 1989. "Using Customized Standardized Tests." *Practical Assessment, Research and Evaluation* 1 (9). Retrieved 28 June 2004 from *http://pareonline.net/getvn.asp?v=1+n=9*.

Winograd, P., S. Paris, and C. Bridge. 1991. "Improving the Assessment of Literacy." *The Reading Teacher* 45: 108–16.

Wisconsin Department of Public Instruction. 1998. *Wisconsin Model Academic Standards for Social Studies*. Retrieved 9 July 2004 from *www.dpi.state.wi.us/dpi/standards/ssintro.html*.

Wise, A. E. 1996. "Quality Teaching for the Twenty-First Century." A special issue of *Phi Delta Kappan* 78: 190–224.

Yatvin, J. 2004. Personal communication on listserv "Literacy for All," 25 August.

Zucker, S. 2003. "Fundamentals of Standardized Testing." *Harcourt Assessment Report*. San Antonio, TX: Harcourt Assessment.

Index